EROTICS & POLITICS

This book aims to provide an interface between the study of sexuality and gender, and in particular between gay men's studies and feminism. In doing so it covers a wide range of issues of concern to gay and feminist movements over the past twenty-five years including gay liberation, lesbianism, sado-masochism, pornography, promiscuity, personal relationships, AIDS and postmodernity. The central focus throughout is on the nature, development and consequences of gay male sexuality and masculinity.

Erotics & Politics is unique in its coverage of a wide range of issues and in the connections it makes between subjects which are typically examined separately.

Tim Edwards is Lecturer in Sociology at Oxford Brookes University.

Critical studies on men and masculinities

Jeff Hearn and David H.J. Morgan (editors)
Men, Masculinities and Social Theory

David Jackson
Unmasking Masculinity
A critical autobiography

David H.J. Morgan
Discovering Men

Jeff Hearn
Men in the Public Eye

Arthur Brittan
The Competitive Self (forthcoming)

Editorial advisory board

EROTICS
&
POLITICS

Gay male sexuality, masculinity and feminism

Tim Edwards

London and New York

First published in 1994
by Routledge
11 New Fetter Lane, London EC4P 4EE

Simultaneously published in the USA and Canada
by Routledge
29 West 35th Street, New York, NY 10001

© 1994 Tim Edwards

Typeset in Bembo by
LaserScript Limited, Mitcham, Surrey
Printed and bound in Great Britain by
Biddles Ltd, Guildford and King's Lynn

British Library Cataloguing in Publication Data
A catalogue record for this book is available from the British Library

Library of Congress Cataloging in Publication Data
Edwards, Tim (Timothy C.), 1963–
Erotics & politics: gay male sexuality, masculinity, and feminism/Tim
Edwards.
     p. cm. – (Critical studies on men and masculinities)
Includes bibliographical references and index.
     1. Homosexuality, Male. 2. Masculinity (Psychology). 3. Feminist
theory. I. Title. II. Title: Erotics and politics. III. Series.
HQ76.E3   1993
305.3–dc20   93–17214
                                                                        CIP

ISBN 0–415–09903–X (hbk)
ISBN 0–415–09904–8 (pbk)

For my mother and in memory of my father

Contents

Acknowledgements

I am deeply indebted to Jeff Hearn for rolling the ball of this book and refereeing the whole game of its writing. Gratitude also goes to the Department of Sociology at Essex University for training me, particularly Ken Plummer, and thanks for the opportunity and support are also due to the Department of Social Science at Oxford Brookes University. Particular love and thanks to my mother for supporting me in so many ways and my much missed father for giving me the strength. Much gratitude and hugs for ideas, comments and continued friendship past and present to Annie, Carla, Huseyin, Maggie, Maxine, Paul, Pauline, Simon and Tom . . . and to Mark for making me think again. Finally, very grateful thanks to Sarah Dann, Gill Davies, Anne Gee, Chris Rojek and all at Routledge.

Introduction

This book began life in 1987 when my main problematic concern was to explain and unpack the complex relationship of sexuality or sexual orientation to identity or gender category and, more particularly, homosexuality and masculinity. I could not and did not and cannot and do not accept that there is no connection. My concern with this connection translates itself academically into a dualistic focus of: first, gay studies, primarily gay men's studies, which have documented the importance of sexuality; and second, feminism, or women's studies, which have primarily documented the importance of gender. Whilst some feminists have attempted to make connections of femininity and lesbianism, many gay male academics have consciously rejected connections of masculinity and gay sexuality, with a few exceptions. In addition, men's studies of masculinity added some insights into masculinity and male experience though frequently excluded full consideration of sexual orientation and heterosexuality as a component of masculine identity.

My concern with the same connections also had a personal translation. I was, and what is more still am, tired of witnessing some gay men's sexism and, more significantly, feeling the full force of it in my personal life with men who seem to find it practically impossible to relate emotionally and sexually to another person at the same time or seek escape routes from emotionality in persistent promiscuity and anti-commitment attitudes or a plain lack of emotional communication and explanation. Importantly, I have also experienced powerful emotional attachments with gay men impossible to achieve with straight men and witnessed constant questioning of gender in certain areas of the gay community, particularly culturally, with exhilarating or simply amusing impact.

The point precisely is that it is indeed difficult to connect gender and sexuality and that the initial intention is also partly personal. There is, though, quite clearly a tension in maintaining or combining academic credibility with more personal or experiential expression. In addition, what this tends to show is not simply the limits of personal experience as much as the masculinism of academe and academic life.

This introduction is divided into two distinct sections or units. The first section or unit, entitled 'The Study of (Masculine) Homosexuality', is a conventional introduction intended to outline the central tenets, style and structure of the text. The second section or unit, entitled 'Technicalities of Construction(ism)' is intended to clarify definitions, intentions and tensions, as well as the central theoretical perspective adopted in the text, primarily for a more academically inclined readership.

The study of (masculine) homosexuality

In this first unit or section I wish to consider specifically the previous study of homosexuality, the perspectives developed from it, and the overall style and structure of the text.

Masculine homosexuality

> The parallel problem that confronts homosexuals is that they set out to win the love of a 'real' man. If they succeed, they fail. A man who 'goes with' other men is not what they would call a real man. This conundrum is incapable of resolution, but this does not make homosexuals give it up. They only search more frantically and with less and less discretion for more and more masculine men and because they themselves are, however reluctantly, to some extent masculine their judgement in these matters is for the most part physical. If you ask a homosexual what his newest true love is like, you will never get the answer, 'He is wise or kind or brave'. He will only say, 'It's enormous'.
>
> (Crisp, 1968: 62)

When Quentin Crisp wrote the above quote in England in the mid to late 1960s, gay liberation had yet to begin. Things, it seems, must have changed. The crunch question, though, is how much, and this is the key issue raised by this book. Undoubtedly, there is now a new gay identity; arguably, a thriving gay subculture; and possibly, a politics of opposition to oppression. Importantly, though, there is still no change in the law, no protection from discrimination against gay men and lesbians and plenty to complain about including Section 28, AIDS and the continued oppression of same-sex sexualities at all levels of society from home to work and from attitudes to statutes.

INTRODUCTION

More significantly, have homosexuals or homosexuality themselves changed and, in particular, is the gay man of today so dissimilar from Quentin Crisp's example?

The primary difference, most writers in the area point out, is political: a post-Stonewall, positive proclamation of being gay after an indefinite history of religious castigation, state criminalisation and medical categorisation (see Adam, 1987; Altman, 1971; D'Emilio, 1983; Plummer, 1981b; Weeks, 1977). However, the struggle against oppression continues and the argument postulated here is quite simple: homosexuality socially and culturally still undermines masculinity, that is to say masculinity is not homosexual and homosexuality is not masculine, and yet of course this does not prevent the attempt personally and individually, or even collectively, to reinvent 'masculine homosexuality'.

Simultaneously, the story of the last twenty-five years has not been one of wild, uncontrolled liberation, but of a continued regulation of sexuality and oppression of gay men and lesbians. Gay men often sought to reaffirm their self-worth and masculinity through the development of specific masculine identities, codes and meanings, and the adopting of a positive, alternative and highly sexualised lifestyle. Negatively, however, this created conformism and led to an over-emphasis upon sex; the problem of intermale intimacy remained. In addition, gay men in the 1970s were often willingly co-opted into capitalist consumerism through the specific developments of their subculture. Later, this lifestyle was threatened personally and politically through the development of the AIDS epidemic as a sexually transmitted disease and as a divisive discourse of desire and damnation. A new sexual identity, sexual subculture, and sexual behaviour was and still is needed to, paradoxically, de-emphasise the importance of sex, whilst maintaining and developing the positivity of gay sexuality as an organising device for an alternative lifestyle. A new gay sexuality will inevitably be developed, as was its predecessor, but it must be achieved with the full, positive awareness of all the issues involved, including feminism and racism as well as an opposition to the social, economic, and political oppression of gay men and lesbians.

The study of homosexuality
The study of homosexuality is heavily and well-documented over the previous century (see Adam, 1987; Altman, 1971, 1982; D'Emilio, 1983; Weeks, 1977, 1981, 1985). It is a study that reconstructs and reclaims homosexuality as an alternative and positive lifestyle, and

[3]

stresses the role of reform movements themselves in making this happen. It is primarily opposed to any attempt to simply apply contemporary concepts of homosexuality to the past and, as it were, expose prior homosexuality in people or society. More importantly, it seeks to show how contemporary developments in the study of homosexuality have shaped our understanding of the past and, in addition, how that past still exerts pressures intertwined with present developments in contemporary society.

In this 'new' social history or study of homosexuality, the particular turning points centre on: first, the rise of the state in the nineteenth century, medically and governmentally, in defining modern sexuality and indeed sexuality itself; second, the social, economic and political pressures and opportunities opened up through the two world wars; and third, the rise of the reform movements themselves culminating in gay liberation and the more or less simultaneous rise of women's movements, black and civil rights protest groups in politicising and recreating sexual, racial and gendered identities. It is particularly significant that the academic studies of sexuality are centrally located in these more political developments and many leading academics today were equally leading activists in the 1960s and 1970s.

There is, though, a difficulty stemming from these developments as, prior to the late nineteenth century and after 1970, the study of homosexuality trails off seriously and it is to this more contemporary question of the impact of these processes that attention is turned here. In addition, the raising of this question is due largely to a generational development as the satisfaction and achievements of a prior generation of activists and theorists come under attack from the dissatisfaction of a current generation of activists and theorists. This is, in itself, pre-mised upon a primarily different set of pressures that include the AIDS epidemic, the conservatism of the state, and an increased sense of international diversity.

So far, two perspectives have primarily been adopted and developed to explain the impact of gay liberation. The first of these positions states that gay liberation was the ultimate result of several centuries of reform movements campaigning for equality for sexual minorities. It therefore expresses, perpetuates and promotes the importance of sexual minorities and erotic diversity. Sado-masochism, paedophilia and non-private sexuality are seen essentially as extensions or expressions of this sexual diversity. The AIDS epidemic represents conversely a concerted conservative attack on this diversity opposed through an identity politics. The second theory of gay

[4]

liberation says that, like all sexual liberation, it was formed by men for men and is about men and male desire. In addition, it was also derived from prior patriarchal practices and masculine socialisation with an indefinite history. Sado-masochism, paedophilia and promiscuity are seen consequently as primary and exemplary expressions of the profound sexism that underlay gay liberation's benign belief in gender breakdown. In addition, AIDS organising is men's organising for men and the only solution is a separatist politics.

These two perspectives or sets of studies are illustrated in a particularly extreme form as poles of a continuum and there is much debate within and between them. The former perspective is developed primarily from the work of post-structuralists and new social historians including Michel Foucault (1978, 1984a, 1984b), Jeffrey Weeks (1977, 1981, 1985) and Ken Plummer (1975, 1981b) as well as many gay male historians, socialist feminists and political activists (see Patton, 1985; Vance, 1984; Watney, 1987). The latter perspective is adopted primarily in the politics of Andrea Dworkin (1981, 1987) and Catharine MacKinnon (1982, 1987a, 1987b) in the United States, and Sheila Jeffreys (1990) and Liz Stanley (1982, 1984) in the UK, as well as revolutionary feminist groups (Coveney et al., 1984).

The proponents of each of these perspectives continuously criticise each other and reinforce or perpetuate a series of highly polarised dualisms of liberalism and radicalism, reform and revolution, sexual politics and the politics of sexuality, explained in detail in the second section of this Introduction. It is important to point out that I do not accept, entirely at least, either position and the purpose of the following chapters is to attempt to develop another or third perspective that recognises the strengths and weaknesses of each of these perspectives.

Style and structure

The text focuses primarily on the gay male community in England and the United States of America. There are two reasons for this: first, the former is my home and therefore well-known to me while the latter is of profound social, economic, and political influence; and second, they tend to dominate the literature and research on sexuality due to the reign of the English language-speaking nations internationally. European empirical, as opposed to theoretical, work in particular suffers in this respect as only recently has it started to attain any translation.[1]

Stylistically, the text attempts a personal-political synthesis in the

[5]

use of various more personal introductions or literary passages juxtaposed with the more academic consideration. It is not my intention, though, to set up a complete personal-theoretical paradigm. Importantly, this kind of technique is not new and has grown in significance through feminism (see Okely, 1987; Smith, 1987; Stanley, 1990; Stanley and Wise, 1983), some men's studies (Cohen, 1990; Jackson, 1990), qualitative methodology and life history (Faraday and Plummer, 1979; Gilligan, 1982; Plummer, 1983; Ribbens et al., 1991) and some, limited gay studies (Greig, 1987; Silverstein, 1977).

The technique is criticised on two counts: first, for its subjective indulgence; and second, for its lack of wider applicability or relevance. The first problem tends to reveal the subjective biases of 'objective' social science, whilst the latter tends to reflect an equal insistence on statistical correlates.[2] Qualitative, small-scale or micro-sociology has a history of running a poor second in funding and status to quantitative, large-scale studies and surveys often seen mistakenly as creating an illusion of validity and social relevance. Nevertheless, it is true to say that such techniques are in their infancy and, consequently, the current text is not wholly sown in either field and mixes personal and political, polished academic and experimental approaches.

The selection of issues for inclusion in the text was carried out according to the criteria of the theory, that is to say gay studies *and* feminism *and* men's studies of masculinity. I therefore do *not* consider any issue in isolation. In addition, whilst the empirical focus is primarily gay male sexuality, many of the points made are more widely applied or applicable to other sexualities and, conversely, ideas and theories other than gay male studies are applied or applicable to gay sexuality.

The first chapter considers the effects of the law reform in Britain and the various State restrictions in America as part of the modern history of homosexuality in combination with the development of the homosexual and homophile movement, culminating in the formation of the Gay Liberation Front (GLF). The second chapter examines the relationships between lesbianism, feminism and gay men in relation to gay and lesbian liberation. The third chapter considers paedophile and pederasty issues as historical constructions in relation to issues of gender and generation; whilst the fourth considers sado-masochism and pornography and, in particular, the relationship of sexuality and power. These four chapters provide the historical backdrop to and develop the sexual-political theory of the text. The fifth and sixth chapters, 'Public sex' and 'Private love' respectively, concentrate on the 1970s development of a specific gay socio-sexual subculture. They could, and should, be seen as axiomatic in relation to the first four. The seventh considers AIDS and the political developments of the 1980s, whilst the eighth looks forward to the new politics of the 1990s under conditions of 'postmodernity'. In conclusion, these eight chapters ultimately form the historical construction and structure of an 'erotic politics', or the politics of personal erotic preferences, discussed in detail in the Conclusion.

Technicalities of construction(ism)

In this next unit or section, I wish to consider more academic questions concerning social constructionist theory, central tensions, intentions, and definitions.

The perspective: the pros and cons of social constructionism

Within the history of homosexuality and the study of sexuality, social constructionism constitutes something of a sociological hegemony as *the* theory of sexuality *per se* and, in particular, homosexuality. The theory at its simplest states that sexuality, far from being 'inevitable', 'biological', or 'natural', is in fact a deeply socially conditioned and dynamic phenomenon that is indeed 'socially constructed' as it does not in itself constitute any kind of separate entity.

The theory developed primarily out of political opposition to Freudian and Darwinian 'hydraulic' or 'essentialist' models of sexuality which see sexuality as an innate and overwhelming drive necessarily controlled or repressed in society. The difficulty with this approach is that it does not account for the variety of sexualities practised differently across time and space in different societies with different social outcomes.

With the rise of the new deviancy theory of the 1960s, attention was also turned not to the phenomenon of sexuality itself, rather to the societal reactions to it and conditions surrounding it. The initial and influential example of this approach was in Mary McIntosh's 'The homosexual role' which turned attention to the 'role' of homosexuality in society as part of a functionalist theory of sexuality (McIntosh, 1968). This was later adapted through more interactive theories of the social construction of sexuality developed in Gagnon

[7]

and Simon's use of 'scripting' to explain sexual learning and sexual meanings, and later by Ken Plummer in explaining sexual stigma (Gagnon and Simon, 1973; Plummer, 1975).

At the same time, European post-structuralism was gaining in popularity primarily through the work of Michel Foucault whose *History Of Sexuality* is now seen as fundamental (Foucault, 1978, 1984a, 1984b). The influence of this theory was then popularised in initially more structuralist terms through the work of Jeffrey Weeks whose unintended trilogy on the modern history of homosexuality is particularly important (Weeks, 1977, 1981, 1985). The perspective is also taken up in some socialist feminists' work, including Gayle Rubin's and Lynne Segal's writing (Rubin, 1984; Segal, 1987).

However, more recently, this social constructionist hegemony has come in for some criticism, not only from revolutionary and radical feminism, but rather more from theoretically advanced analyses. These include David Greenberg's colossal history of homosexuality which also offered a critique of social constructionist theory, Diana Fuss's influential post-structuralist feminism, Steven Epstein's political commentaries, particularly in relation to the AIDS epidemic, and an overall discussion of the issues in the 1987 Amsterdam conference 'Homosexuality, Which Homosexuality?' (see Altman et al., 1989; Epstein, 1987, 1988; Fuss, 1989; Greenberg, 1988). The criticisms they, and I, make amount to a theoretical-empirical-political trinity:

Theoretical criticisms
The most simple point here is that social constructionism lacks a proper theory of agency and structure or determination (see Epstein, 1987). This situation varies with the type of social constructionist theory, that is to say interactionist approaches primarily emphasise the agency of the constructing whilst more historical approaches emphasise the structuring of the constructed. The difficulty in either case, though, is the lack of analysis of the overall question of who constructs who, how and why, and with what implications.

Empirical criticisms
Social constructionist theory is premised empirically on social anthropological and new social historical study. Studies particularly include anthropological analysis of the North American Berdache and Margaret Mead's studies of Samoan society, Foucault's inversion of Victorian history, Alan Bray's analysis of Medieval and Renaissance society, and Jonothan Katz's historical account of American society

(see Bray, 1982; Foucault, 1978; Katz, 1976; Mead, 1977; Ortner and Whitehead, 1981). These studies highlight the significance of variation in sexual practices and attitudes across time and space and therefore promote the importance of the social, as opposed to the natural or individual, in these processes in particular. Critically significant though these studies are, they are still hardly exhaustive of the whole of time and space. Particularly significant are the continuities across time and space in the near universal oppression of same-sex identities, if not same-sex practices, and the overwhelming oppression of same-sex feeling in western societies (see Altman et al., 1989). The variation in responses is therefore limited from damnation to mild legitimation, yet never includes full parity or acceptance. Most importantly, the point of continuity of oppression requires explanation it tends not to receive in these, or other, studies.

Political criticisms
Social constructionist theory is criticised as sexist in its primarily gay male focus and racist in its western focus (Coveney *et al*, 1984; Stanley, 1984; Trumbach, 1989; Wieringa, 1989). However, each of these situations is not intrinsically or necessarily the case and may potentially lose importance within a modification of social constructionist theory. The real difficulties, then, centre on: first, an issue of power which endlessly slips into control or regulation; and second, a lack of analysis of subjective experiences of oppression (Van Den Boogaard, 1989; Schippers, 1989). For example, try telling a victim of rape it helps to know it was 'socially constructed'. Importantly, whilst social constructionism offers the potential to say that what is constructed is deconstructed and then reconstructed, this has yet to appear in practical or political terms. More importantly still, social constructionism can slip into conservative ideology as the notion of 'curing' homosexuality returns with the equal notion that the homosexual can 'corrupt' or construct others in the name of social constructionism, due to equal elements of constructionist and essentialist thinking in the opposition surrounding gay sexuality (see Epstein, 1988).

What this situation in total amounts to is a messy and complex oscillating from essentialism to constructionism within the theoretically limited confines of each. The crunch is also that it is, in itself, another dualism in a series of studies already sweating under the weight of at least one too many. The theory proposed here is therefore 'critically constructionist' as it accepts central tenets of

[9]

constructionism though with a rather more critical viewpoint upon its complexities and limits.

Gay studies/women's studies/men's studies

To make such an argument as outlined earlier demands more than a mere résumé of gay studies. Gay studies, that is to say gay men's studies, has traditionally found it difficult to come to terms with the importance of gender as well as sexual identity. The reason for this situation is clearly located in a fear of effeminate stereotypes particularly predominant in the 1950s period prior to gay liberation. The problem has primarily been dealt with by bunching lesbianism and feminism together and therefore leaving out attention to the gendering of gay men or by ignoring gender, feminism and lesbianism lock, stock and barrel.[3]

One, problematic, exception has been the study of gay male clone culture or machismo where the interconnection of gay sexuality and masculine gender identity is particularly clear (Bersani, 1988; Blachford, 1981; Edwards, 1990; Gough, 1989; Marshall, 1981). A second, and equally problematic exception has been the rise of separatist lesbianism so blindingly against gay men's gender sexism that lesbianism almost becomes a by-product of a particular kind of cultural feminism (Coveney et al., 1984; Jeffreys, 1990; Stanley, 1982). Lesbian feminism has paid more attention to the connections of gender and sexuality, though, in the form of femininity and lesbianism (Daly, 1979; Rich, 1984). Feminism has similarly had a lot to say, mostly critical, concerning women's experience of male sexuality (for example, Dworkin, 1981, 1987). This is not the same as an analysis of masculinity, though, and there is a clear tension of internal (male) and external (female) perspectives on the issue, primarily explored through the men's studies of the 1970s and more recently in the 1990s.[4]

The difficulty concerns the reconciling of gender studies (traditionally studying men and women) with women's studies (usually studies of women only) as gender studies in the 1970s tended to generalise and gloss over sexual inequalities and, more recently, have tended to simply collapse into women's studies of women.[5] In addition, men's studies as a reaction to second-wave feminism on various levels were critical of masculinity in many ways, though profoundly uncritical of the role of sexuality in masculine identity, particularly the component of heterosexuality, and excluded consideration of gay studies' significant critique of the naturalness of (any) sexuality (see Carrigan et al., 1985).

[10]

The difficulty here, then, is in trying to draw on three different sets of studies or perspectives when the tensions within as well as across them are so colossal. Consequently, it is not my intention to simply stick them together, rather to find interfaces of conflict or consensus on certain issues as they occur historically.

Tensions, intentions and definitions
In this section, I wish to set out some of the main tensions that dominate the rest of the text as well as some of my main intentions and definitions.

Tensions
First, I would highlight three tensions or dualisms that tend to dominate the academic literature concerning gender and sexuality:

(1) Liberalism vs. radicalism: the first of these concerns the extent to which change and progress is located within or outside of the existing social, economic or political system. Liberalism seeks to maintain yet ameliorate the existing system for certain citizens, or merely amend the system to maintain certain aims and therefore change the system from within; whilst radicalism sees the system itself as the problem and seeks to change the system itself from within and without in whatever way works.

(2) Reformism vs. revolutionism: the previous tension is partly reflected in the second tension of reformism and revolutionism, or the primarily political question of creating rights and equality within a given system or the attempt to counter-culturally and ideologically impose an alternative system. This is also partly a question concerning socialism or the extent to which the sexual and/or gender order can change within the present capitalist system. These first two tensions or dualisms are well-known to anyone active, directly or indirectly, politically and academically.

(3' Sexual politics vs. politics of sexuality: the third dualism of sexual politics and the politics of sexuality is perhaps the most important and one which is unpacked in Chapter 2. The distinction is one of an emphasis upon seeing sexuality as a site or heightened example of gender oppression or upon seeing sexuality as a site of oppression in itself within an overall social system. Gay male studies have traditionally aligned

[11]

themselves with the latter and feminism with the former, although the distinction is not as hard and fast as this, as some socialist feminism in particular supports a politics of sexuality approach (see for example, Vance, 1984).

These tensions are the outcome of academic and political developments which are still continuing today. It is not my intention to take sides or even to seek resolutions to these tensions, rather to expose their sticking points and contradictions.

Intentions

Other tensions are related to the intentions of the text which are tiered on several levels. On the first level, the text is simply a critical overview of contemporary sexual-political history, paying particular attention to gay liberation. On a second level, the text critically seeks to find an interface of gay sexuality with gender identity, academically, in the form of an interface of gay studies with feminism and, personally, through the use of personal opening introductions. In addition, though, I am not trying to set up a new personal-theoretical trajectory or standpoint, rather to simply acknowledge that many theoretical or political points do have a personal aspect or origin. Third, the text most ambitiously seeks to dismantle some assumptions common within gay studies and feminism and produce an analysis or perspective which is neither gay affirmative nor pro-feminist, rather gay affirmative *and* pro-feminist. This ultimately paves the way to an agenda for an erotic politics as a potential political strategy and an academic standpoint.

Definitions

Part of developing this alternative standpoint also involves some specific or different definitions of primary concepts. I use the concept of sexuality to refer to sexual orientation or sexual preference only whilst the term gender merely refers to masculinity and femininity (or androgyny) only. The terms gay community and gay studies primarily refer to the gay male community and gay men's studies though may apply to the lesbian community and lesbian studies. Similarly, the terms gay and lesbian studies and the gay and lesbian community refer to both groups equally. Conversely, discussion of lesbians and the lesbian community does not include reference to gay men or the gay male community. More conventionally, I use the term gay to imply a post-gay liberation politically identified identity, whilst the term homosexual merely means same-sex feeling or an identity pre-gay liberation. In addition, the terms social, economic and political are used frequently to refer to three conceptually distinct, yet in practice connected, spheres of life: first, social values, practices and ways of living; second, economic modes of production, capitalism or other monetary exchange systems; and third, political parliamentary or personal ideologies. These three areas are commonsensically inter-linked yet conceptually distinct. The cultural sphere refers primarily to that which is predominantly left out of the other three, particularly including the arts, advertising, consumerism, the media and philosophical ideas and is of primary importance to the theory of postmodernity. Postmodernity theory is considered more fully in Chapter 8.

CHAPTER 1

Coming out, coming together

Coming out is a modern concept, yet its practice involves levels of difficulty that have a very long history: fears of rejection, isolation, confusion, categorisation, of making the wrong decision, of the limits of identity. Coming out for me was a slow, often painful, often confusing, sometimes exhilarating process of experience: not a sudden development. My parents suspected I was not the latest edition of contemporary heterosexual conformity soon after I entered primary school as I stubbornly dumped footballs, played with little girls instead of little boys, and developed a talent at drawing pictures. Consequently, homosexuality was a possibility prior to puberty, a probability during adolescence as girlfriends never did appear, and definite, if difficult, after it. The difficulty was my infatuation with women emotionally and my constant hankering after first one man and then another sexually. Isolation ensued. The solution of sorts came to me, like many others of my middle-class, well-educated generation, in going to university. As an undergraduate, I joined the gay soc and went on the scene and, as a postgraduate, I threw the closet door open completely, launched myself into gay studies and proclaimed myself as an openly gay student and class teacher. The support of a gay supervisor, other gay or lesbian lecturers and students and, overall, a tolerant or 'right on' department more than helped. I also stopped living in households where there was less than support or acceptance of homosexuality which usually meant living with other gay men. Following this through into the 'real world' of work and 'making it' as a single man with discrimination and without some of the economic benefits of heterosexual coupledom is a problem, not insurmountable, but a problem . . .

Homosexuality is perceived to be a 'problem' for society. Similarly, society is perceived to be a 'problem' for homosexuals and homosexuality. Something, apparently, has to be done about them and something, consequently, has to be done by them about the problems imposed upon them, and this is the double bind of this book.

[14]

The making of the modern homosexual

> Homosexuality in this culture is a stigma label. To be called a 'homosexual' is to be degraded, denounced, devalued or treated as different. It may well mean shame, ostracism, discrimination, exclusion or physical attack. It may simply mean that one becomes an 'interesting curiosity of permissiveness'. But always, in this culture, the costs of being known as a homosexual must be high.
>
> (Plummer, 1975: 175)

The state does not create homosexuality, yet it does seek to construct its significance, regulate and control it and indeed, all sexuality, though most vehemently male homosexuality. Male homosexual practices have occurred across all centuries in all societies, yet the male homosexual identity and more particularly the gay man and the gay community are a more recent phenomenon.[1] Importantly, the universality of male homosexuality has received the most culturally specific of societal reactions from mild legitimation to wild damnation. Male homosexuality has, however, never received an acceptance, parity, or an equality with heterosexuality. The irony of identity politics is that in creating an opposition to state oppression, the state's power to define and regulate sexuality is inadvertently increased; yet not to have an identity is to retreat into defeat, retire into obscurity, or even vanish into invisibility. Consequently, the question becomes one not of 'identity or not' but of 'what identity, where, why and how'? Most of the contemporary literature on sexual politics and male homosexuality sees identity as a culturally specific necessity and the question of causality or consequence constantly collapses into a mere lauding of identity, or at least a plurality of identities, *per se*.[2] It is to this question, then, of the hows and whys, rights and wrongs, pros and cons, of identity which I will most particularly consider here.

The history of homosexuality

> Homosexuality has existed throughout history, in all types of society, among all social classes and peoples, and it has survived qualified approval, indifference and the most vicious persecution. But what have varied enormously are the ways in which various societies have regarded homosexuality, the meanings

[15]

they have attached to it, and how those who were engaged in homosexual activity viewed themselves.

(Weeks, 1977: 2)

The history of homosexuality is highly loaded with anachronistic, technical and interpretive difficulties on several levels. First, in the question of definition and conceptualisations of sexuality, as already pointed out, they are culturally specific and located in time and space. Consequently, what's 'gay' today wasn't yesterday or isn't in another society and so on. Second, this leads on to a question of reinterpretation of the past, or even reinvention, when the actors concerned are silenced and can no longer speak and give their meanings and interpretations of themselves and their situation. Third, this leads to a difficulty concerning actual sources which increase in sparsity and speciousness the further afield one steps or the further one rewinds the clock.

However, a couple of texts in particular have tried to provide an overall perspective on the whole history of homosexuality: first, David Greenberg's *The Construction of Homosexuality* (1988); and second, Duberman et al.'s edited collection *Hidden from History* (1989). The difficulty of each lies in the potential loss of perspective across such a wide canvas. Consequently, the question then centres on more specific studies of sexuality and these include work on the Greco-Roman empire's forms of sexual practice (Eglinton, 1971) and Medieval and Renaissance England (Bray, 1982).

Moreover, far and away the most well-documented period of history is that of approximately the past one hundred years in England and America and, to a slightly lesser extent, Europe, primarily through the work of new social historians (Adam, 1987; Altman, 1971, 1982; D'Emilio, 1983; Katz, 1976; Weeks, 1977, 1981, 1985), all of whom share varieties on the same socially constructionist perspective on sexuality and tend to highlight similar sets and points of development although they may emphasise the importance of different points in time and space.[3]

To summarise this study, the history of homosexuality in western society over the previous century is crudely classified here, using my terminology, into five interrelated phases or developments: damnation, criminalisation, medicalisation, regulation, and reform. Moreover, there is perhaps a sixth developing at present following the medico-political impact of the AIDS epidemic (see Chapter 7). Importantly, all of these phases or developments not only interact and connect, they, to an extent at least, coexist and are all in evidence, alive and kicking, in today's contemporary society. The question centres then, more on the rise and fall of these developments and of their dominance or decline. Consequently, artificial as they are, they remain valid heuristic devices.

Damnation

The history of the sacred control of sexuality is sparse to say the least and distinctly anachronistic, though nonetheless often considered significant.[4] Consequently, the rise of Judaeo-Christian religions and, in particular, Protestantism and Catholicism, is often seen as instrumental in forming some of the first moves in legitimating certain forms of sexuality and condemning others, fostering fears and fuelling hostilities towards those 'other' sexualities.

This essentially started with the Reformation of the Church in the early part of the second millennium. In aiming to control and regulate its own wayward activities it inadvertently led to later control and regulation of activities throughout the rest of the society. Specific codes and condemnation depended on the conditions of the particular doctrine in question, though what they all had in common was a series of prohibitions against non-procreative forms of sexuality such as sexual pleasure *per se*, prostitution, extramarital sex, and (male) homosexuality in the form of same-sex practices and particularly sodomy. Women's sexuality was controlled more through marital mores, male power and prostitution, and effectively rendered non-existent unless directed towards men, although the persecution of witches in the fifteenth and sixteenth centuries is frequently regarded as indicative of control of women's sexuality.[5] Consequently, this meant that homosexuality was a sin, an abomination, a crime against nature and worthy of damnation. It is important to point out, though, that this applied to practices and not people: there were no 'homosexuals' and practices were also defined retrospectively as 'homosexual' in terms involving same-sex relations and, in particular, sodomy.

Criminalisation

From 1885 to 1967 all male homosexual acts and male homosexuality in England and Wales as set out in law were completely illegal. The criminalisation of male homosexuality came with Section 11 of the Criminal Law Amendment Act of 1885 which sought to reaffirm moral and social order within an outbreak of concern over national identity in the uproar over Home Rule for Ireland and the decline of the Empire, city lifestyles and contamination, and the overall political perception of sexual depravity. Male homosexuality was one target among many, the others particularly including prostitution, soliciting, and an outcry over public decency and public health following the Contagious Diseases Acts of the 1860s. Underlying all of this were patterns of development in industrialisation, urbanisation and social stratification. The working class were increasingly militant, middle-class women involved in purity campaigns were increasingly opposed to male sexuality, and cities were creating their own problems in maintaining order and decency in anonymity.

Prior to the Amendment, the only act of law which applied in any way directly to homosexuality was the law on sodomy, part of the 1533 Act of Henry VIII, a law which was applied with varying degrees of vigilance in convictions and sentences due to the need to produce proof of entry and ejaculation, a situation which was worsened in the early nineteenth century when Sir Robert Peel dropped the need to prove ejaculation and reinstated the death sentence in 1826. Curiously, sodomy was still an ill-defined concept, on occasions conflated with concepts of procreation, contraception or oral sex. The death sentence was effectively outlawed from the 1930s onwards having been removed from the statute book in 1861 and replaced by hard labour, particularly for those in the armed services commonly seen as a particular problem in maintaining social order due to the ideologies of contagion and seduction surrounding confined same-sex environments.[6] The death penalty was, however, only dropped completely in the nineteenth century to make way for a wider net of state regulation of sexuality.

Medicalisation

More or less simultaneously with the criminalisation of male homosexuality, came its medicalisation. Whilst homosexual practices had existed for centuries, the notion of a specific homosexual person did not appear until the late nineteenth century when a Swiss doctor, Karoly Maria Benkert, formally coined the term in 1869 and it developed into more common parlance in the 1890s. At the same time, clinical psychology was expanding its role as a science seeking to explain human variations in sexuality through experiments and studies of patients in terms of medical-psychological models of causality. Krafft-Ebing's *Psychopathia Sexualis* (1886) was a classic in this sense as a series of clinical case studies used to develop a scientific understanding of sexuality. Consequently, a whole series of codes and

[18]

categories were created to cover every perversion, fetish and sexual turn-on, from fetishism to sado-masochism, and from precept to practice. Significantly, sexual orientation in itself and sexual orientations were in the making and these included homosexuality. Havelock Ellis, the most significant sex scientist in England at the time, created the notion of *Sexual Inversion* (1897) used to define male homosexuality in a similar way to Karl Heinrich Ulrich's coining of the term 'Urning' or 'Uranian' in Germany to categorise the situation of having a 'feminine soul in a male body'.

In addition, the problematic implication of this was the conjunction of male homosexuality with effeminacy, conflating sexuality and gendered identity. Thus, these theories tended to, on one level, pathologise the homosexual as someone sick or medically ill or in need of treatment: 'If the law and its associated penalties made homosexuals into outsiders, and religion gave them a high sense of guilt, medicine and science gave them a deep sense of inferiority and inadequacy' (Weeks, 1977: 31).

This similarly also led to governmental regulation of sexuality, particularly in high places, and the Oscar Wilde trials of the late nineteenth century were a prominent example of a political moral panic simultaneously stigmatising, pathologising and regulating the newly defined male homosexual as part of maintaining the status quo of sexual and class inequality.

Regulation
The two world wars created a crisis economically and socially in re-creating national wealth and reasserting social order. In addition, they had contradictory effects on homosexual communities. On one level, they inadvertently fuelled the homosexual community in creating the opportunity for furthering same-sex relations within the confines of specific collectivities.[6] However, on another level, the second world war led to the decimation of some gay communities, particularly in Germany under the Third Reich and concentration camps where the pink triangle was used to signify homosexuality and implied a high placing on the list of exterminations and, moreover, meant above-averagely barbaric behaviours against homosexuals nationwide documented powerfully in Richard Plant's *The Pink Triangle* (1987). The pink triangle is now an international gay and lesbian symbol of both grieving for lost brothers and sisters and of opposition to oppression.[7]

[19]

The Wolfenden Committee and its report in 1957, recommending the decriminalisation of male homosexuality and imposing in turn its regulation through 'privatisation' (i.e. legalising it in private only) and limiting the age of consent to twenty-one, therefore protecting innocent minors and children, was a reaction to the problem of reasserting social order as part of an economic and political moral panic. The lead up to Wolfenden was one of increasing change: gradual acceleration of economic growth, the changing form of family life to more and smaller households, the increasing participation of women in the workforce, the separation of sex from procreation through the developing production of contraception finalised in the pill in the 1960s, and the development of sexual consumerism, marketing and recreation.

In addition, a political time bomb went off when Burgess and Maclean, two known homosexual diplomats, defected to the Soviet Union. On top of this, the high public profile of the Montagu-Wildebloode trial created a political panic and an explosion of consciousness and concern over sexuality, particularly in high diplomatic places.

Similarly, Kinsey and his associates' notorious reports and publication of *Sexual Behaviour in the Human Male* in 1948 created an outcry concerning the surprisingly high prevalence of male homosexual activities. These activities took place in conjunction with the increasingly efficacious use of policing systems and agents provocateurs in controlling the developing male homosexual community, particularly in large cities and London, leading to an alarming increase in male homosexual prosecutions.[8]

Thus, the Wolfenden Committee in turn sought to preserve moral decency and protect the innocent from corruption. Importantly, the laws on prostitution and paedophilia were also tightened up as in the Amendment of the previous century. Consequently, it was a highly loaded ideology of tea and sympathy combined with an objectification and curious collusion of male homosexuality, prostitution and paedophilia as particular 'social problems'.

Reform
The paradox of the criminalisation, medicalisation and state regulation of sexuality, and particularly male homosexuality, was to produce those sexualities as entities and identities around which individuals could define themselves and others and what is more, with sufficient initiative, form collectives according to that identity. Consequently,

the nineteenth and twentieth centuries had also seen an escalation in sexually defined collectivities taking advantage of city anonymity to form meetings, groups and social gatherings in the form of an underground network of wink of eye and word of mouth. These meetings, groups and gatherings were prone to any kind of intrusion from the outside world from which they sought to separate themselves or reclaim space from, in the form of economic difficulties, individual attacks and raids of premises. Their function was, and is, mostly socio-sexual rather than political, though, on top of this, as part of the same simultaneous counter-reaction to the same series of social, economic and political processes, some of them did develop into politically motivated middle-class reform groups.

The paradoxical collusion of medical and state definitions is critical in these processes as those scientists who medicalised male homosexuality and invented the category were often the same men who sought to oppose the criminalisation of that category. Consequently, J.A. Symonds, Havelock Ellis and Edward Carpenter each produced writings which not only sought to explain sexuality in medical scientific terms, they also sought to normalise homosexuality and promote and campaign for reform. Magnus Hirschfeld in Germany had used the idea of a 'third sex' to term the situation of a male–female, masculine–feminine combination in one body, and Edward Carpenter in England had similarly used the idea of an *Intermediate Sex* (1908). These men, though, were equally important parties in setting up the Society for Law Reform premised on the idea that if one could not change a medical condition one should at least ameliorate its social position. Thus, the British Society for the study of Sex Psychology (BSSP) was set up in 1914 with Edward Carpenter as its president seeking to provide a forum for study and a political collectivity. This collectivity and work expanded on to an international scale with connections to parallel developments in Germany where Magnus Hirschfeld had set up a Scientific Humanitarian Committee for sexual reform in 1897, and, in 1928, the World League for Sexual Reform (WLSR) was established.

The problems these groups faced in terms of social and political opposition were enormous and a measure of the depth of the oppression of homosexuality at the time. Moreover, the problems within these groups were problems which are repeated today in tensions between liberalism and radicalism, reform and revolution, the crunch being the attempt to maintain middle-class respectability and produce acceptability as well as personal protection against permanent

[21]

oppression and potential persecution. The validity of science was ultimately the main means of providing legitimation for the reform of the law on male homosexuality. However, it would require an ironic inversion of debates about public decency to produce the final reform. Moreover, Wolfenden, as part of an economic and political moral panic as previously outlined, inadvertently provided the final step in defining male homosexuality as a social problem thus producing similarly social, as opposed to sacred or medical, solutions. Consequently, it fuelled and fed the conditions for reform and the Homosexual Law Reform society was set up in 1958 by A.E. Dyson and others of academic distinction. Thus, pressures, props, scripts, actors and conditions in place, the stage was set for . . .

An act of tolerance

Law reform came, at last, to England and Wales in 1967. When it arrived, mild and aetiolated, the walls shoring up society did not collapse.

(Weeks, 1977: 156)

The 1967 Sexual Offences Act was an act of tolerance, compromise and reform, not of acceptance, victory and revolution. The legislation, derived from over a decade of intense discussion, merely legalised male homosexual activities in England and Wales, excepting Scotland and Northern Ireland. Moreover, the merchant navy, armed forces and diplomatic services were all excluded and declaration of homosexuality was, and is, sufficient evidence for unconditional dismissal.[9] The most important points of all though were: first, the age of consent set at twenty-one, five years higher than the heterosexual equivalent; and second, the restriction of activities to 'in private', thus still ensuring that laws continued to cover issues such as gross indecency and public order.

In addition, the definition of 'in private' was particularly strict, referring to any activity where a third party was present and not necessarily in the same part of the property. Consequently, if you and your partner were over twenty-one at home alone and kept the curtains closed and the noise down you were within the law; if anyone saw you, if you were caught so much as holding hands on entering the front door, you were not. What is more, the situation is still exactly the same, or worse, twenty-five years later.[10]

Thus, the underlying ideologies behind both Wolfenden and the final law reform were not the liberation of homosexuality but its regulation under a different guise. As if finally seeing the paradox of producing such highly visible and definable groupings, the attempt was made to reinvisibilise homosexuality by taking it out of the statute book where possible without losing a grip on public decency. The difficulty for the guardians of decency and order, though, was that the wheels of a militant community were already set in motion over a century ago and it was all far too late . . .

Gay liberation

> Gay liberation transformed homosexuality from a stigma that one kept carefully hidden into an identity that signified membership in a community organising for freedom.
>
> (D'Emilio, 1983: 247)

Gay liberation began in Britain in 1970 but it was born in the United States a year or so earlier, built on the foundations of the reform movements first developed in the previous century. Consequently, its impact was profound and deeply political though only interpreted as all the more important in comparison with its past. Its most primary impact was upon coming out and in creating a new politics centred around identity which were set to dominate the 1970s and the 1980s. Particularly important in this are UK–USA comparisons.

UK–USA comparisons
North America's position as the 'superpower' of western society and as the epitome of consumer capitalism, individualism and freedom of expression invoking imagery of the 1950s American dream, glamour, fame, California and Hollywood, created a connection of America at the level of individual fantasy and social ideology with particular forms of sexuality, including gay sexuality (see Hearn and Melechi, 1992). The sheer size and diversity of the United States, geographically and culturally, temporally and spatially, presented particular problems for the maintenance of social, economic, and political order. In addition, and moreover, of profound importance in this are the processes of industrialisation and the development of city life in re-creating the separation of 'public' and 'private' as discrete spheres and as a set of increasingly sectarian distinctions through which the

simultaneous processes of sexual diversification and specialisation could operate.

Particularly significantly, the McCarthy era of 'commies and queers' in the 1950s, an interesting association in itself illustrating the ideological connection of capitalism and some forms of homosexuality, was an important example of a domineering attempt to reassert control in the face of this increasing diversity. This was not directed so much towards the 'doing your duty' and 'stiff upper lip' puritanism and Protestant Work Ethic historical traditions in the UK, as much as an aggressive assault on the association of maleness, physical power and patriotism. This has an important relationship with the comparative UK–USA constructions of masculinity in terms of mind–body dualisms of repression and expression, stereotypically exemplified in the form of masculinity implied in a cold bath (Britain) or a hot shower (America):

> The list is endless – and the requirements exacting. Men stand up straight, queers go limp. Men walk firmly, poofs just prance about. Men are tough (this is a Nixon favourite), fags and bleeding heart liberals are soft. Men are cool – particularly under fire – while cissies become hysterical. Men go into the army, nervous nellies stay at home.
>
> (Hoch, 1979: 86)

Whilst intensely masculine male sexuality was and is socially acclaimed in America in its endless production of highly sexualised heroes from Cary Grant to Kevin Costner, male homosexuality was and is still severely castigated as a sign of weakness.[11]

However, reform movements, as in England and Europe, were developed in opposition to the oppression of male homosexuality in the United States. The formation of the Mattachine Society, a development of an overall homophile movement dating back to the Bachelors for Wallace group founded in 1948 who supported the Progressive Party candidate in California Henry Wallace, by Henry Hay in 1951 at Los Angeles, California, was an immensely closeted affair carried out along the structured lines of Communist secrecy. It primarily sought to develop a positive homosexual identity in terms of state parities with heterosexuality as the oppression of homosexuality in the United States varies significantly from state to state legally and socially. Similarly, the Daughters of Bilitis group was formed in San Francisco in 1955 to fight for some rights of lesbians.

Moreover, though, the Homophile Movement, although larger, more strongly organised and more powerful, as a whole suffered similar problems of liberal respectability as in Britain. D'Emilio says, quite convincingly: 'Although the discontinuities between pre- and post-Stonewall eras are glaring and undeniable, the tendency of liberationists to dismiss their forbears has obscured how much they owed the homophile effort and how much it achieved' (D'Emilio, 1983: 240). This is true, though it is also a measure of the intensity of the oppression of homosexuality in North America that the Homophile Movement still did not achieve more.

Importantly, male homosexuality in America remains in a paradoxical position due to the scope of practices and constraints across states: the positive developments surrounding sexuality in parts of California and New York contrast sharply with the severe vilification of homosexuality in the deep South and central states of America. Consequently, it is not surprising that gay liberation began and developed to its peak in New York and San Francisco, not Florida and Ohio; or that whilst many gay men emigrated to such states in the 1970s, the United States as a whole is still deeply hostile towards homosexuality.

The Stonewall Rebellion and the formation of the Gay Liberation Front

On Friday June 27, 1969, shortly before midnight, two detectives from Manhattan's Sixth Precinct set off with a few other officers to raid the Stonewall Inn, a gay bar on Christopher Street in the heart of Greenwich Village.

(D'Emilio, 1983: 231)

The Stonewall Inn, a backstreet, unlicensed centre for blacks, 'scantily clad go-go boys', drag queens, and drug trafficking, was a regular target for police raids. Police raids of homosexual premises were not uncommon and, in fact, they had been increasing in frequency and vociferousness since the second world war. The difference was that this time the blacks, go-go boys, and drag queens fought back. Quite literally, limp wrists turned into fists. Graffiti, fighting, raiding, vandalism, and looting followed and the Stonewall Inn on Christopher Street was soon burned to the ground in defiance of the police and in a grand and glorious, riotous assertion of gay power. Within a month, the Gay Liberation Front (GLF) was formed. It was started in the

[25]

West Village, New York, and within weeks was spreading like wildfire through every major city and state in North America.

It is particularly easy to see this as a sudden and totally unexpected development and it is important to point out though that, conversely, America was already politically 'highly inflammable' and ready and waiting for the spark that was Stonewall: 'The Stonewall riot was able to spark a nationwide grassroots "liberation" effort among gay men and women in large part because of the radical movements that had so influenced much of American youth during the 1960s' (D'Emilio, 1983: 233).

These movements and groups particularly included the civil rights movement, the student movement, the women's movement, peace movements, black group protests developing out of the political activism of Martin Luther King, and the overall opposition to Vietnam in the wake of political controversy concerning the Kennedy assassinations.

The crucial distinction between the Mattachine Society in America or the reform movement in Britain and gay liberation was the assertion of self-worth, the validity to be oneself privately and publicly. Slogans included: 'Gay is good', 'Gay is proud', 'Gay is love', or even 'Blatant is beautiful'; symbols of an exhilaration borne out of reaction to centuries of repression. Consequently, gay liberation also signalled the birth of 'being gay' as the word 'gay' was used as a blatant assertion of positive self-evaluation over the medical, pathologised label of homosexual. For example, writers for the New York pamphlet 'Come Out' proclaimed: 'WE ARE GOING TO BE WHO WE ARE'.

Coming out was consequently reconstructed to mean 'coming out' (of closets) and 'coming together' (in unity). The terminology was a deliberate, double ambiguity: coming (sexually), coming out (personally) and coming together (politically). The conjunction of the personal and political was no coincidence and was developed from a similar conjunction with other political groups, particularly women's groups, who sought to prove that 'the personal is political'. As a result, coming out was now seen to work on three levels rather than merely one or two: first, telling oneself that one is attracted to the same sex and homosexual or gay in identity; second, telling others who are of the same identity in a safe, usually homosexually exclusive space; and third, and here there is the difference, telling the wider and usually straight society of family, friends and workplace.

This tripartite approach to coming out developed into a similarly triple-tiered approach to oppression perceived as practised on three levels: first, in discrimination in relation to inequality at home or at work in terms of rights, opportunities and protection; second, in coercion or hostility including raids and assaults; and third, most controversially, the notion of tolerance as a form of oppression as opposed to an acceptance of difference. This factor was partly rooted in radicalism and an opposition to the liberalism of the 1960s and partly in the tension of reform and revolution.

It was also an attack on the previous reform movements which had 'merely' sought to attain equal rights for homosexuals rather than transform the whole of society, and also on the growing wave of 1960s permissiveness that was perceived to simply smooth over homosexuality as part of hippy-type culture and refused to recognise the structural inequalities and difficulties surrounding gay sexuality. Controversy centres on whether this criticism of previous reform movements was indeed correct or fair given the deeply oppressive conditions these groups operated under as illegal as well as stigmatised citizens and, moreover, it ignored the question of their contribution to gay liberation through providing many of the props, scripts and sites through which the new movement could operate and develop (D'Emilio, 1983).

The development of gay liberation on an international scale was equally rapid in spreading to Europe and England, located in the interpersonal connections of the previous century that were already made, and the post-war developments of international communications and transport systems were also important.

Gay liberation in Britain

The Gay Liberation Front (GLF) began life in Britain when a meeting was called at the London School of Economics (LSE) on 13 October, 1970, by Aubrey Walter and Bob Mellors who had recently visited the United States. One year later, a GLF Manifesto had been made following the formation of the 'Come Together' pamphlet and a London group formed including: David Fernbach, Tony Halliday, Mary McIntosh, Jeffrey Weeks and Elizabeth Wilson, among others.

The aims were in many ways the same as in the United States, though on a much smaller scale and with a somewhat more rationalised, particularistic approach. Dominant concerns included democratic organisation, gender bending or radical drag, and an assault on certain institutions including, most importantly, the family, education and the media, all seen as equally sexist, heterosexist and oppressive. The opposition to this oppression took the form of 'think ins', 'sit ins',

[27]

demonstrations, and 'alternative' social functions, including con-
sciousness-raising. The Manifesto was put into practice through such
group practices and soon meetings were topping five hundred at the
peak of attendance waves. However, within another year, the Gay
Liberation Front was all but defunct.

A unity of many contradictions

> The individualism which weakened GLF as a movement was
> for many people its greatest achievement.
>
> (Weeks, 1977: 206)

The Gay Liberation Front had been flung together with an essentially
centripetal force and it ultimately flew out and diversified with an
equally centrifugal force. This factor is in fact at the crux of the
contradictions in current politics of sexuality as, positively, the effect
on thousands of young men and women growing up or coming out
in the early 1970s was profound and led to a whole series of networks
of social activities and services founded on a new politicised identity.
The difficulty lay, and still lies, in the overwhelming fragmentation of
the movement into less powerful sets and groups which, when faced
with a concerted attempt to impose some form of oppression such as
in Section 28 or even AIDS, find it very difficult to form long-term,
coherent or collective action.

The reasons for this situation are not difficult to see: first, gay
liberation in asserting the personal is political as its maxim heightened
individual differences and threw them into the heated political arena;
and second, this then centred on two interrelated differences. The
first of these differences lies in the distinct tension between liberalism
and radicalism. A good example of this is the simultaneous overlap
and separation of the Gay Activists Alliance (GAA) and the Gay
Liberation Front (GLF) in the United States of America: 'The Gay
Activists Alliance seeks to find acceptance in present society: the Gay
liberationists are committed to a transformation of that society'
(D'Emilio, 1983: 116).

If this was the situation in the United States of America, the
equivalent situation in England was in the tension between the
liberationist GLF and the more rights-centred CHE (Campaign for
Homosexual Equality) which had developed more directly out of the
original reform movements.[12] Moreover, as numbers were often
small, members often felt torn or oscillated between the two.

There was, however, a second issue. This centred on the question of sexuality itself, seen as some form of political opposition *per se*, or only political as part of or in conjunction with some other form of more structural social, economic and political opposition. The latter standpoint was primarily derived from socialism and was voiced and practised through those already involved and active in socialist movements. The Gay Liberation Front did involve some socialist ideals, particularly at the level of opposition to the family. More importantly, though, it also set up a conflict with the more traditional, party-politically oriented Left, perceived correctly often as not as equally heterosexist in theory and in practice, seeing gay sexuality as an adjunct to the greater cause of class revolution rather than as a valid issue in itself.[13]

Conflict over whether to create an alliance with the Left and if so how far and in what way to take it was a particular point of contradiction and, in practice, conflict erupted over the perception of gay culture itself, often seen as ghettoised and playing a part in consumer capitalism and exploitation. In addition, though, it was also seen as performing an important function as a safe, same-sex, exclusive, socio-sexual meeting place for the developing gay community. The attempts to provide alternatives, for example LSE discos, were successful early on though ultimately fell apart through lack of funding and the overall collapse of the Gay Liberation Front.

Further conflicts and contradictions were likely and started to ensue later over class and race as the early gay liberation activists were mostly, or more or less solely, middle class, well-educated and white. However, the other and most fierce of all contradictions, sexism, was and is the most fundamental of all and forms the focus of the next chapter. To sum up, then, gay liberation was ultimately a unity of many contradictions. In addition, these contradictions around sexuality and politics, race and gender set up the main parameters of discussion for succeeding chapters.

Conclusion: coming out, coming together

For let there be no confusion: the very concept of homosexuality is a social one, as one cannot understand the homosexual experience without recognising the extent to which we have developed a certain identity and behaviour derived from social norms.

(Altman, 1971: 2)

Coming out is a modern concept; yet its practice has a long history. The history of homosexuality is, in a sense, essentially contradictory as the universality of homosexual practices is counterpoised with the cultural specificity of homosexual identities and homosexual communities. Moreover, a further contradiction concerns the simultaneous reform and regulation of male homosexuality through the development of an identity and community in conjunction with medical, legal and state regulation concerning that identity and community. Consequently, in coming out one creates an identity and in coming together one creates a community, and in creating an identity or a community, one also creates and facilitates the foci for the opposition and oppression of that identity and community. Yet not to have an identity or a community in a culture which otherwise actively and passively assumes and normalises heterosexuality as a complete totality and an entity, is to collapse into complete partiality or even non-entity.[14]

The question then centres on the development of that identity through the practices which oppress it and the opposition to those practices and that oppression and, on top of this, to consider the question of the causes of that identity and community, its consequences, its practices and its implications. Previous consideration of the issue has tended to stop at or collapse into the first point of identity per se.[15] Importantly, the purpose of the next seven chapters is to start at that first point and develop to the second point in the question of what identity, where and how and with what implications. To say it is a sexual or political identity is only the starting place.

CHAPTER 2

Sexual politics and the politics of sexuality

My first encounters with feminism were confusing and conflicting: it often seemed to me that masculinity could be as problematic as femininity but this could not be reconciled with men's social, economic and political oppression of women. The problem, though, was that my own resistance to the traditional male sex role and lack of conformity to the expectations of masculinity required explaining and this seemed to impinge upon my sexuality. I clearly did not occupy the same position in relation to women as many men did or at least as I perceived them to do. In addition, my developing homosexuality led me to reconsider men and masculinity in terms of my personal relationships with them. Men could clearly be as problematic as some feminist women made them out to be; I became feminist identified: demonstrations of traditional masculinity and machismo were denounced as divisive, conformist, and even downright misogynist. It made little difference if they were gay or straight, in fact the sexual objectification of some aspects of the gay subculture was worse. However, I was also still aware that many gay men were struggling to come to terms with themselves and their sexuality and some forms of judgemental feminism seemed to damage the situation. In addition, I could not account for the fact that I was still attracted to some forms of masculinity sexually and it was easy to see the alternative positive aspects of gay culture and casual sexual encounters in supporting the development of individual sexuality. Moreover, it became clear that such encounters were not necessarily as masculinist as they seemed and involved affection, consideration, even intimacy. Furthermore, this was not completely incompatible with other states of consciousness or political conviction. However, certain contradictions remained unexplained. In particular, the combination of feminist and gay identification was becoming problematic. Was it or was it not possible to successfully combine them? Consequently, can one create, or put together, a sexual politics with a politics of sexuality? These are the questions, and others, which I shall attempt to answer in this chapter. The personal and the political remain as complex as ever.

The primary purpose of this chapter is to explore and examine the impact of feminism upon gay (male) liberation and lesbianism, both

[31]

academically and politically, although feminism will also inform many
of the subsequent chapters. This chapter is divided into three parts:
first, a discussion of the historical construction of contemporary
interfemale sexuality and lesbianism, as opposed to male homosexuality as outlined in the previous chapter; second, a consideration
of the academic and political tensions at the centre of certain conflicts
within feminism and, indeed, some gay men's studies concerning
sexuality; and third, a consideration of how these tensions then apply
more specifically in practice to interfemale and intermale or lesbian
and gay male sexuality and sexual relations.

Introduction: historical construction

Invisible women

> The truth is that if male homosexuals are the 'twilight men' of
> twentieth century history, lesbians are by and large the 'invisible
> women'.
>
> (Weeks, 1977: 88)

If the primary problem for gay men has been one of the oppression
resulting from overt visibility, the primary problem for lesbians has
been the oppression resulting from covert invisibility. Lesbianism has
never been illegalised though it has been both bitterly attacked and
medicalised.[1] There are several perspectives taken to explain this
situation, all derived from various forms of second-wave feminism:
first, that definitions of women's sexuality are male-controlled and
consequently it is seen as orientated solely towards men or simply
non-existent; second, that it is part of the reproduction of men's rights
in a sexual patriarchy; and third, that it is a product of the development of modern capitalism in producing a public–private split and
consigning women to the private sphere. More importantly, history
is conspicuously masculine, his story. However, women have sought
to recover their past, their roots, their story.

The development of the visible lesbian

Any attentions to women have tended to be, at best, attempts
to constrict them within male models, thus duplicating on a

smaller scale the kinds of work done on gay men, or at worst, footnoting or appendixing mention of women in studies only concerned with men.

(Faraday, 1981: 112)

The majority of literature and evidence concerning 'homosexuality', a supposedly non-sex-specific term, until recent developments within second-wave feminism, was written by men, about men, for men. Whilst homosexual men were increasingly creating underground socio-sexual contact networks and developing an academic understanding of themselves through sexology in the latter part of the nineteenth century, although this was still deeply oppressed and pathologised, women with same-sex feeling still tended to face a silenced non-existence. The domestic development of the private sphere did, however, give some women the opportunity, particularly if they were middle class, to develop 'romantic friendships', well-documented in Lillian Faderman's *Surpassing the Love of Men* (1981), and to start to raise their consciousness and relate to other women on this more covert level.

One of the earliest overt assertions of lesbian existence started in 1928 with the publication of Radclyffe Hall's *The Well of Loneliness*, a novel achieving visibility through notoriety, a court case, and a public scandal comparable with the trials of Oscar Wilde at the end of the previous century. The book's central theme is the life history of Stephen, a tomboy-like, 'masculine' woman who develops a powerful attachment to the pretty, 'feminine' Mary. This relationship is at the heart of the story, quite literally, which ends in tragedy with the marriage of Mary. The 'butch/femme' stereotype is patently present and problematic, but the book was beginning to bring about a visibility of lesbianism in Britain.[2]

Lesbianism was also becoming increasingly visible later in the United States through the development of what Jonothan Katz (1976) calls 'passing women', usually upper-class women who dressed up and 'passed' as men in society, and he points out:

Despite their masculine masquerade, the females considered here can be understood not as imitation men, but as real women, women who refused to accept the traditional, socially assigned fate of their sex, women whose particular revolt took the form of passing as men.

(Katz, 1976: 209)

[33]

In addition, the first and second world wars forced and freed women to relate to other women as opposed to men. This was also partly induced through a more than significant gender differential in the population during and after the wars.[3]

Of profound importance in understanding these processes is the undulating development of the modern women's movement, dating back to the beginnings of industrialisation and the publication of Mary Wollstonecraft's *A Vindication of the Rights of Women* in 1792. The more overt development of the modern women's movement tended to dip in the early to mid-nineteenth century and then developed again through the sexual purity campaigns of the late nineteenth century, culminating in the political activism of the Pankhurst sisters in forming the Women's Social and Political Union (WSPU) in 1903 and leading the Suffrage Movement, eventually securing the vote for women in 1928.[4] On a more covert or individual level, however, women's struggles against sexism have of course been more or less continuous. Significantly, then, the primary impact of these early developments in forming the modern women's movement, apart from attaining certain rights, was to start to raise the consciousness of women and to start to aid an understanding of their oppression. In addition, though, it also started to define and construct the notion of a specifically female sexuality, qualitatively different from men's in terms of a fuller, more sensual and, in fact, very powerful set of feelings, as distinct from the more directive 'drives' of male sexuality. This, in turn, raised the question of the ultimate potential of an interfemale sexuality. Thus, modern lesbianism was beginning to be born.

In addition, many groups and organisations were beginning to be formed by women as well as men. For example, Faderman (1981) points to the importance of literary groups and circles in the late nineteenth and early twentieth centuries in providing the opportunities for women to meet other women of similar sexual or romantic persuasion and also to start to find a voice as well as a room of their own.[5]

Women were, however, at this time also increasingly confronted with the medicalisation of their sexuality through the same rise of science and sexology in the late nineteenth century that had defined male homosexuality outlined previously in Chapter 1.[6] Importantly, similar conflicts developed over the definition of female sexuality as women sought to define themselves as other than female variants on a male theme. Homosexuality implicitly meant male homosexuality and interfemale sexuality was often defined as female homosexuality, implying the same, primarily sexual, terms of precept and practice.[7] Particularly importantly, this sometimes also implied an exposing of women's same-sex feeling across time and space or a continuity of interfemale experience set up in opposition to 'compulsory hetero-sexuality' (Rich, 1984).

Women's groups developed in the post-war period in Europe and the United States in opposition to these processes primarily through the facilitation of feminism. For example, the Daughters of Bilitis (DOB), founded by Del Martin and Phyllis Lyon in San Francisco in 1955 and slightly later in 1958 in New York by Barbara Gittings, formed a parallel development to the formation of the Mattachine Society and an assertion of the dual oppression of femininity and deviant sexuality: the double bind of the lesbian position. In addition, *The Ladder* developed out of this group as a pamphlet aimed at supporting women with same-sex feeling through education and adjustment of these women to fit in with society. Not surprisingly, then, *The Ladder*, which had been established in 1956, collapsed in 1972 under the impact of second-wave feminism.

The formation of gay liberation offered a further opportunity for lesbians to assert their existence. They were often eager to join in gay liberation and ally themselves with gay men, partly out of exploitation of the situation for themselves and partly out of empathy with gay men. 'Gay' initially literally meant gay men and gay women. Within months, though, this statement was being undermined and divisions between gay men and lesbians were becoming chasms; the common cause of supporting an oppressed sexuality was soon seen as naively optimistic due to different sets of interests:

> In being part of the word 'gay' lesbians have spent untold hours explaining to Middle America that lesbians do not worry about venereal disease, do not have sex in public bathrooms, do not seduce small boys, do not go to the baths for flings, do not regularly cruise Castro Street, and do not want to go to the barricades fighting for the lowering of the age of consent for sexual acts.
>
> (Altman, 1982: 179)

In addition, gay men's 'radical drag', a deliberate gender bending, was easily seen, rightly or wrongly, as degrading to women. Gay men, however, often felt maligned and moralised against as an unnecessary

[35]

addition to what remained for them a very significant stigmatisation of their sexuality and sexual expression. Moreover, if gay men were to challenge traditional notions of monogamy and masculinity, then promiscuity and effeminacy offered themselves as very direct alternatives.[8] The question was consequently raised as to the extent of the congruence of lesbian and gay men's experience, or even its existence: 'For gay men the question has fundamentally been about sex, about validating a denied sexuality. In recent discussions on lesbianism, on the other hand, there have been heated exchanges about the necessary connection of a lesbian identity to sexual practice' (Weeks, 1985: 201). As a result, the twin developments of feminism or the women's movement with lesbianism or women's same-sex feeling led to a dualism of positions on the issues of women's, and men's, sexuality and the relationship between lesbianism and feminism.

The second wave of feminism, defined through the works of Simone de Beauvoir (1953), Shulamith Firestone (1970), Betty Friedan (1963), Kate Millett (1971) and Juliet Mitchell (1971), had in turn redefined femininity and the position of women in relation to wider social, economic, and political changes. These consisted in the UK, more positively, of women's increasing participation in the work-force, contraception and some, limited, legislative protection in the Equal Pay Act of 1970 and the Sex Discrimination Act of 1975; and, more negatively, the maintenance of social, economic and political structures of inequality and the persistence of men's oppression of women in nearly all spheres of life.

The influence of second-wave feminism was to problematise the feminine, mothering and the family as repressive institutions and to assert the right to education and work as equal opportunity and equal outcome for women, and to demand freedom from harassment, abuse and exploitation. The slightly later, and particularly American, attack directed specifically at sexuality by Brownmiller (1975), Griffin (1979), and Dworkin (1981) concerning pornography and rape as the theory and practice of the oppression of women, led to the development of a distinct rejection of all male values and activities, in turn creating a politics of separatism: the woman-identified-woman (Morgan, 1977). Moreover, in America, a new, politically motivated perspective developed through the Radicalesbians groups, instigated in the ideas of Ti-Grace Atkinson who argued that lesbianism was to the women's movement what Communism or socialism was to the labour movement (Atkinson, 1974).[9] It became clear that there were two (or more) feminisms and, in addition, this led to the development of a dualism between lesbians pre-feminism and lesbians post-feminism and different forms of combining lesbianism and feminism. More broadly, the problematic relationship of lesbianism and feminism, for some connected and for some separated concerns, echoed a wider series of tensions that in sum make up a sexual politics and a politics of sexuality and the purpose of the next section is to explore these tensions.

Inner tensions

Put most simply, sexual politics are primarily defined as the study and practice of, or opposition to, gender oppression, and the politics of sexuality are defined as the study and practice of or opposition to the oppression of sexuality. These are essentially ideal types and it is important to point out that the distinction is heuristic. The difficulty remains the immense conflict that has tended to develop around the relationship or separation of sexuality and gendered identity. Consequently, this distinction creates the first tension.[10]

Gender oppression vs. sexual oppression

Sexuality, then, is a form of power. Gender, as socially constructed, embodies it, not the reverse. Women and men are divided by gender, made into sexes as we know them, by the social requirements of heterosexuality, which institutionalizes male sexual dominance and female sexual submission. If this is true, sexuality is the lynchpin of gender inequality.

(MacKinnon, 1982: 19)

The tension of gender oppression versus sexual oppression is primarily one of emphasis. For some women (and men) gender, or maleness–femaleness and masculinity–femininity, is the primary mechanism through which women's (and some men's) sexuality is oppressed and sexuality is important only as a heightened example, site, or lynchpin of gender oppression. For example, male sexuality is seen as socially controlling or more simply as power over women in the form of sexual violence or rape. Primary exponents of this position include most radical feminists (see Brownmiller, 1975; Morgan, 1977; Millett, 1971), though some see sexuality as located in a more materialist or

Marxist context (see Delphy, 1984; Firestone, 1970; MacKinnon, 1982, 1987a, 1987b), most more cultural feminists (Daly, 1979; Griffin, 1979, 1981) and nearly all revolutionary feminists including Andrea Dworkin (1981, 1987) and the work of Sheila Jeffreys (1990) and the Women Against Violence Against Women (WAVAW) group.[11]

Primary exponents of the politics of sexuality point out alternatively that sexuality is itself a system of oppression operated semi-autonomously of gendered identity:

> Sex is a vector of oppression. The system of sexual oppression cuts across other modes of sexual inequality, sorting out individuals and groups according to its own intrinsic dynamics. It is not reducible to, or understandable in terms of, class, race, ethnicity, or gender.
>
> (Rubin, 1984: 293)

Most importantly, they point to the dominance of heterosexual, procreative or monogamous sexuality over homosexual, fetishistic or promiscuous sexuality. Consequently, gay male sexuality is seen more sympathetically as part of a political structuring of deviant sexualities and erotic minorities, whilst the gender oriented or sexual political perspective is fiercely denounced as morally conservative and an anti-sex discourse. In addition, Gayle Rubin in 'Thinking sex: notes for a radical theory of the politics of sexuality' asserts: 'A radical theory of sex must identify, describe, explain, and denounce erotic injustice and sexual oppression' (Rubin, 1984: 275). Whilst Gayle Rubin is one of the main proponents of this position, most gay male writers adopt this perspective including Ken Plummer (1975, 1981) and Jeffrey Weeks (1985, 1986) and some more socialist feminists are also sympathetic towards it including Cindy Patton (Patton, 1985; Patton and Kelly, 1987), Lynne Segal (1987, 1990) and Carole Vance (1984).

Sexual domination vs. Sexual variation

The second tension of sexual domination versus sexual variation is again a difference of emphasis connected directly to the tension of gender and sexual oppression. A position emphasising sexual domination points to the importance of sexuality as a site of dominance of men over women in a multitude of ways including sexual definition and conception as well as sexual action and practice, particularly including sexual violence. Alternatively, an emphasis upon sexual variation seeks to deconstruct the idea of any central sexuality and sees validation of sexual diversity as critical theoretically and politically. Proponents of these positions are essentially the same as in the previous tension alternatively explicated as the conflict of pleasure and danger. For example, Carole Vance in her influential edited collection entitled *Pleasure and Danger: Exploring Female Sexuality* (1984) which came from the (in)famous Scholar and Feminist IX conference 'Towards a Politics of Sexuality' held at Barnard College in 1982, states:

> Sexuality is simultaneously a domain of restriction, repression and danger as well as a domain of exploration, pleasure, and agency. To focus only on pleasure and gratification ignores the patriarchal structure in which women act, yet to speak only of sexual violence and oppression ignores women's experience with sexual agency and choice and unwittingly increases the sexual terror and despair in which women live.
>
> (Vance, 1984: 1)

The problem, though, lies in trying to simultaneously juxtapose the two aspects of sexuality: pleasure *and* danger.

Sexual sameness vs. sexual difference

The third tension of sexual sameness versus sexual difference essentially echoes the second tension, though this time more politically. An approach emphasising the importance of sexual sameness points to sexual continuities across time and space and seeks to oppose this through an oppositional politics or an imposition of practices and concepts precisely opposite to the perceived uniform conformity. For example, Adrienne Rich in an important paper, 'Compulsory heterosexuality and lesbian existence', proposes a particularly 'female' concept of sexuality: 'I perceive the lesbian experience as being, like motherhood, a profoundly female experience, with particular oppressions, meanings, and potentialities we cannot comprehend as long as we simply bracket it with other sexually stigmatised existences' (Rich, 1984: 228). Importantly, she proposes two new concepts of inter-female sexuality or lesbianism, the lesbian existence and the lesbian continuum:

> Lesbian existence suggests both the fact of the historical presence of lesbians and our continuing creation of the meaning of that

[39]

existence. I mean the term lesbian continuum to include a range
– through each woman's life and throughout history – of
woman-identified experience; not simply the fact that a woman
has had or consciously desired genital sexual experience with
another woman.

(Rich, 1984: 227)

Similarly, women's sexuality is often seen as an 'essence', or at least as
a separate 'entity', as opposed to a part of all sexuality. It is also seen
primarily as a political opposition to other forms of sexuality, particularly male sexuality, including gay male sexuality.

Conversely, a perspective of sexual difference seeks to validate
sexual difference in order to undermine any kind of sexual sameness
which is equated with sexual dominance. Radical feminists have
attempted to put the former into practice, whilst most socialist feminists and many gay male activists tend to emphasise the latter. It is
particularly important to point out that these three tensions do *not* add
up to, theoretically, a constructionist–essentialist tension or, politically, a liberal–radical dichotomy. For some proponents of sexual
politics, the importance of gender, dominance and sexual sameness
still implies social construction and for some proponents of the
politics of sexuality, sexual variation and erotic difference represent
radical political issues.

In sum, an emphasis upon gender oppression, sexual domination
and sexual sameness potentially compiles a sexual politics whilst an
emphasis upon sexual oppression, sexual variation and sexual difference tends to lead to a politics of sexuality. These tensions are, of
course, on one level at least, necessarily essentially false and contradictory. Gender oppression is an aspect of sexual oppression and vice
versa, whilst sexual domination necessarily relies on some degree of
sexual variation or relations of difference. In addition, various
attempts to transcend or implode these differences have developed
since, particularly as part of post-structuralist theory (see, for example:
Bordo, 1990; Grosz, 1987; Haraway, 1990; Irigaray, 1985; Marks and
DeCourtivron, 1981; Nicholson, 1990). The implications and limits
of these perspectives academically and politically are discussed
primarily in Chapter 8. Importantly, although theoretically contradictory and interdependent, these tensions have still dominated and
informed gay male and lesbian academic writing and political activism,
creating two further tensions centred on related, yet differing, concerns.

Lesbianism–feminism (misogyny) and homosexuality–masculinity (homophobia)

The purpose of this next section is to explore and examine the implications of the various tensions previously outlined in practice, primarily for lesbians and gay men. For lesbians, these tensions tend to boil down to the balancing and integrating, or not, of sexual orientation and political conviction, namely lesbianism and feminism; and for gay men the problem becomes one of balancing and integrating, or not, sexual orientation and gender identity, due to the primarily related yet differing mechanisms of oppression, misogyny and homophobia, that operate in relation to lesbians and gay men respectively.[12] It is particularly important to point out that these are still *tensions* in operation and not simply *positions*. As a consequence, activists and theorists alike are unlikely to consistently 'fit' uniformly into any one category, yet struggle to gain equilibrium whether as lesbians or gay men.

Lesbianism–feminism (misogyny)

Lesbianism and feminism are related, as already outlined, but should not be equated. Consequently, whilst for some lesbians, their lesbianism is primarily an expression of their feminism, for others their feminism is more a facilitation of their lesbianism. This problematic tension of lesbianism and feminism is partly a question of political conviction, reflected in different identities and life histories, and partly an issue of life history and identity reflected in politics: in short, the interplay of the personal and the political. Consequently there is, theoretically at least, a distinct qualitative difference between a female who develops lesbian feeling and later becomes a feminist to facilitate that feeling; and a feminist who, possibly having been heterosexual, becomes a lesbian out of political conviction. Significantly, whilst for some women the two issues are essentially confused and interlinked, for others they are quite distinct and it follows that there are lesbians who are not feminists and feminists who are not lesbians, but some women who are both. This problematic tension of feminism and lesbianism later developed into unpleasant personal and political conflicts in the 1970s and 1980s, and: 'The result has been a rupture amongst self-identifying lesbians between those who see themselves first and foremost as feminists, who see their politics as reflected in their lesbianism: and those who identify as lesbians whose political expression may or may not be feminism' (Weeks, 1985: 202).

The primary problem facing lesbians, all lesbians, is misogyny or the oppression of women's sexuality, particularly an autonomous women's sexuality separated from men's, and this includes gay male misogyny. Jalna Hanmer argues: 'Even though gay men face discrimination in society, it does not reduce the structural and personal privilege their maleness gives in relation to women' (Hanmer, 1990: 30). However, this separation of discrimination against gay men and gay male misogyny is not entirely correct. Whilst some gay men may occupy privileged positions which may in turn oppress women this is not necessarily the case and they do so primarily at the expense of their sexuality as any gay man in any position who 'comes out' runs the risk of losing his male privileges of jobs, career, housing and so on. On top of this, gay men do not occupy the same socio-structural position as straight men in terms of social policy, taxation or insurance, as single gay men and gay male couples do not receive the same economic or social perks as single straight men or married couples. The complete evidence of gay men's superior or privileged socio-structural position to women then, systematically ignoring everything to do with homophobia or discrimination, in sum amounts to their higher and more disposable incomes maintained at the expense of their sexuality.

The central issue or difficulty here is the attempt to separate completely sexual politics from the politics of sexuality rather than see these as interacting tensions. It is often said that lesbians deal with 'two' problems, of being women and being lesbians in a male-dominated and heterosexist society, whilst gay men only deal with 'one' problem, namely homophobia against their gayness and not their maleness. For example, Jalna Hanmer points out: 'Women are primarily oppressed as women, whether lesbian or heterosexual, but gay men are oppressed as sexual deviants' (Hanmer, 1990: 30). Whilst this seems to make common sense, it consistently ignores the entangling of gender and sexuality as gay men and lesbians are both primarily oppressed for being the 'wrong kind of men' (effeminate, fearful and anti-family) and the 'wrong kind of women' (overly aggressive, assertive and argumentative) respectively. Consequently, misogyny and homophobia become part of the same problem.

Nevertheless, the evidence for gay male misogyny does not end here and extends primarily into more experiential territory. A primary and polemical example of this perspective is Liz Stanley's paper

SEXUAL POLITICS AND THE POLITICS OF SEXUALITY

'"Male needs": on the problems and problems of working with gay
men', reproduced after presentation at a radical feminist conference in
the late 1970s (Stanley, 1982). She starts:

> Once upon a time I experienced my relationships with gay men
> as a paradigm of what 'liberated relationships' between women
> and men might be like. Now I find it difficult even to think of
> gay men without a groan, without thinking that in some
> respects they are more sexist, and certainly more phallocentric,
> than many heterosexual men.
>
> (Stanley, 1982: 190)

Liz Stanley suffered considerable disillusionment through her involvement with the Manchester CHE group, and primarily condemns gay
men for what she perceives as phallocentric, pro-capitalist and hypo-
critical practices from the viewpoint of this experience. These criticisms
come from Stanley's witnessing of gay men's use of cruising, clubs and
meeting places to form often casual sexual contacts. Consequently, the
policy adopted is primarily separatist, whilst paradoxically still seeking to
control that which it separates itself from in a futuristic 'feminist' society:
'Its achievement would entail the end of the lifestyle of the average,
sexist, phallocentric gay man. It would provide less opportunities for
them to fuck each other, and fuck each other over. And so they resist it'
(Stanley, 1982: 212).

In addition, Liz Stanley has since produced academically advanced
work on feminist epistemology, often with Sue Wise (Stanley and
Wise, 1983; Stanley, 1990). This is applied in a later article highly
critical of the theoretical foundations of 'radical' gay men's studies
(Stanley, 1984). Gay men's studies are seen as 'deductive' or theoretically distanced from 'real life', in itself a somewhat masculinist or
male perspective. Moreover, the work of Ken Plummer and Jeffrey
Weeks, derived from Gagnon and Simon and Michel Foucault respectively, is also criticised as a kind of hijacking of feminism to fit in
with a particular politics of sexuality stripped of an analysis of power
or personal experience. Consequently, rape and sexual violence and,
more generally, gay men's sexism and many feminist ideas are left out
as not fitting into their theory. 'The theory' is in fact a particular kind
of social constructionist politics of sexuality which Stanley effectively
exposes as a sexist 'attempt to produce a theory of sexual politics
stripped of feminism and any analysis of power other than that which
is seen to oppress adult gay men' (Stanley, 1984: 61).

[43]

Joyce Layland (1990) has also written interestingly on the contradictions of mothering a gay son, witnessing simultaneously discrimination against gay sexuality and the power of the gay male community in dominating, parodying or simply excluding women in organisations and groups, drag and camp culture, and clubs and bars, respectively.

Similarly, Sheila Jeffreys in *Anticlimax: a Feminist Perspective on the Sexual Revolution* (1990) severely criticises the sexual revolution and permissiveness of the 1960s and early 1970s as a series of male supremacist sexual practices oppressive to women. For example, contraception is seen as oppressive to women in undermining their sexual autonomy to simply say 'No' and in allowing men more rather than less sexual freedom. Moreover, she criticises the gay movement's sexism: 'Gay liberation, I suggest, after an initial heady commitment to feminist principles, became a movement for male gay liberation, incorporating principles which are at total odds with the concept of women's liberation' (Jeffreys, 1990: 145). This proposition is premised upon a series of perceptions or conflations concerning gay male sexuality and the practices of promiscuity, paedophilia, sado-masochism, transvestism and transsexualism, as all of these practices are perceived to eroticise power and inequality.[13] Consequently, gay sexuality is seen essentially as sexist sexuality.

This particular perspective on sexuality makes the important point that gay men are not necessarily immune from practising sexism through virtue of their gayness. Nevertheless, there are several particular difficulties worth discussing. First, it can often slide into an adoption of a simplistic or structural functional account of sexuality, explained simply as a process of socialisation, that pays very little attention to agency or meaning. Second, the perspective is already very dated as it is centred on the sexual attitudes and practices of the 1970s as previously outlined, and it is, in its entirety, pre-AIDS. In addition, it is limited in terms of its scope to only a small minority of a minority group of gay men who took part in such practices, in turn particularly contextually located within specific American and European cities at a particular point in time, thus undermining some of its more sweeping points, although some of these points may, taken in context, still stand up to critical scrutiny (see Chapter 5). This also contrasts sharply with the work of other writers who have pointed out that such practices are not necessarily as phallocentric or as crudely sexist as they seem and, more particularly, are not incompatible with the simultaneous maintenance of personal relationships or other political convictions, whilst the practice of phallocentric acts or the eroticisation of power does not necessarily determine, impact upon, or reflect political consciousness (Bristow, 1989; Watney, 1987; Weeks, 1985). Third, this perpsective commonly leads to a neglect of gay men's resistances to these practices (Gough, 1989; Shiers, 1980; Stoltenberg, 1989). Consequently, it is a somewhat oversimplified perspective upon a more complex phenomenon. Moreover, it is important to point out that not all feminists share the same view of gay male sexuality. Gayle Rubin's radically different view on sexuality has already been cited and Lynne Segal in *Is the Future Female? Troubled Thoughts on Contemporary Feminism* (1987) provides a slightly more up-to-date critique of the radical feminist perspectives and more specifically develops a cautiously sympathetic perspective on issues of gay sexuality in *Slow Motion: Changing Masculinities, Changing Men* (1990). She points out:

> It would be quite wrong to suggest that gay men have solved the problems of exploitation and oppression within sexual encounters and relationships. It is right, however, to believe that, amongst men, it is gay writers and activists who have devoted most time to addressing them.
>
> (Segal, 1990: 153)

and also applies this perspective to the AIDS crisis.

In addition, though, there are also several difficulties with this perspective. First, one difficulty lies in the more practical application of this alternative perspective to lived experiences and, in particular, to sexual violence and sexual power, two issues it has tended to slide over in a sea of variations and contextualisations. Second, there is a difficulty in defusing the significance of gender in sexuality as a central mechanism through which the oppression of women and indeed gay men may operate. Third, there is a tendency also to slide into a slightly individualistic 'live and let live' perspective that slips into simplistic prescription. Thus, this perspective on sexuality, primarily developed as a reaction to radical feminism, is in need of further development (Hanmer, 1990; Vance, 1984).

In sum, in more extreme form, these two perspectives may also add up to a sexual politics and a politics of sexuality on gay male misogyny, as underlying these discussions are tensions concerning gender and sexuality, gay men's similarity or difference to other men, and political questions of power and oppression. In particular, the impact

[45]

of feminism upon gay men or the gay male community is raised as an important issue and underpinning this is the relationship of homosexuality and masculinity discussed in the next section.

Homosexuality–masculinity (homophobia)

Gay men and the gay male community occupy a complex political position in terms of sexual politics and the politics of sexuality, and a similar set of paradigmatic problems to lesbians beset gay men and the gay male community. For some gay men, their gayness is a way to challenge masculinity, personally, through nonconformity to certain roles and identities and, politically, in an adoption of a different social-structural position, particularly in relation to women; whilst for other gay men, their gayness is simply sexual, having sex with other men whilst in all other respects retaining a traditional masculine identity, set of activities and socio-structural position in society.

Significantly, the study of gay and/or male sexuality in relation to wider issues of gender identity is, generally, gallingly lacking although its significance is conversely and constantly increasing in relation to issues of sexual violence, sexual practices and sexually transmitted diseases including AIDS (Edwards, 1990). Starting with the mollies and molly houses in the eighteenth century, if not the Greco-Roman emphasis on young males' femininity, male homosexuality has had a long association with effeminacy. More recently, the development of drag queens and camp culture commercially brought effeminacy into the public sphere of pubs and clubs but both gay liberation and the women's movement brought about a newer awareness of gender and identity.

The gay male community, particularly through the Gay Liberation Front, began to develop different approaches to the presentation of gay sexuality and gendered identity, dividing ultimately into a dualistic continuum of first, 'effeminists' who self-consciously sought to denounce and drop all displays of traditional or stereotypical masculinity partly out of personal expression and partly out of political alignment with feminism; and second, what I shall call 'masculinists', or a cult of proponents of gay male machismo that took traditional or stereotypical forms of masculine display, posture or dress and pushed them to the extreme out in the open, partly as a positive expression of sexuality and partly as a counter-reaction to the stereotypes of effeminacy that had dominated the previous century at least (Marshall, 1981).

Ultimately, it was the 'masculinists' who dominated the 1970s and whose precepts and practices set up the parameters of the discussion in succeeding chapters (see Kleinberg, 1987). Furthermore, 'effeminists' and effeminacy, as well as camp culture, came under attack from feminists who saw these postures and practices as, explicitly, exploiting and attacking femininity and, implicitly, expressing misogyny. Similarly, 'masculinists', machismo and macho culture were also criticised as sexist and it seemed gay men in the 1970s were essentially in a 'no win' or Catch 22 situation in relation to feminism and gender identity.

In the 1980s, some gay men began to argue against this conflation of gay sexuality and misogyny, asserting instead that misogyny should be conflated with homophobia, a problem from which, in practising, was something women and lesbian feminism were far from immune. Ultimately, though, homophobia was set to develop into a centre of political controversy located in the same, or at least similar, tensions of sexual politics and politics of sexuality. Consequently, the question became one of conflict and/or congruence between lesbians and gay men according to identification and politics in precept and practice.

At the centre of these concerns was clone culture, clearly located in the question of connection or not of masculinity and homosexuality:

> Homosexuality is now signified by theatrically 'macho' clothing (denim, leather and the ubiquitous key rings) rather than by feminine style drag; the new 'masculine' homosexual is likely to be non-apologetic about his sexuality, self-assertive, highly consumerist and not at all revolutionary, though prepared to demonstrate for gay rights. This, one might note, is far removed from the hope of the early seventies liberationists who believed in a style that was androgynous, non-consumerist and revolutionary.
>
> (Altman, 1980: 52)

As a result, few areas of the history of homosexuality have aroused such severely heated and hot-headed hysteria as the hype surrounding the 1970s cruising gay clone whose identity and sexual practices, despite potential collapse at least through the impact of the AIDS epidemic, are constantly recounted and castigated as sexist misogyny or proclaimed as the triumph of sexual pleasure over conservatism.

Most of the criticism, and indeed some of the counter-criticism, has come from women and feminists. Nevertheless, men and gay

[47]

studies have increasingly had something to say on the issue of gay male misogyny. John Stoltenberg (1982) in a stinging attack on gay male sexuality and sado-masochism, starts:

> I do not know of a movement for liberation that has betrayed its revolutionary potential so soon after its inception as the male-dominated movement for the liberation of 'gay people.' Instead of acting upon the recognition – available in feminist writings for some time – that the stigma of being queer origi- nates in the male supremacy of culture, which stigmatizes all females and all that is 'feminine,' most gay males have chosen a completely reactionary strategy: seeking enfranchisement in the culture as 'really virile men,' without substantially changing or challenging their own misogyny and male-supremacist convictions.
>
> (Stoltenberg, 1982: 124)

Less polemically and more academically, Michael Kimmel (1990) develops a perspective on the importance of sexual scripts and sexual learning in application to male sexuality and male sexual practice seen as social constructions located within a wider context of patriarchy. Consequently, the cruising clone is seen as a conformist, as opposed to an opponent, to masculine sexual scripts: 'They [gay men] are not "perverts" or "deviants" who have strayed from the norms of mas- culinity, and therefore brought this terrible retribution [AIDS] upon themselves. They are, if anything, over-conformists to destructive norms of male behaviour' (Kimmel, 1990: 109). Despite making a potentially useful connection, the problem or difficulty with this perspective is that it has the tendency to almost medically re- pathologise the gay male and gay male sexuality as 'hyper conformity' or simply 'hyper sexuality'.

Slightly differently, Jamie Gough (1989), having acknowledged the sexist implications of some aspects of gay male sexuality, points to the importance of the oppression this imposes on gay men themselves in conformism to sexual performance and sexually fetishistic stereo- types: 'Masculinity as a sexual fetish is, therefore, oppressive not simply for dictating a certain norm, but for demanding something which cannot be achieved' (Gough, 1989: 121).

This point is supported in John Shiers' deeply personal and pole- mical article 'Two steps forward, one step back' where he outlines the oppressive difficulties imposed upon him as a young man coming out on the 1970s gay scene whilst trying also to maintain his socialist convictions. Consequently, initially: 'Understanding sexism and the oppression of women seemed like the key which unlocked the prison gates' (Shiers, 1980: 140). Following this through, though, he noticed the tension of maintaining left wing or socialist feminist convictions with starting to develop a positive gay sexuality and supporting it in practice through the gay scene, often seen as misogynist in its male-only or male-dominated management strategies. He notes: 'We valued our gay social lives more than the principle of outright opposition to misogynist male managements' (Shiers, 1980: 143). However, he later realises the limits to the tolerance of male homosexuality as:

> In other words, if we are good boys, who are prepared, perhaps after an initial coming out fling, to settle down with a nice man in quasi-marital bliss, then we may be tolerated (provided that we are reasonably discreet, particularly in front of the children; do not scream in the street at night or wake up the neighbours with distasteful rows about who forgot to buy the KY) as an uncomfortable but essentially harmless departure from the norm.
> (Shiers, 1980: 147)

As a consequence he also points to the political importance, potentially at least, of asserting sexuality as sexual pleasure *per se*. It is apparent, therefore, that there is a dual, not single, issue of gay men dealing with their own misogyny or sexism and the way it also oppresses them with the issue of society's constant and omnipresent heterosexism, the most brutal brunt of which is homophobia. To put the problem another way: 'Gay men are caught in the double bind of being told that we are not men yet being expected to behave as men' (Humphries, 1985: 74).

This situation led in the 1970s to the development of attempts to ape and mock masculinity. The most extreme and infamous form of these was the primarily American development, already partly outlined, of clone culture where a series of traditional images of masculinity from cowboy to construction worker were adopted in an over-the-top, overconformist form that was, on occasions, self-conscious and effectively slightly silly. Consequently, traditional images of masculinity could possibly be mimicked and undermined. The difficulty was that this could also lead to conformism and an internalisation of some extreme forms of masculinity, particularly

[49]

sexually, and the problem remains the ambiguity within these images as: 'To be sure, gay masculinity is not, in any simple way, "real" masculinity, any more than camp is "real" femininity. It is more self-conscious than the real thing, more theatrical, and often ironic' (Gough, 1989: 121).

This ambiguity or theatricality has been ignored by proponents arguing that misogyny is the dominant paradigm of gay male sexuality, yet it is primary to the arguments made by proponents of homophobia as the prime paradigm of gay male sexuality. Gregg Blachford (1981), for example, points to the importance of reproduction *and* resistance to dominant ideology in gay male sexuality, asserting: 'In this reproduction of the sexual objectification that even goes beyond that characteristic of heterosexual casual encounters, one is not challenging the ideology of male dominance in our society and its resulting homosexual oppression' (Blachford, 1981: 191). Yet he also notes: 'many of those who don these "costumes" may have no real desire actually to take on the associated characteristics of virile masculinity' (Blachford, 1981: 201) as essentially 'masculinity and femininity are just roles to be donned or shunned at different times' (Blachford, 1981: 197). The difficulty with this perspective, though, lies in its attempt at having the cake and eating it as a given individual act cannot attack and assert sexuality at once. A central, and related, tension concerns the extent to which the sexualisation of masculinity is in itself seen as subversive primarily because images of masculinity are not supposed to be sexually objectifying but obviously and deliberately are made to be so by many gay men.

Essentially, the issue is that separation or connection of sexuality and gendered identity as a sexually serious act is not *necessarily* a serious gender identity, or is it? Leo Bersani (1988) points out that this process is more problematic and more complex as masculinity is a seriously important part of male same-sex sexuality, saying: 'Parody is an erotic turn off, and all gay men know this' (Bersani, 1988: 208). The primary example of this is the much-proclaimed complaint that the often-picked-up American clone look-a-like hunk promptly loses all his sex appeal when starting up a conversation concerning Jane Austen or Verdi's opera! Importantly, then, gay male sexuality never ceases its identification with, its longing for, its resistance to or, in short, its relation to male sexuality and masculinity. Consequently, in loving the masculine one is not masculine and constantly asserts its potential collapse:

Gay men's 'obsession' with sex, far from being denied, should be celebrated – not because of its communal virtues, not because it offers a model of genuine pluralism to a society that at once celebrates and punishes pluralism, but rather because it never stops re-presenting the internalized phallic male as an infinitely loved object of sacrifice.

(Bersani, 1988: 222)

The question is also raised constantly as to the connections and implications of this process for the precepts and practices of homophobia and/or misogyny. Craig Owens (1987) argues against the idea of a 'homosexual monopoly' as an example of homosexual misogyny and argues for the integration of misogyny and homophobia through the concept of the 'homosocial' and, in conjunction, attacks certain feminist criticisms of gay male misogyny as premised upon homophobic bases, pointing out: 'the myth of homosexual gynophobia remains perhaps the most powerful obstacle to a political alliance of feminists and gay men' and that 'the "function" of this myth . . . is to obscure the profound link between misogyny and homophobia in our culture' (Owens, 1987: 219).[14]

On a more political level, Joseph Bristow (1989) provides a blistering polemic against lesbian proponents of gay male misogyny. He begins by distinguishing and defining misogyny as 'men hating women' from homosexuality 'men loving other men' (Bristow, 1989: 54) and goes on to argue that homophobia is a clumsy concept amalgamating the problems of lesbian and gay men into one lump, proposing:

Sexual fears about lesbians and gay men manifest themselves differently. Lesbians, for example, are at the receiving end of misogyny, which can come into operation to enable men to control a situation whether at home, at work, or in the street. Gay men can indeed be the agents of this kind of appalling sexual hatred. Furthermore, 'homophobia' is not a precise analytic tool when discussing kinds of anti-gayness that surface now and again in feminist writings, particularly those written from a radical lesbian-feminist perspective. Feminist fears of gay men may not be altogether unrelated to general fears of gay men. However, feminist objections to aspects of gay culture derive from a politics which some gay men would claim to share.

(Bristow, 1989: 57)

[51]

This makes the important point that women, lesbians and feminists are not immune by virtue of being women, lesbians or feminists or all three, from perpetuating or promoting the pervasive problem of homophobia. Bristow's liberalism is backed up by arguments, again, about ambiguities in gay male sexuality, asking as gay clones 'are we really men' or simply 'clones' or 'leather *queens*' (Bristow, 1989: 64)? Using Sedgwick's (1985) argument that homosociality is based on homophobia, homophobia becomes primarily a heterosexual problem which benefits heterosexual men and oppresses homosexual men. Underpinning this whole polemic is the principle of sexual pleasure if not sex *per se* as a source of profound fear and fascination and gay male sexuality as, in a sense, the sexiest or sex-ist of all sexualities is central in this, as: 'We are – to the heterosexual world – walking definitions of sex. We *mean* sex', and he concludes: 'One of these days the world will find out what we have already discovered – that homophobia and misogyny, and not the lifestyles of gay men, are central to the problems of our society' (Bristow, 1989: 74).

The point at the end of the day would seem to be that what is being dealt with is not gay male misogyny or lesbian homophobia, or indeed misogyny or homophobia as practised by lesbians, gay men or the whole population, but misogyny *and* homophobia. Gay men, then, occupy a quite unique position. They are men and yet also relate to men as their primary emotional and sexual subjects. Consequently, they are equally likely to act as sexist men or to suffer from the acts of other sexist men.

Conclusion: sexual politics and the politics of sexuality

Gay men and lesbians are two parallel armies with the same enemy: heterosexism which is part of a system of the dominance of 'male' values over 'female'.

(Mitchell, 1980: 56)

There is no way, absolutely no way, in which our interests can be said to be the same. Gay men, perhaps more than any other men, ally themselves with the activities and products of sexism. More than any other men they choose to act and construe

themselves, and each other, in ways dominated by phallocentric
ideologies and activities.

(Stanley, 1982: 211)

What is not recognised is that while both lesbians and gay men
are not 'heterosexual', heterosexuality itself is a power relationship of men over women; what gay men and lesbians are
rejecting are essentially polar experiences.

(Faraday, 1981: 113)[15]

Gay liberation's benign belief in gender breakdown soon turned out
to be gender blindness. This breakdown formed the basis for lesbian
feminism's criticism of gay male misogyny and some gay men's
criticism of lesbian erotophobia. Problems, polarities and differences
developed out of this breakdown into what I have called sexual
politics and the politics of sexuality. In particular, the construction of
interfemale sexuality developed in conjunction with the rise of the
women's movement and feminism, whilst gay male sexuality similarly
developed as part of the development of the gay male community,
academically and politically. Questioning the construction of these
identities and sexualities creates insights into their causes and outcomes. More importantly, this develops potential opportunities for
deconstruction and reconstruction of sexuality, gender and identity as
dynamic, not static, entities.

More politically, the difficulty centres on the practicalities of such
processes in a deeply heterosexist culture perpetuating inequalities in
gender *and* sexuality. Consequently, it is necessary to recognise that
gender and sexuality operate as oppressive hierarchies, as sexual
politics and the politics of sexuality. Politically, this has tended to lead
to attempts to oppose sexual politics or the politics of sexuality, and
impose the opposite. It is important to point out, though, that in
recognising gender and sexual inequality, theoretically as well as
politically, one has to recognise sexual politics *and* the politics of
sexuality.

It is also particularly important to point out that sexual politics and
the politics of sexuality constantly connect and it is this connection
that raises the question of individual identification. Consequently,
homosexuality undermines masculinity yet empowers femininity so
that whilst the openly gay male often loses some of the privileges of
masculinity in terms of identity, discrimination and domestic power,

the lesbian may gain some of the privileges of masculinity through increased independence, at least personally, from the primary though not the only oppressor, *heterosexual* masculinity. Identification is also critical as an indication of political intention as neither male or female homosexuality implies any political persuasion *per se* until it is opened up to societal discrimination. In sum, if one does not have an overt sexual identity in a society where heterosexuality is omnipresent, one essentially passes as heterosexual with all the political implications that implies for males and females.

Male homosexuality tends to be primarily oppressed by homophobia, and lesbianism tends to be primarily oppressed by misogyny. Importantly though, gay men also suffer from their own and others' sexism and misogyny, and lesbians, probably increasingly, suffer from some forms of homophobia. The problem, then, is primarily one of emphasis or degree, and identity has become sexual, political and gendered. In addition, it is also generational and aged or age-related, and this is the focus of Chapter 3.

CHAPTER 3

Gender and generation

One reason for the inclusion of this chapter was personal. When I was younger, older men fairly regularly leered at me on trains and in toilets and later, when coming out, I was often put into uncomfortable positions when men much older and physically stronger than me obviously objectified me sexually and started to get 'heavy'. I have since also had a few affairs with older men who I did consent to, or even seduce: the first insisted I shut up as I was destroying the virginal image he had created; and the second in the end said he couldn't have sex with me properly as he preferred casual sex to more personal or intimate sex and, from our friendship, he knew me too personally.

Definitions of childhood

As homosexuality has become slightly less open to sustained moral panic, the new pariah of 'child molester' has become the latest folk devil to orchestrate anxieties over the political, moral and interpersonal life of western societies.

(Plummer, 1990: 231)

Pederasty is a contentious issue. It is otherwise called Greek love, man and boy love, or even the love of youth. Furthermore, there are immediate problems of definition. Is it separable from paedophilia (the love of children in general). Is it 'sexual'? Is it incestuous? When is a man not a boy and when does a boy become a man? Where does the growth of youth fit into this? Is all intergenerational sex 'child abuse'? Are all paedophiles or pederasts 'child molesters'? Does the question of consent or seduction reconstruct the issue? Is it power, control, inequality – or all three?

There are no set universal answers to these questions as they are essentially context-related historical constructions. In addition, the definitions and constructions of childhood sexualities are a contentious issue in social science as pederasty (usually defined as homosexual,

post-pubertal sex with boys) is often confused and conflated with
paedophilia (often defined as heterosexual, pre-pubertal sex with boys
and girls). The muddying of these distinctions is criticised as a social
science as well as lay value-laden confusion:

> In contemporary Western society, intimate and sexual relations
> between men and boys are considered as criminal, unlawful,
> pyschologically deviant and damaging to the boys involved,
> regardless of the emotional contexts in which they occur. By
> almost exclusively studying these relationships as forms of sexual
> abuse, the social sciences have narrowed our view of the subject.
> (Sandfort et al., 1990: 5)

Consequently, whilst there are clearly qualitative and context-related
distinctions across gender, class and race categories, there are clearly
also distinct continuities in age structuration in studying intergenerational sexuality; and pederasty is not, perhaps, so separate from
paedophilia. The primary point of this chapter is, where appropriate,
to create connections across these categories.

As the categories are themselves hard to define, creating connections across these distinctions is necessarily difficult. There are
clearly sharp contrasts across age and sex and according to sexual acts,
the context in which they take place and the nature of the particular,
parental or non-parental, relationship. For example, the implications
of a father secretly fondling his three-year-old daughter are radically
different from a homosexual molestation across two generations on a
train, again different in turn from mutual adolescent play in the toilets
at school. Clearly, there is also a question of societal context as our
reactions to such situations are not necessarily the same as in other
societies or, more simply, the same as those of our grandparents.

In this chapter, in attempting to more specifically take on the
contextual associations of Western European or American society,
one might say there are five key factors to consider in any analysis of
intergenerational sexuality: first, the physical and psychological age of
the parties involved and hence the degree of age difference; second,
the gender and sexual orientation of the persons involved and their
interactive variations; third, the overall context in which the sexual
activities take place whether at home, work, school and in or out of
private; fourth, the actual sexual activities involved varying from
fondling to full vaginal or anal intercourse; and fifth, the most difficult
to define of all, the actual interpersonal nature of the relationship,

parental or nonparental, and the implications of this. Thus, it is quite clear that the variety and scope of potential intergenerational sexual situations or relationships is vast. This vastness of variation, however, may mask or cover significant continuities, particularly in relation to questions of inequality, and it is the primary purpose of this chapter to expose, sensitively, these continuities, paying particular attention to pederasty or intergenerational intermale sexuality.

Constructions of childhood sexuality

Pedophilia, like homosexual behaviour, has existed universally, and has been variously treated in different societies.

(Gay Left Collective, 1981: 58)

Like homosexuality, pederasty was and is practised across continents and centuries, whilst the identities, forms, norms and values attached to it have constantly changed. The starting place for this process is usually cited as the Greco-Roman practice of pederasty or pedagogic eros, usually called 'Greek Love'. Eglinton's *Greek Love* (1971) is a monumental attempt to understand and validate Greek love within a historical context. Consequently: 'Despite many attempts by apologists for homosexual acts between adults to justify them by appealing to the example of the ancient Greeks, the adult homosexuality of today has little in common with Greek attitudes or practices' (Eglinton, 1971: 3). It is perhaps a measure of the oppression of male homosexuality that so much mileage has been made out of the association of Greek love with contemporary homosexuality. Conversely, Eglinton sees Greek love as a solution to a social situation, as opposed to a social problem, primarily in terms of functionalism. Most importantly, *kalokagathia*, a state of fine mind in fine body, is developed through a paternal preparatory process. It is, consequently, a question of conformism. In Sparta, young men had 'inspirers' or soldiers chosen by their fathers to be responsible for their development into heterosexual manhood. In addition, oral sex was seen as a preparation for vaginal penetration and older male identification performed the function of forming codes of conduct and instilling 'masculine' virtues alongside nationalism. The ultimate intention of all of this was the formation of fearless soldiers. Thus, the most important point to grasp is the sharp contrast of this conformity with

[57]

the extreme nonconformity of 'child molesting' male homosexuality, thus illustrating the importance of historical processes in constructing attitudes and sexual practices.

The Christian tradition was central in changing the definitions of all homosexualities. With the rise of the Roman Empire's oppression of all forms of non-procreative sexuality and sexual pleasure, *kalokagathia* died an ignoble death: 'Their ideal was victory over pleasure, of whatever kind' (Veyne, 1985: 27). Male homosexuality, as non-procreative sexual pleasure *per se*, was never simply socially, economically, or politically validated. In addition, Christianity tended to increase the oppression of pederasty as the educational function was increasingly undertaken in Church doctrine in monasteries.

Similarly, other societies have had and continue to have differing views concerning intergenerational sexuality given, in particular, varieties concerning age of consent laws, which are generally lower in Europe.[1] For example:

> For the Melanesian peoples, who hold that the insemination of boys is *necessary* for them to attain sexual maturity, the antipedo-phile complex is inconceivable, and for many societies where sexuality is an integral component of the pedagogical relation-ships of older and younger men, current Western attitudes would be thought puzzling or reprehensible.
>
> (Adam, 1987: 152)

Such anthropological evidence illustrates the varieties in practices and codes of sexuality across time and space, although there is also significant continuity in the fact that male homosexuality as sexual pleasure *per se* never was, or is, socially accepted as: 'In all these cases sexuality is made to serve purposes and aims other than sexual satisfaction and procreation' (Bleibtreu-Ehrenberg, 1990: 21).[2]

Moreover, there was no child molestation; there were no 'children' as we now know them. There is also no child molestation in many non-western societies today as there are no 'children' as we know them.[3] It was with the rise of industrialism and Victorian capitalism that there came the creation of 'childhood', initially as a middle-class phenomenon. Working-class children were still appall-ingly exploited in the early development of intensive capitalist expan-sion, though with increasing economic efficiency the demand for work decreased and the dependency of children increased, and childhood as a middle-class phenomenon gradually became a general norm. Thus, it is essential to see childhood as constructed historically.

One could also say that this marked the transition from pederasty *per se* to paedophilia, given the invention of the increasing dependence of each of the sexes and the increasing consignment of boys as well as girls to the private sphere as: 'In a real sense, pederasty was defeated by the invention of paedophilia – and not to the discovery of adult traumas brought on by infantile sexual experience, but to the creation of modern childhood' (Moody, 1981: 148).

Moreover, the concept of 'childhood innocence' developed as part of nineteenth-century Victorian ideology concerning children which constantly cast the child as a completely passive victim and, in addition, as part of the development of a particular taboo on childhood sexuality: 'Since at least the eighteenth century children's sexuality has been conventionally defined as a taboo area, as childhood began to be more sharply demarcated as an age of innocence and purity to be guarded at all costs from adult corruption' (Weeks, 1985: 223). Popular examples of this process include the fairy tales of Hansel and Gretel, Little Red Riding Hood, the Pied Piper and even the sweet-seller in the Disney Film *Chitty Chitty Bang Bang*, all of which cultivate a stereotype of a malevolent and molesting adult preying on childhood innocence, partly premised on fact, as children were exploited as cheap workers and pimped into prostitution, and partly on fiction, in the creation of mythic and colourful characters.[4] However, Freudian psychoanalysis then reconstructed childhood as sexual, thus setting up a contradiction of innocence versus sexual knowingness within the current discussion of children.[5]

The increasing success of capitalist expansion in the twentieth century had freed children from previous slavery, though it had also led to an increase in domestic dependency and state control through age of consent laws. The growth of compulsory education was crucial in reinstating, as well as extending, the dependency of children still further, and the growth of the caring professions, in particular social workers, sought to protect rather than empower children. This dependency, as we shall see, is a crucial issue in children's vulnerability to abuse and exploitation. In addition, the longitudinal impact of these developments was to increase parental control and responsibility and to exacerbate both by the publication of Bowlby's and Dr Spock's books in the 1950s.[6]

With the development of sexually permissive ideologies in the

1960s it was, to an extent at least, inevitable that attitudes towards intergenerational sex should become slightly more relaxed and allow the possibility of a debate on the subject which should, perhaps, be seen as more 'progressive' than none at all. Thus PIE (Paedophile Information Exchange) was formed in 1974 with Tom O'Carroll as its chairman in order to destroy mythology surrounding intergenerational sexuality, encourage its social acceptance, provide support for its proponents, increase contact networks and promote reform of age of consent laws. PAL (Paedophile Action for Liberation), formed almost simultaneously as a more militant counterpart to PIE, was overly optimistic concerning its opposition, consequently collapsing into PIE almost immediately. In North America, the Boston-Boise Committee successfully resisted state intervention, making significant gains and forming the North American Man Boy Love Association (NAMBLA) in 1978.

However, the simultaneous rise of fundamentalist and familial ideology in the form of Anita Bryant's 'Save Our Children Campaign' in Florida in 1976, the Kiddie Porn panic of 1977 in the United States and the attack in Canada on the Body Politic's article 'Men Loving Boys Loving Men' in 1978, whilst Mary Whitehouse continued to campaign against all forms of pornography and non-procreative sexuality in the UK, created a very severe counter-reaction against the slight easing of negative attitudes towards intergenerational sexuality. As a result, PIE was met with riotous hostility culminating in the criminalisation of Tom O'Carroll, imprisoned for sixteen months for 'corrupting public morals', whilst PIE without its leading proponent collapsed.

This process is mostly interpreted as part of a perspective of moral panics in which the media played a central part. Plummer (1981) points out: 'This whole period of moral outrage – in which course the press played a leading role – provides a clear instance of the degree of public hostility awaiting paedophile organisations that attempt to change the orthodox viewpoint' (Plummer, 1981: 127). The media had, it was said, successfully exploded, distorted, and indeed created the 'child molester', Esther Rantzen's 'Child Watch' being the latest in a long line of innocent childhood constructions. In addition, it was difficult to conceive of Cleveland ever developing into its present pinnacle of crisis without the media incentive: 'Each panic shows the typical profile, with the escalation through various stages of media and moral manipulation until the crisis is magically resolved by some symbolic action' (Weeks, 1985: 224). LaFontaine (1990), however, further facilitates an understanding of the Cleveland Crisis as a context-related conjunction of ideological factors including an undermining of the traditional family, parental authority and autonomy through state interference and institutional conflict. Consequently, colossal sympathy was evoked for parents, whilst social workers were castigated and children simply silenced.

The latest discussion of satanic or ritual abuse, where children are involved, or even killed, in occultist sacrifices, takes the sensational aspects of the issue and conflates this with concerns over the validity of children's 'stories'. Currently, the question of care is also raised as stories leak out concerning cruelty to children in care institutions contrasted with the critical sanctity of childhood innocence.

Moral panic perspectives clearly and successfully deconstruct factors surrounding the issues and show how they develop into crises, though they do not explain the constant lay and academic concern with childhood sexuality that has developed from a particular moral panic into a permanent and dynamic panic that has conflated the pederast with the paedophile, imploded incest into childhood sex, turned child lovers into child molesters, molesters into abusers, and abusers into ritual abusers with abundantly little analysis of practices, precepts or childhood opinions. In addition, an added difficulty lies in the conflict of the deconstruction of childhood innocence and adult molesters with the necessary recognition of children's often very real suffering.[7]

Radical perspectives on paedophilia and pederasty

No one will dispute that the age taboo is much more a proscription against gay behaviour than against heterosexual behaviour, can one seriously imagine a gay male version of 'Lolita' or 'Pretty Baby'?

(Tsang, 1981: 8)

Any perspective on paedophilia or pederasty is on the whole 'radical' unless it is a downright condemnation. The discrimination against gays and homosexuality is sometimes relatively trivial compared with the vitriolic and draconian attacks on paedophiles and pederasts. Prosecution, prison, and physical assault are common reactions and standard treatment. The majority of gay men are not pederasts,

[61]

though the popular press's perception and promotion of them as 'child molesters' is crucial in creating the association. Furthermore, this forms one of the reasons for the gay movement's often vacillatingly hostile reaction to intergenerational sexuality: having fought for a grain of social, economic, and political equality or respectability, they were hardly likely to invite a return to abuse by association. This situation is, thus, saddening but understandable. It is also probably a measure of the post-Stonewall precariousness of the status of gay sexuality.

A radical defence

It is the purpose of this section to provide a critique of pro-paedophilia and pederasty perspectives. The case of these perspectives is premised primarily upon three points, and particularly important is Tom O'Carroll's *Paedophilia: the Radical Case* (1980). First, as a self-confessed pederast and activist, O'Carroll seeks to demystify intergenerational sex and present a case for opposition to its oppression. O'Carroll is quite convincing in deconstructing paedophiles and pederasts as other than 'monsters' and 'molesters'. In addition, he gives evidence to support the point that the media stereotype of the child molester is mostly unsupported. For example, most pederasts or paedophiles are known to the children concerned and, in addition, the acts they practise are commonly not physically violent and involve consent. The children concerned are also often older than the media say, often nearer adolescence than childhood or infancy. Tom Reeves, also a self-confessed pederast, points out:

> I am positively turned off by the notion of molesting someone. I sometimes fail, to be sure, but I aim at allowing my young lovers to express their own real desires and feelings. I am usually turned on by their seduction of me, and turned off by any hint that they feel molested, coerced or even cornered.
>
> (Reeves, 1981: 27)

Importantly, this position is supported by other evidence, including child abuse studies (LaFontaine, 1990) and studies of intergenerational gay sexuality (Sandfort et al., 1990). Controversy, however, centres on the validity of some of these studies (see *Journal of Homosexuality*, 1990, 1/2). The problem remains: 'The disparity in size and power between parent and child creates a *potential* for abuse' (O'Carroll, 1980: 167). Thus, abuse is not inevitable, but isn't this potential sufficient reason for concern? Tsang states:

The primary issue, it should be made clear is not the right of men to have sex with boys. Rather the real issue is the liberation of young people so that they are empowered to make their own decisions regarding all aspects of their lives, including their sexuality.

(Tsang, 1981: 10)

This leads on to the second point, that of the denial of childhood sexuality through age of consent laws and indeed the lack of sex education, particularly in relation to gay sexuality where ignorance reigns supreme until experience takes its place. This primarily rests on the notion of an individually and psychologically repressed, as opposed to a socially, economically, and politically oppressed, childhood sexuality. This does not necessarily lead to biological determinism but does inevitably imply some kind of psychodynamic theory and most of O'Carroll's perspective is derived from Freud and Stoller.[8] Children are deeply oppressed sexually and there are obvious examples of this such as in the stigma attached to masturbation. Does this mean, though, that children need overt sexual experience with adults? This all too often turns into the adult's right to have sex with children, rather than vice versa, and: 'One noticeable aspect of the current debate is the relative absence of children's voices' (Presland, 1981: 74).

However, the voices of some young men and boys would seem to point to some evidence for the repression thesis. Thus, for example, Mark Moffett feels: 'Man love is also something which has helped thousands of boys discover their own sexuality and get in touch with what they really feel' (Moffett, 1981: 14). He also points to the oppression of childhood sexuality through the lack of power to provide consent and the perpetuation of sexual powerlessness through a lack of sexual learning. Similarly 'Youth Liberation believes that children should have the right to control their bodies' (Youth Liberation, 1981: 47) and the JCGT (Joint Council for Gay Teenagers), following the lead of the gay youth movement, points out: 'The purpose of this response is straightforward: it is to make it clear beyond doubt that young homosexual people of both sexes are a reality and are, in our society, demanding recognition and positive support, not legal sanctions' (Joint Council for Gay Teenagers, 1981: 84). Consequently, the question is raised as to the justification of intergenerational sexuality. In other words, why men or why not another boy or youth? This is an area where some form of sexual

[63]

freedom is probably more justified in the sense of being freed from stigma, and here we are probably dealing with both homophobia and erotophobia. The problem is also one of ageism or sexual discrimination on the basis of age alone.

This develops into the third point, that of the continuity of the idea of Greek love in helping young people, particularly young men, to recognise their sexuality and mature through the guidance of an older man. For example, Eglinton argues: 'Greek love, when handled responsibly (whether or not institutionalised as it was in ancient Greece), helps tide an adolescent boy over an essentially difficult period in his life, when his relationship with the world hangs in the balance' (Eglinton, 1971: 78).

However, this would seem ultimately to highlight problems concerning contemporary paternal practices within the family if, as this statement implies, the father is frequently inadequate on this level; then the issue still lies primarily with improvement of paternity. Importantly, Jeffrey Weeks points out: 'This position is obviously paternalistic and is also anti-homosexual; for it is not the gay nature of the relationship that is stressed, but the age divide and the usefulness of the experience for later heterosexual adjustment' (Weeks, 1985: 226).

Alternatively, Pat Califia points out that this process may also have positive implications for homosexual development: 'Boy-lovers and the lesbians who have young lovers are the only people offering a hand to help young women and men cross the difficult tension between straight society and the gay community' (Califia, 1981: 144). This isn't, in fact, quite true as the lesbian and gay youth movement provides this very function, at the same time operating an upper age limit for members, and other organisations and groups for young gay men and lesbians do exist as already evidenced.

Underlying these issues is the thorny problem of whether gay sexuality can be indeed facilitated or 'promoted' as the idea that one can help young gay people is deeply intertwined with the idea of dirty old men 'corrupting' young people. Help and corruption are ultimately inseparable as two sides of the same coin. This conceptual coin flipping also parallels the tension of empowerment versus protection and pleasure and danger that has developed within feminism concerning children's and women's sexualities.[9]

A radical attack
Pederasty has come under considerable criticism and attack from

fundamentalists, familialists and second-wave feminists. It is, however, incorrect to equate feminism with simple anti-pedophilic moralism as some gay men imply.[10] There is perhaps, though, a danger here which Gayle Rubin alludes to: 'If we are not careful, we will be using feminist politics to rationalize and perpetuate harmful stereotypes that originate not in feminism, but in our puritanical heritage' (Rubin, 1981: 110).

The more structural issues surrounding paedophilia and pederasty are, however, attributable to and constructed through second-wave feminism forming the first of three most important points. In exposing the power of men as a central concern, the paedophile or pederast has come in for criticism as a prime proponent of patriarchal paternalism. Kate Millett asserts: 'Sex itself is presented as a crime to children' (Millett, 1984: 218). Thus, in a sense, Millett is perhaps in some agreement with the proponents of the pro-paedophilia and pederasty perspectives. However, the vulnerability of children to abuse is the central issue:

> But the main point about children and relationships between adults and children is that children have no rights. They have no money. Because they have no money, no status, and no place to go, their dependence becomes emotional and psychological as well. Few relationships equalling the dependency of childhood can be found in human society.
>
> (Millett, 1984: 221)

Or more simply: 'If your father rapes you, he also feeds you' (Millett, 1984: 217). Consequently, Millett asserts that paedophilic and pederastic relationships founded on inequality are not easily condoned. This is due, however, to a series of social structures and institutions and not to the essential nature of gendered and generational relations:

> Intergenerational sex could perhaps in the future be a wonderful opportunity for understanding between human beings. But conditions between adults and children preclude any sexual relationship that is not in some sense exploitative. This is not actually the fault of the adults involved, but of the entire social structure.
>
> (Millett, 1984: 223)

Consequently, she does advocate support for children's sexuality independently, personally and in relationship to themselves and each other. Most feminists have, however, simply refused to support paedophiles or pederasts on personal or institutional levels, for example, in reaction to PIE or NAMBLA, as part of opposition to patriarchal practices.

This, then, leads on to the second most important point, that children cannot consent, according to or in the sense of an adult definition, an essential ingredient to the proponents of intergenerational sexuality. This is due to a question of inequality at the level of individual subjectivity as well as more objective social structural factors. If a child, as already stated, is essentially ignorant sexually, regardless of whether they even have a sexuality of their own, which is a separate issue, then it is clearly difficult to see how they can consent to what they do not understand at the same level and in the same way as their potential adult partners. On top of this, what is 'sexual' for a child is very likely not the same, or perhaps even very similar to, what is 'sexual' for an adult: 'Childhood sexuality should be regarded as different from adult sexuality not only because of physical differences, but also because of differences in knowledge and understanding of sexual activities and their consequences' (Ennew, 1986: 61).

This raises a third and more contentious issue within feminism, namely the degree to which child sexuality is paralleled and explained through the same dynamics that oppress women's sexuality. Consequently, for Diane Russell: 'The truth that must be faced is that this culture's notion of masculinity – particularly as it is applied to male sexuality – predisposes men to violence, to rape, to sexually harass, and to sexually abuse children' (Russell, 1984: 290). Russell has since been criticised by other feminists for being 'heterosexist, homophobic and ageist' (Califia, 1981: 139) partly because of the dubious nature of her statistics and her insistent claims that gay men, rather than heterosexual men, rape men and that male–male rape is a far lesser problem than male–female rape. Importantly, given the profoundly limited and contentious nature of any statistics on sexuality and sexual abuse, it is some wonder as to why they are used at all in any analysis of sexuality.[11]

Florence Rush in *The Best Kept Secret* (1980) provides a more theoretically advanced analysis that prioritises gender as a central issue and the association of women with children as crucial:

They have shared the same minority status . . . Together they have been idealised, romanticised, infanticised, trivialised,

sexualised and desexualised . . . Since both women and children
have been lumped together as helpless, dependent and powerless,
they even share the same 'feminine' gender and consequently
both have been sexually used and abused by men.

(Rush, 1980: 170)

This is a most important, though contentious, point counterpoised
with an opposed perspective:

The problem is that, although some feminists are correct to state
that children and women are oppressed by the same forces, they
fail to comprehend that the form oppression takes for children
is different and that the repression of 'ageism' compounds the
repression of sexism.

(Ennew, 1986: 58).

Moreover, it is dangerous to assume that women, through their own
oppression, are somehow immune from oppressing children, particularly in their powerful position as mothers, and there is some
evidence that, although it is less common, women do oppress and
exploit children sexually (LaFontaine, 1990).[12] Similarly, this does not
necessarily help to explain the sexual exploitation of boys, albeit by
men, as well as girls.[13] Thus, the difficulty with this perspective is that
it ultimately perpetuates a simplistic gender dualism that masks a more
complex reality.

In conclusion to this section, there is clearly a tension of issues
concerning intergenerational sexuality. Advocates of its cause state,
quite correctly, that children are not on the whole violently assaulted,
that paedophiles and pederasts are not child molesters and childhood
sexuality is deeply oppressed. Moreover, second-wave feminists have
pointed to the importance of power and inequality in compounding
this oppression and raised the question as to whether a child can
indeed ever consent in any situation of such personal and political
inequality. This first results in a difference of emphasis on generation
or gender in constructing and constricting childhood sexuality respectively; not gender and generation as distinct yet interconnected
factors in childhood sexuality. Second, generation is generally used to
explain inequalities in gay sexuality and gender is generally used to
explain inequalities in straight sexuality. As a result, one solution to
this situation is to try to consider gender and generation and gay
sexuality.

[67]

Gender, generation and gay sexuality

Whereas a male homosexual is invariably seen as a potential child molester, and a lesbian pedophile identity is socially non-existent because it presupposes an autonomous female sexual identity, the image of an older woman initiating a young man fits in with traditional male fantasies of woman. At the same time the deflowering of the young virgin has a special place in male mythology.

(Gay Left Collective, 1981: 57)

The primary purpose of this section is to consider the connections across categories of age, gender and sexual orientation, discussed in the introduction to this chapter, particularly in relation to inter-generational gay male sexuality.

Gender is generationed and generation is gendered. In addition, these interrelations operate on three levels. First, physically, whilst a female of fifteen or sixteen is not markedly different from a female of twenty-five or thirty and is essentially physically a woman, male physical maturation comparatively tends to take much longer. A male may start to reach puberty anywhere from the age of ten to nearer fifteen and the development of full reproductive capacity, pubic hair and a deeper voice all accompany frequent rapid height development. All these factors also stand as culturally specific signifiers of mascu-linity and as a marked separation from femininity. More importantly, males still continue to develop physically until well into their twenties and consequently, other signs of masculinity including musculature, broad shoulders and, in particular, chest hair often do not develop fully, if at all, until a male is in his early or even late twenties. It is therefore quite likely for pronounced physical differences to exist between a male of even twenty-six or twenty-eight, let alone a lot older, and a male of eighteen or nineteen.

As these physical signs are also endowed with significant social connotations of masculinity, in terms of prowess, power and virility, the likelihood of physical intermale inequality is consequently quite high and leads potentially also to eroticisation of such physical differ-ences. This eroticisation also depends in part on the extended nature of the development for males, as opposed to females, as the younger male frequently feels a yearning for maturity into 'real masculinity' that seems to take an eternity and he is therefore, regardless of sexual

orientation, often drawn into wild hero worship or downright adoration for males who develop earlier in these respects or who are
simply older. In addition, endless and increasing media representations of males as mature, macho and masculine or immature,
wimpish and effeminate create confusions and complications. Distinct
blurring does indeed also occur over this issue as masculinity is so
delicately premised on, for many males, the simply unattainable, and
therefore becomes an object of otherness or of desire.

This process similarly works in reverse as, once a male has matured,
attained the muscles and a smattering or more of body hair, he can
never return to adolescence and for some men this then leads to a
yearning for lost youth which in turn conflates into a yearning for
youths *per se*. More importantly, males increasingly lose sexual status
as they grow older. The most salient or important point, then, is that
one is simply not dealing with equals through virtue of the same male
gender, rather one is dealing with a hierarchy of masculinities. These
masculinities are also dualistic and unequal in relation to the second
two factors of gender–generation connection.

Second, differences exist psychologically and experientially, that is
to say the younger man or youth by virtue of being younger is less
experienced and less knowledgeable. This inevitably puts him at a
disadvantage unless he has significant physical advantage in other
respects as, for example, in the 'young buck and old ram' mythology.
At the level of sexuality, this is particularly apparent as there is an
appalling lack of sex education.[14] Consequently, also given the active
as opposed to passive role of male sexuality, the adolescent male is
frequently in the position of yearning for sex without having a clue
how to go about it and, on top of this, finding his whole identity as a
developing male dependent upon it. It is at this point that the role of
father figures or simply elder males play an important part in helping,
or not, the younger male. However, given the competitive, not
nurturant, nature of masculinity, this situation is open to exploitation
and is at the very least a power relation premised on simple inequality
in intellect and practice.

Third, and most clearly, structural factors are also at work in
creating very significant inequalities between older and younger men.
The most important point here is economic: one can only earn very
little until one is sixteen and until the age of twenty-one salaries are
not even on a parity with elders for the same occupation. On top of
this, the hierarchical structuring of salaries according to age and
experience permanently puts younger men in a situation of running

behind older men until retirement. This is, of course, cut across by class, as the working class tend to make more money earlier and the middle class tend to make it later, yet, as an overall part of the capitalist system, age operates as a significant structure of inequality.

Consequently, as so many aspects of life are dictated through financial concerns, options are more closed for the younger male, who is usually unable to finance his own accommodation in particular, and more open for the older male. Also, one cannot learn to drive independently, let alone own a car in the UK, another sign of 'having made it as a man', until one is seventeen with a licence of one's own. All these factors add up to significant dependency, also associated with femininity and not masculinity, as opposed to independence. Importantly, a youth's title is not technically 'Mr' until eighteen, his class and position is dictated by his father's or guardian's and he cannot vote, get credit, or even buy his own drinks until eighteen (twenty-one in some night-clubs). Thus, all these factors constitute the basis for considerable inequality between males of different ages with certain crunch points particularly emerging in the early teens (puberty), late teens (rights), and late twenties (physical maturity).

Furthermore, as all these factors also have their part to play in the development of socially sanctioned masculinity, there are clear connections at the level of gender and generation: 'It was not the masculine character of the boys which kindled the love of men: it was the physical resemblance to women as well as his psychic shyness, demureness and need for instruction and help' (Rush, 1980: 171). Gay male writers have, however, on the whole tended to underestimate, underwrite, or totally ignore issues of intergenerational sexuality and its connections to the gay community. Consequently, when they have tried to deal with the issue it has tended to lead to defensiveness and an uncritical insistence on consent as undermining all else when consent involves the right to say 'no' as well as 'yes'.[15]

It is quite clear, then, that despite the divisiveness of consent statutes and legislation in illegalising young gay men's consent in any situation and in criminalising an older partner irrespective of context, that this is not the end of the story of the connections of gender, generation and gay sexuality as applied to the practices of the gay male community. Importantly, much of this depends on the status of adolescence as opposed to childhood in society as: 'Like childhood, Western adolescence is regarded as a "special" era, with its own needs, problems, artefacts, economics and language' (Ennew, 1986: 24). The story does not end here either, as this tends to generalise the issues of gender and generation across heterosexual and homosexual categories. Significantly, the three levels of differences outlined earlier are still a part of wider structures of masculinity, inequality and their connections to gay sexuality.

First, physical factors have their part to play in intermale sexual relations as the younger man is likely to be physically weaker, unless the older man is indeed very much older, and this leaves him primarily more open to sexual violence. He is also likely to be idolised and objectified as both 'less of a man' and 'more of a man' as he is, on the one hand, feminine with smooth skin, shiny hair and fewer physical signs of masculinity and yet is also likely to be at his most unproblematic sexual peak, and both factors are often idolised and sought after by older gay men. Moreover, Tom Reeves provides an example of this process in speaking of his own sexual preferences: 'It is self-consciously homosexual, but it is directed at boys at that time in their lives when they cease to be children yet refuse to be men' (Reeves, 1981: 27).

Second, psychological factors play a particularly important part: homosexuality more than heterosexuality depends upon experience for learning, and consequently initial sexual partners, once on the gay scene in particular, are likely to be older, and indeed, wiser. The crucial issue here is that early sexual relations often do not develop, as do their heterosexual counterparts, within the context of a relationship, but rather within the context of more casual encounters, and this often constitutes the fear and fascination factor of many early encounters. Such factors have implications across the gay community as a whole as young men, similarly to young women who resist this process in attempting to take control of sexual situations and decisions, are often known as 'prick teases'; whilst older men who particularly seek out the young and inexperienced are known as 'chicken hawks', which effectively stereotypes the two parties equally. Similarly, virgins are particularly sought after by some men and are also particularly vulnerable to physical abuse and: 'A male virgin is thus similarly ambiguous, and this ambiguity is not only one of status but also one of sexual identity' (Ennew, 1986: 54).

These are problems the gay community has often both ignored as too difficult, and reacted violently against as reactionary politics. One exception in this process of silencing the issue is Michael Alhonte's article 'Confronting ageism' (1981). Speaking directly from personal experience, he asserts that adults avoid the real issues: 'Instead, they seem to concentrate on a boy's right to have sex, which often translates to their right to have sex with boys' (Alhonte, 1981: 156). Furthermore, this translates into gendered notions of sexuality as the masculine–feminine, active–passive distinction isn't dead yet: 'The idea that a teenage boy might enjoy something other than the "submissive" role is also foreign to many men' (Alhonte, 1981: 157). On top of this, stereotypes proliferate: 'Boys are cast as the young, ingenuous protégé or the streetwise, butch, jock punk. They are considered either utterly innocent or falsely cocky and self-assured . . . Men, on the other hand, are considered stable, omniscient, and self-reliant' (Alhonte, 1981: 157). This then becomes objectification as: 'Too many men adore boys as abstract sexual beings, but refuse (or are unable) to deal with them as people' (Alhonte, 1981: 158).

The situation is exacerbated by the third factor of the inevitable economic imbalance between the independent man and the wholly dependent boy. This affects the costs of dates, ability to make arrangements, problems of parental conflicts *et cetera, ad infinitum*. In short, a socially, economically, and politically structured inequality: a problem of paternalistic male dominance. The final result is that: 'They find me old enough to screw but not old enough to talk to' (Alhonte, 1981: 188).[16]

This position is of course counterpoised with evidence for children's and youth's sexual desires as outlined earlier. Finkelhor (1990) criticises this evidence, though, saying that the views of the youths change over time, leading to increasingly negative evaluations. In conclusion, whilst the young gay man may indeed have desires and designs on older men and may indeed set out seduce them, he remains in a physically, psychologically and structurally inferior position steeped in stereotypes, practices and codes of socially approved masculinity: the all too easily oppressive linkage of gender, generation and gay sexuality.

Conclusion: gender and generation

Gender identity is clearly distinct from a sexual identity; a sense of being a boy or a girl is not directly linked to a sense of being heterosexual, homosexual, sado-masochistic or paedophiliac, which usually comes later. Nevertheless, given the centrality of gender identity as an organizing feature of social life it is very likely to shape sexual identity.

(Plummer, 1990: 241)

In this chapter I have primarily attempted to examine some of the connections across age, gender and sexual variations. Social constructionist and, in particular, moral panic theories whilst pointing out the importance of historical processes in shaping contemporary hype and hysteria around the issue, tend to contradict the difficulties of real or lived experiences. Importantly, feminism has profoundly highlighted the importance and significance of gender or, more particularly men, in perpetuating the problem. Moreover, gay male academics have often pointed to the importance of more positive sexual experiences and the oppression of young people's sexuality. Significantly, though, the difficulty lies in the gaps or the lack of connection of these two issues. Consequently, in the next section, I considered the connections of gender and generation in structuring gay male sexuality and sexual practice. Similar points of connections can, I expect, apply to heterosexuality which operates an age hierarchy as much as a gender dichotomy. The empowerment of children, all children, and young people as opposed to simply parental or adult-defined protection of 'innocence', then, is of paramount importance. The problem, though, is not monolithic maleness dropping out of the sky in parachutes but a specific, often western or capitalist, system that reifies male sexuality and male dominance and stratifies and structures masculinities accordingly. In addition, these are the issues under consideration in the next chapter on sado-masochism and pornography. Consequently, in conclusion, it is essential to consider the full significance of connections of masculinity and sexuality, identity and maturation, gender and generation.

CHAPTER 4

Sado-masochism, masculinity and the problem of pornography

Few gay men, myself included, have failed, on occasions at least, to fantasise and/or practise sexual activities concerning submission to a dominant 'masculine' man. Such sexual fantasy and/or activity may imply masochism and indeed sadism as the 'masculine' man does indeed dominate. To what extent, though, such activities or fantasies actually constitute masochism or indeed a sado-masochistic identity depends on definition. The distinction, though, of 'normal' non-sado-masochistic from 'deviant' sado-masochistic gay male sexuality, in itself stigmatised as deviant, is not entirely or continuously clear and whilst most gay men will often admit to a desire for dominance or submission they will only do so in the company of their own kind and usually with a defensive sense of camp comedy. Coming out as a sado-masochist or simply as a lover of 'masculine' men is indeed a second coming out for the already-out gay man.

The definitions and derivations of sado-masochism

The definitions and derivations of sado-masochism are not entirely clear or distinct. Sadism most commonly refers to the inflicting of pain to achieve sexual gratification and is derived from the extensive writings and practices of the French count, the Marquis de Sade (1740–1814). Masochism most commonly refers to the necessary sufferance of pain in achieving sexual gratification and is similarly derived from the work of Austrian novelist Leopold von Sacher-Masoch (1836–1895). Krafft-Ebing in *Psychopathia Sexualis* (1886) later defined the activities of sadism and masochism in more medical and scientific terms and the construction of sado-masochism is in many ways similar to the construction of male homosexuality though murkier and more distorted through a lack of any really valid evidence or study (see Chapter 1).

The construction of sado-masochism as an identity was therefore not in evidence until at least the nineteenth century and current understanding of the concept and practice is perhaps premised more upon contemporary developments in the 1970s and 1980s, although the practices of sadism and/or masochism in all likelihood have a lot longer history and a greater cultural diversity.

Sado-masochism may possibly be seen as most importantly premised on the developments of industrialism and capitalism due to the separation of home from workplace thus creating a private sphere where such activities could take place and, in particular, the rise of a class society as the earliest evidence of such activities is clearly located in the upper-class use of prostitution and 'rough trade' (Macnair, 1989). In addition, the construction of authoritarian identities through the rise of the state in the nineteenth century was crucial in creating current 'sadistic' and 'masochistic' identities and roles. In particular, the development of the mental–manual distinction and associations of cleanliness and dirtiness facilitated through class distinctions, partly dependent on the affordance of proper sanitation and hygiene, is one clue to the current context of sado-masochism.

More importantly, the medicalisation and in particular psychoanalytic analysis of sado-masochism through the work of Freud, the sexologists, and a whole host of followers including Alfred Kinsey, started to define sadism and masochism as identities rather than simply practices (see Chapter 1).

In addition, the institutionalisation and exploration of sexuality *per se* in the 1970s, as well as increased media and state intervention, led to the conflation of sadism and masochism theoretically and in practice, as proponents were quick to point out that they practised sadism *and* masochism. They were, therefore, 'sado-masochists' and small networks and groups developed around the identity in the 1970s in large cities in order to make contacts and facilitate community development. More importantly, perhaps, sado-masochism in America in particular was increasingly institutionalised through specifically developed pubs and clubs, specialising as both meeting places and centres of sexual activity, providing on occasions highly stylised locations and scenarios including dungeons and darkened rooms.[1]

Moreover, though, with the increased media publicity of sado-masochism and openness of its proponents in gay and lesbian communities, this led to a particularly heated debate on the subject,

[75]

concerning its sexual political implications, pros, cons, merits and limits. Most importantly, this discussion is characterised as a quite unparalleled polarisation and dualism of perspectives that would seem at least to be completely irreconcilable and premised on the most fundamental of differences.

This discussion and conflict is not, however, one which is characterised as being between feminists and gay men as simply critics and advocates of the position respectively. Sado-masochism is conversely often centred on conflicts in feminism over the right to promote sexual pleasure and the obligation to prevent sexual danger. Moreover, for some feminists, particularly those in the San Franciscan SAMOIS sado-masochist community, sado-masochism represents the ultimate rejection of femininity as 'nice girls' essentially 'don't do it', whilst for other feminists sado-masochism represents the ultimate cop-out in feminine passivity.[2]

This partly depends on a difference in implications concerning lesbian or straight women's sexuality as lesbian sado-masochism is not necessarily the same as straight sado-masochism. Thus, the implications concern the oppression of sexual minorities as well as women, as Rubin points out: 'The anti-S/M discourse developed in the women's movement could easily become a vehicle for a moral witch hunt' (Rubin, 1984: 299) whereas Nichols et al. state: 'We believe that sado-masochistic impulses are created and sustained by events and images within our society, and that sado-masochistic behaviour reproduces and therefore condones many of the power imbalances and destructive features of our lives' (Nichols et al., 1982: 138).

Similarly, the gay male community is sharply divided over the merits and limits of sado-masochism and its political implications for gay male sexuality. Consequently, rather more complexly, the discussion centres on four theoretical and political tensions or paradigmatic dualisms that reveal sado-masochism not to be so much a separate category of sexuality as much as an extreme and polarised example of the whole of sexuality and, indeed, the debates and discussion on sexuality.

The meanings and implications of sado-masochism

SM has also become an issue of major sexual political controversy in various radical movements, with both the feminist and gay and lesbian movements sharply divided about the merits of such activities.

(Weeks, 1986: 80)

The meanings and implications, personally and politically, of sado-masochism are premised primarily upon four interlinked paradigmatic dualisms.

Desire/damnation

In essence, the bottom-line issues of the debate, as they have been articulated, are the repressive intolerance of sexual minorities versus the incompatibility of feminism with power and/or violence in personal relationships.

(Rian, 1982: 45)

Sado-masochism is simultaneously a damned desire and a desire for damnation. Does, then, a desire for damnation undermine that damnation or even provide opposition to it, or merely reinforce that damnation? This issue has given the gay male community as many headaches as the women's movement, who were quick to point out that such role playing or oppression potentially at least reinforced the real oppression of women in society. Similarly, some men in the gay male community noticed that sado-masochistic acting potentially perpetuated the oppression of male homosexuality through active–passive dualisms and the debasement and degradation of oneself and one's desire for other men: 'The proliferation of sado-masochism is the major internal threat to gay freedom, comparable only in destructiveness to the impact of repressive laws and persecution by cops. The basis of both is the same: self-hatred' (Rechy, 1977: 253).

This works in two ways according to the loathing of self involved in masochism and the loathing of the other in sadism and, in each case, self and other are homosexual. Therefore, for John Rechy: 'The ritual of S & M embraces the straight world's judgement, debasement, hatred and contempt of and for the homosexual' (Rechy, 1977: 257). Sado-masochists themselves, though, often see such activity as a positive expression of sexuality and point to its cathartic qualities in alleviating guilt and stigmatisation:

It takes images of masculinity, the use and abuse of power, and the values of creativity, and it pits them against the perils of

[77]

human arrogance and the realities of human limits. It creates from all of this an experience that is cathartic, ecstatic and spiritual.

(Mains, 1984: 21)[3]

The significance of this, though, depends on the second dualism.

Repression/oppression

The case for S/M oscillates constantly between an essentialism of sex, power and pleasure, and a relativism which suggests that in certain circumstances 'anything goes'.

(Weeks, 1985: 239)

Sado-masochism opens up and polarises the extent to which sexuality *per se* is repressed and therefore is potentially liberated and liberationary or is oppressed and therefore is potentially neither liberated nor liberationary in itself. This issue of course centres on the infamous dualism of essentialism (repression) and constructionism (oppression) polarised further through the double stigmatisation of sado-masochism, highlighting a more pragmatic problem, as if one accepts that sado-masochism is an oppressed and stigmatised sexuality does one highlight its repression which supports its practice as liberation or its oppression which ultimately simply pulls it apart?

As a result, proponents and critics alike of sado-masochism are not consistent on this point. For example, Mains points out in essentialist terms: 'Vital to self-acceptance, and central to the leather mythos is a reconciliation of the human and the animal' (Mains, 1984: 29). In contrast with this, though, sado-masochism is perhaps quite unique in proposing and practising constructionist qualities of sexuality as it 'acts out' sexuality in a theatrical, scripted and role-playing way; yet its sexualised seriousness for its proponents appears to undermine this whole position.[4] In addition, the difficulty here is that as much as sado-masochistic sexuality and sexual practice is clearly 'constructed' in its identities and role playing, it is also of necessity serious to succeed sexually. Sado-masochistic sexuality, whilst perhaps appearing to parody or play with ideas concerning sex to an outsider, necessarily also relies on a serious individual internalisation of sexual fantasy for its insiders: laughter isn't sexy.

[78]

Sex power/power sex

> Does it expose and parody the order of power in society – or
> does it mimic and reinforce it?
>
> (Macnair, 1989: 147)

Sado-masochism in eroticising power and inequality quite clearly polarises the whole issue of the relationship of sex and power; the extent to which sex *per se* is power or the extent to which power is sex, thus leading on to the extent to which sado-masochism 'plays with power' or 'perpetuates power' and the extent to which power lies within or outside of sex. The perspective adopted interlinks with the previous point as essentialists will stress the power of sexuality and constructionists the sexuality of power. Importantly, the centrality of sex in sado-masochism is in question as to what extent is sado-masochism 'sexual' at all, as so much of its activity is concerned with power play rather than sexuality or sexual pleasure as: 'Sado-masochism is as much an irreducible condition of society as it is an individual "sexual preference" or lifestyle: indeed, sado-masochism reflects the power asymmetries embedded in most of our social relationships' (Linden et al., 1982: 4).

Consciousness/consent

> The S/M debate, by breaking a taboo on what could be said or
> done, has made it possible to think through again the impli-
> cations of sexual needs and sexual choice amongst consenting
> partners.
>
> (Weeks, 1985: 240)

To what extent does sado-masochism dictate or reflect wider consciousness or sexual politics; to what extent is this factor affected or not through consent? Proponents of sado-masochism are at pains to point out that sado-masochism is consensual. This therefore raises the question of whether this undermines its impact on consciousness or the extent to which sado-masochists otherwise act 'sado-masochistically'.

There is no clear evidence that sado-masochists are any more likely to vote Conservative, express or practise fascist opinions or actions, or take out anything at all out on other people; what little evidence does exist shows that they are often over-averagely educated, middle-class, and often slightly timid people who find self-fulfilment and

[79]

power for themselves only through their sexuality.[5] However, can one maintain politically right-on convictions while whipping someone or wearing a Nazi uniform without feeling a little confused or guilty? There is also a question here of civil and individual liberties in that does one have the right to kill or injure someone or be killed or injured by someone because you or they 'consented' to it and does an outside body such as the state have any right to say anything about it?[6] The problematic premises of these questions undermine any attempt to provide simple answers. However, the state, which frequently seeks to legitimate conformist forms of sexuality and reinforce definitions of deviancy, is clearly unequivocally not the institution with the solutions, as evidenced in the example of Operation Spanner.[7]

Sado-masochism, masculinity and male dominance

> Masculinity is a known, unquestioned fact.
>
> (Mains, 1984: 15)

I very much doubt if any of these questions about sado-masochism will be answered by attempting to come down off one side of the fence and prove one perspective triumphant over the other. Neither, I suspect, will it be solved by merely carving a midway route of balance between them for what is at stake are a whole series of highly individually and socially ingrained dualisms concerning sexuality that are probably at best pulled apart for the artificial minefields that they are rather than perpetuated. To attempt to do this, then, requires more detailed examination of the nature and meanings of sado-masochism and, in particular, its connections to masculinity as 'the fantasy of erotic domination permeates all sexual imagery in our culture' (Benjamin, 1984: 292).

Initially, it is perhaps necessary to try to define and consider exactly what sado-masochism and sado-masochistic practices are and constitute. The first distinction centres on one of acts and identities. Sado-masochism is perhaps more than any other sexuality premised on a particular linking of sexual acts and practices with codes, dress and identity. Identities are necessarily dualistic in that a sadist needs a masochist and a masochist needs a sadist to define himself ultimately as a sadist or a masochist.[8] This commonly turns into the master–slave dualism or sometimes a top–bottom dualism although this is often confused with simple active–passive dualisms as well. To properly enact this dualism one also necessarily needs to look the part, that is, to dress accordingly. This most commonly involves the use of leather, the most reified of 'dominant' dress codes, as this most readily infuses 'animal' and 'naturalistic' associations with heightened sexual signification. In addition, leather is usually worn in its entirety i.e. cap, jacket, vests/shirts, bands, underwear, trousers, and boots. The use of various individual leather items in contemporary popular culture, in particular jackets, is a source of some confusion although the entire leather look is unequivocally 'sado-masochistic'. Leather, though, is often combined with denim, most particularly Levi's jeans, and here the confusion with gay clone culture and indeed popular culture is particularly noticeable. It should also be said that this imagery is profoundly 'masculine' rather than 'feminine' in its design and associations and this is often the source of its eroticism for its proponents and its damnation for its opponents.

Whilst the leather/denim look is dominant, this is not entirely separable from the adoption of other types of dress with sufficiently male, dominant, and/or authoritarian associations. These include a whole array of uniforms, and American police and military effects are particularly common. Most importantly here, the nearer one can approximate complete authenticity to the original, the greater the prestige and the eroticism. This also creates more confusion with corporal punishment (CP) where uniformed physical punishment is meted out as the primary source of sexual excitement. These practices are of course also partly dependent on economic and practical access and status as such clothing is expensive and, in its more extreme forms, not readily accessible in the high street other than in very large cities and it is otherwise attained privately or through mail order. In addition, religious, legal or educational dress are also used occasionally.[9]

Consequently, the nature of the dress is not nearly so significant as its connotations in terms of masculinity, authority or power. It is also particularly important to point out that dress codes are often far more significant for the masochist regarding the sadist than vice versa and the masochist may dress similarly or in simple opposition to the sadist.

Sado-masochistic activities are commonly perceived to rank along a continuum according to the degree of pain, humiliation or degradation involved. Therefore, at the 'softest' level this involves mere dominant and submissive role playing, perhaps including dressing up,

[81]

according to codes of personal taste, and involving the same sexual acts as involved in 'vanilla' or non-sado-masochistic sex, though with clear lines of distinction of activity and passivity in all cases. Various other acts come into play as one continues through the continuum which also constitutes a sexual script of activities progressing from 'softer' to 'harder' in a given scene or series of acts. These acts frequently include issues of degradation in the master or dominant partner urinating or defecating on the slave or submissive partner and this may also escalate to enforced urine drinking or faeces eating, being slapped or hit, tied up or chained, gagged or forced to do traditionally unpleasant things including bootlicking or being forced to crawl around on all fours on a lead. The dominant partner or master will also metaphorically or literally 'strip' the submissive partner to the point of exposure or loss of privacy. Verbal communication is kept to a minimum other than for the master to verbally abuse the slave and for the slave to beg and/or plead. It is at this point that a distinction usually starts to occur between 'soft' and 'hard' sado-masochism as such a ritual will lead either directly to vigorous sexual activity or alternatively to the infliction of pain on the slave. If sexual acts occur this will usually involve a heightened distinction of activity and passivity as the slave is *forced*, often physically, to carry out certain sexually passive acts including cock sucking, arse rimming and very hard fucking. The slave as finale to all this will then usually have to clean up the effects.

If, alternatively, pain and torture are involved this can include bondage, shaving or cutting of hair on the head or body, use of clamps, pinches, pins or needles sometimes inserted into the genitals themselves. The ultimate sado-masochistic act though, and the one over which the most controversy ensues, is fist fucking or the insertion of a whole fist into the rectum. Apart from the crossing of a whole new dimension of pain threshold, this act also involves total trust in and submission to a master who at this point has the power to potentially internally rupture the slave or ultimately kill him.

The most important point in this discussion, then, is that there is clearly no one uniform phenomenon called sado-masochism and the acts and identities involved vary in nature, meaning and extremity from denim to Nazi uniforms and from mere role playing to life-threatening situations.

Moreover, the importance of masculinity as a source of eroticism underlies all these situations: 'Thus, the analysis of pornography indicated that sado-masochism, that is, interpersonal psychic and/or physical violence as a source of sexual pleasure, was a male phenomenon. Male sexual violence was the ultimate expression of masculinity' (Eisenstein, 1984: 123). Particularly apparent is the importance of masculinity in structuring sado-masochistic activities and situations. The sadist is usually unequivocally 'masculine' in connotation and the masochist is usually unequivocally 'feminine' in connotation (Benjamin, 1984; Dworkin, 1981).

However, difficulties do occur as first, master and slave are not necessarily male and female and may operate according to male or female same-sex sexuality or in heterosexual reverse. Moreover, meanings are sometimes muddled as masochists can on occasions maintain or increase 'masculine' status through their capacity to take pain, humiliation and degradation in greater and greater doses or generally play their role well:

> Presented thus gay male SM seems to have a striking similarity to those rites of passage by which a boy becomes a man in many primitive societies; rituals sometimes involving institutionalised man–boy relations, and sometimes involving the demonstration of strength through the acceptance of pain.
>
> (Macnair, 1989: 160)

More importantly, though, one cannot escape the importance of the reification of male dominance in some form and it is this which most concerns sexual political activists. In particular, this concerns inter-female sado-masochism as the question is consequently raised as to whether this adoption of masculine dress, posture and identity, even to the level of dildoes, is adding to wider female masochism or hijacking masculinity for women.

The question is raised also as to exactly how distinct sado-masochism is from all or vanilla sexuality in terms of codes, meanings and sexual activities. Very many gay men and indeed straight men appeal to other men and women in view of their 'masculinity' often signified or added to through 'dominant' dress codes and practices including leather jackets, jeans, certain ways of standing, walking and talking. Exactly how distinct, then, is the desire for a lover's nip or pinch, to dress up, to have an occasionally very hard fuck, an odd experimentation tied to the bed posts, to talk dirty, and so on, from sado-masochism? 'In short, the "SM phenomenon" is not so radically different in its political implications from the phenomena of "deviant" sexuality in general' (Macnair, 1989: 161). Or, indeed, all sexuality. What one is perhaps really dealing with is a continuum and not a separation or series of distinct categories.

If a distinction is in existence it most significantly centres on a question of pain *per se* as a source of sexual pleasure. For many people, gay or straight, this is perhaps something of a cut-off point. Most importantly of all though, until further study is carried out in an area fraught with emotive and mindless attempts at politically motivated support or criticism and a complete lack of valid investigative analysis or sociological study, there is perhaps little one can say without worsening the situation and: 'The heat in the debate is not there because SM poses us with radically new questions, but because it reminds us of old questions and old debates which we have not, as yet, managed to resolve' (Macnair, 1989: 161).

In the following section, I wish to consider some of these questions more specifically in relation to the gay male community, primarily through an analysis of gay male pornography.

Gay male sexuality, sado-masochism and the problem of pornography

An apartment. A tall, slim, fit-looking young man walks into a room with few furnishings save for a covered settee, a chair, a table, a pile of books and what looks like a collapsed set of shelves and cracking plaster. It appears warm and sunny and the man wears only an old T-shirt and jeans and is attempting to tidy up. The doorbell rings, he opens the door and in walks another white, young, well-built man carrying a toolbox and wearing a white T-shirt and a tightly-fitting old pair of Levi's. 'Hi,' he says, 'you want some shelves fixed' – his suntanned face smiles – 'Yeah,' the other guy replies, 'they fell down last night, I'm hopeless!' Light mutual laughter, silence. 'Right, well I'll get to work then,' says the workman who puts down the toolbox, takes out a small set of portable steps, climbs them and begins to work. The workman's T-shirt is cut tight across his chest and back and he is clearly muscular, whilst his jeans snugly hug a large button-stretching bulge. Time passes; he works up a sweat. The apartment owner hands the workman a long, cool drink, while looking up at him. 'Cheers,' the workman says and looks directly back, swallows the drink quickly, smiles lightly, turns, and starts working again. The apartment owner pauses, watches and steps over to the workman, saying 'Hey, you look like you need some help with that.' He reaches to help lift the shelf with one hand whilst with the other he reaches between the workman's thighs into his

[84]

crotch from behind. The workman turns, smiles knowingly, and says 'Sure' in a long, low Californian drawl. The apartment owner squeezes the workman's swelling crotch and starts pulling open the buttons of his jeans. The open flies reveal a set of sweating, white briefs barely concealing enlarged genitalia and the apartment owner pulls them down quickly to reveal a very large cock which he pulls a few times and then takes in his mouth. 'Yeah, suck that cock' the workman says and puts his hand in the hair of the apartment owner forcing his head down on to his erect cock, 'Mmn, you like that don't you?' His genitals are large and glisten with the apartment owner's saliva. They speak no more except for the repetitions of the workman's 'Mmn, yeah', 'Suck that big dick', or 'Show me how much you like it'. The sexual action becomes more frantic, the sucking more forced, dominated by sounds of 'Oh yeah!' until the workman suddenly pulls out his cock and ejaculates, groaning loudly and repeatedly as his semen spurts over the apartment owner.

The workman now commands the apartment owner to 'Lick my ass' and he turns and parts his legs. 'Oh yeah,' he says, 'that feels good, really lick my ass.' The apartment owner has now opened his own jeans and is masturbating his own above-averagely large cock. 'Get over the table,' says the workman to the apartment owner and, as he does so, the workman yanks down his jeans and pushes him down and over the table, looking at his bare ass which the workman begins to finger. 'Do you want me to fuck your ass, tell me you want me to fuck your ass,' the workman says, and the apartment owner moans and says: 'Oh yeah, fuck my ass'. The workman masturbates his cock until it stiffens once again and begins to push it into the waiting ass-hole. 'Oh yeah, ah—' moans the man on the table as the shaft of the workman's cock enters his ass-hole. He begins fucking him rhythmically getting faster and faster as his balls bang against the apartment owner's ass. The workman slaps the apartment owner's ass and says: 'C'mon, tighten that ass-hole', and 'Oh yeah, that feels good.' His face contorts as the rhythm and slapping increase until he pulls out his cock and ejaculates repeatedly onto the apartment owner who masturbates himself, sweating and groaning, to a hasty orgasm.

What this passage represents is entirely fictional. It is, though, instantly recognisable, to anyone appropriately acquainted with such films, as a typical example of an American gay male pornographic film. American pornographic imagery and indeed American imagery generally is some of the most popular and pervasive in all film formats on the international market and this particularly includes the market of gay male pornography. Such pornographic imagery and sexual action is also otherwise commonly known to the gay male community as the 'suck-rim-fuck' storyline.

[85]

Deconstructing the meanings of such pornography is necessarily a complex and multifaceted task taking into account such factors as audience, context and selective personal interpretation. Nevertheless, three factors are, I think, particularly apparent and predominant in much gay male pornography or sexual imagery, marketing and consumption as a casual glance at the classified section of *Gay Times*, for example, also illustrates.

First, there is an issue of contextual transgression which is central to all gay male pornography and indeed a lot of its heterosexual equivalents, as an apparently normal and non-sexual scene, such as having the handyman in to do a few repairs, is turned into an intense sexual scenario. The intensity of the sexuality and sexual action is of course linked to the very fact of this transgression. Transgression is also an essential and significant ingredient in all gay sexuality, considering the general societal assumption of heterosexual normality, so much so that a gay sexual scene is therefore transgressive on a second and greater, societal level.

Second, there is significant emphasis placed upon the eroticisation of inequality or dominance as, for example, the workman dominates the other man through the use of physical force and coercive orders, although this domination is partly undermined through the other man's overriding provocation and consent. Nevertheless, in identifying with the apartment owner one is clearly led into an eroticisation of the workman's domineering manner.

A third and linked factor underlying all of this is the simultaneous eroticisation and valorisation of masculinity as part of this process. The workman primarily dominates through his physical and psychological masculinity: his muscles, the size of his cock, his physical presence, and his authoritative orders. In addition, this whole factor is heightened in the masculinity of the context – his workmanship. Importantly, this factor dominates most gay male movies where the same or similar sexual activities take place on construction sites, in school rooms, locker rooms, prisons and other places where male-to-male contact, male exclusivity or masculine association is often significant. These three factors of transgression, eroticisation of inequality, and valorisation of masculinity are also at the centre of feminist and gay male academic discussion of pornography.

Feminists in the 1970s and 1980s widely criticised pornography as degrading to women in sexually exploiting them and showing them as willing participants in primarily male fantasies. Few disputed these claims academically and the far more contentious issue centred on the claim that such imagery perpetuated the rape and sexual exploitation of women or even directly created it. Andrea Dworkin (1981) asserted that pornography was the epitome of male power over women, whilst Robin Morgan's slogan 'pornography is the theory, rape is the practice' (Morgan, 1977) led to a widespread adoption of anti-pornography campaigning in the women's movement culminating in attempts to impose complete censorship.[10] Importantly, though, some socialist feminists asserted that such claims limited women's sexual autonomy (Coward, 1982; Segal, 1987; Vance, 1984; Wilson, 1983). The women's movement remains sharply divided over the merits and limits of these viewpoints and it is not my intention here to try to answer these questions, rather to locate the wider connections of this issue to the conflicts surrounding gay male pornography.

Gay male academics, like some socialist feminists, have challenged the more radical feminist view of pornography as less applicable or simply inapplicable to gay male sexuality on three counts: first, through the differing role of gay male pornography in validating a stigmatised sexuality; second, in the differential context and meaning of gay male pornography due primarily to a question of a gender similarity of men producing films of men for men; and third, through the differential status of the pornography itself due to severe censorship laws particularly applying to the importation of pornography often necessary due to the lack of variety, quality or quantity of pornography freely accessible in Britain (see Blachford, 1980; Watney, 1987; Weeks, 1985).[11]

The question is consequently raised as to the degree of similarity or difference of gay male pornography to all pornography. For example, Michael Kimmel says: 'Straight men and gay men have far more in common about their sexuality than we might at first suppose' (Kimmel, 1990b: 11). Scott Tucker, however, writing an article after consuming some pornography, says: 'Gay male pornography is a capitalist industry like any other, but it has served to affirm the sexuality of many gay men. To that extent it is a real and positive part of gay male culture' (Tucker, 1990: 269). This also sets up another example, then, of the conflicts of sexual politics with the politics of sexuality (see Chapter 2). In addition, it seems to me that this also raises three further questions for discussion: first, the overall relation of viewer and viewee; second, the overall position of pornography as part of or in society; and third, the limits and perhaps potential of gay male pornography following on from this.

There is quite clearly a qualitative difference in the viewer–viewee relationship when the persons concerned are of the same, not different, gender. The difficulties here, though, are: first, that whilst this may imply greater equality there is still a strong tendency, as we have already seen, to eroticise inequality within same gender parameters or to hierarchicalise competing masculinities; and second, following on from this, for some writers there is an implicit implication of power over femininity in this which makes gay male pornography more similar to straight male pornography in gender terms than at first it might seem (see Dworkin, 1981; Dyer, 1989). Moreover, though, the central issue is still not the merely implicit oppression of women, more the explicit oppression of certain types of masculinity in these images and pornography or, more simply, men's sexism against men.

More significantly still, this process is then juxtaposed with the oppression of male same-sex sexuality at a societal level which is constantly played upon in the pornography as the passive or powerless partner is always perceived as more primarily homosexual while the active or powerful partner's sexuality is perceived to transgress from straight to gay and, in addition, the gay consumer of the pornography is led to identify with the pre-given gay partner in eroticising the transgressive straight to gay partner due to the camera's construction of the passive partner as subject and the active partner as object.

The particular issue or problem, then, is not so much gay male pornography *per se*, rather more the societal relations that construct the specific form of the pornography. In an ideal society, gay male pornography could potentially provide an added validation of sexual diversity and yet, in the reality of sexual inequality, it primarily reproduces limited representations of masculine sexuality.

A secondary factor often considered here is the extent to which gay male pornography then reflects 'real' gay sexuality. Stoltenberg says: 'The values in the sex that is depicted in gay male sex films are very much the values in the sex that gay men tend to have' (Stoltenberg, 1989: 249). However, there is a contradiction here as these values may very well not actually reflect gay sexual practice as no evidence is provided, though equally they may very well reflect sexual fantasies as otherwise the pornography would not sell or succeed.[12] The difficulty, though, as with sado-masochism, is that a lack of particularly qualitative research in the area leaves these highly eroticised yet secret issues in sexuality hidden whilst wide open to profound misinterpretation and political posturing.

Conclusion: sado-masochism, masculinity and the problem of pornography

Sado-masochism and pornography do not so much represent exceptional forms of sexuality as much as provide heightened examples of all sexuality. As a result, academic and political discussion also tends to reflect this process in polarising issues of diverse yet damned desires and the constant nagging questions of sexual violence and inequality that are never very far away. What is curiously lacking, though, is a considered analysis of the status of gay sexuality in this, usually only seen as central in sexual diversity and stigma. Moreover, the problem is the profoundly limited forms of gay male sado-masochism and pornography which are constantly all too clearly caught up in processes of eroticising gendered and sexual inequality. Consequently, the question is raised then as to why these particular forms of gay male pornography and sado-masochism which, as we have seen, are limited in their eroticisation of masculine dominance rather than sexual diversity, still apparently appeal to so many gay men when the implicit images of gay men in sado-masochism and pornography are primarily more negative than positive. I suspect the answer to this question lies again in a societal context of inequality surrounding gay sexuality which pornography, in particular, can successfully play upon and eroticise. As every fantasy must necessarily have some grain of reality in it to succeed, it is to this question of the eroticisation of the inequality of gay sexuality, not simply eroticised inequality *per se*, or an eroticisation of oppression, that I turn to in the next chapter.

[89]

CHAPTER 5

Public sex: the eroticisation of an oppressed position

Sexuality is without the importance ascribed to it in our contemporary society (western capitalist); it is without that importance because it does not exist as such, because there is no such thing as sexuality; what we have experienced and are experiencing is the fabrication of a 'sexuality', the construction of something called 'sexuality' through a set of representations – images, discourses, ways of picturing and describing – that propose and confirm, that make up this sexuality to which we are then referred and held in our lives, a whole sexual fix, precisely; the much-vaunted 'liberation' of sexuality, our triumphant emergence from the 'dark ages', is thus not a liberation but a myth, an ideology, the definition of a new mode of conformity (that can be understood, moreover, in relation to the capitalist system, the production of a commodity 'sexuality').

(Heath, 1982: 3)

The primary purpose of this chapter is to explore the implications of public or non-private sexuality personally, socially and politically. Consequently, it is divided into two central parts, the first concerned with codes and identities and the second with contexts and acts, and each of these is in turn located within an analysis of wider discussions, tensions and debates.

The public sex debates I

Few subjects arouse the same degree of fear and fascination as sexuality conducted outside of privacy or private contexts or, more simply, public sex. Consequently, the prohibitive feeling that sex should be or can only be conducted properly 'in private' is, it seems, deep-seated. On top of this though, the definitions of privacy shift and have only relatively recently developed into their paranoid and policed state, primarily through the separation of home from workplace in creating public and private spheres combined with the artificial consignment of sexuality to the private sphere for procreative purposes only. More importantly, the development of cities into open, anonymous networks of potential catwalks is a major factor in creating the contexts for non-private sexuality. I call it 'non-private' as the paradox of public sex is that it constantly seeks to protect itself in corners, in darkness, and around doors due to constantly increased state surveillance, and it consequently equally constantly oscillates from apparent non-privacy into comparative privacy. The concepts of public and private are of course more complex than this, both conceptually and particularly in practice, but the central problem is that in relation to sexuality, the concepts of public and private become sharply demarcated and circumscribed within deeply political debates about social acceptability, liberation and decency and, indeed, it is the primary purpose of this chapter to explore and examine these debates.

The definitions of privacy set up via the state over the previous century are frequently confusing, centred on value notions of decency, order and peace; yet the definition of privacy used in the 1967 Sexual Reform Act was surprisingly, or perhaps not so surprisingly considering its primary target groups of gay men and prostitutes, specific and precise in criminalising almost everything and every kind of gay sexuality outside of adult consenting sex at home with only two parties present. Particularly importantly, a paradox develops as it is this very same targeted group of gay men who have most flagrantly and defiantly flouted all convention and found, created and constructed the most sophisticated ways of practising non-private sexuality within and around the confines of state surveillance throughout the previous century and particularly in the 1970s. Consequently, a series of tensions is set up between prohibitors and proponents of public sex and the public sex debates centre initially on three paradigmatic tensions between liberation and regulation, between opposition and oppression, and between counteraction and co-option.[1]

Liberation and regulation
The most obvious of these debates is the tension between liberation and regulation as public sex is often seen by its proponents as liberating personal or individual inhibitions and opposing politically and collectively heterosexual ideology; yet equally clearly public sexual activity is

constantly regulated through legal and state restrictions and cannot necessarily be said to be able to be liberationary (see Lee, 1978; Rechy, 1977).

Opposition and oppression

This problem of liberation and regulation leads on to the second tension between opposition and oppression as public sex is obviously oppressed through surveillance yet opposes this opposition through the persistence of its practice. Particularly importantly, it remains oppositional in terms of dominant sexual mores of decency and privacy (see Hocquenghem, 1972; Mieli, 1980).

Counteraction and co-option

On top of the previous point, a further problem develops concerning the extent to which public sex is a counter-reaction to primarily capitalist city developments or conversely the point to which it is simply co-opted into the mechanisms of corporate capitalism through the development of profitable subcultures and ultimately ghettos of gay sexuality. This leads on to a second question of the extent to which gay sexualities and subcultures are co-opted into dominant or mainstream sexual cultures. This was evidenced in the 1980s as Levi's jeans, high-energy disco and various art forms started to get taken in and taken over as part of advertising, TV and city lifestyled sexualities (see Altman, 1982; Gay Left Collective, 1980; Mitchell, 1980; Mort, 1988; Shepherd and Wallis, 1989).[2]

These three tensions will set up the parameters for the discussion that follows: first, of codes, definitions and identities; and second, of conduct, contexts and acts used in public sexual activity.

Codes, definitions and identities

A tall, white, well-built man walks anonymously along an American city street. He has short, close-cropped, sandy-coloured hair, faded through exposure to the sun, and wears a well-trimmed moustache. His clear-coloured eyes stare dead ahead, simultaneously seeing and ignoring, maintaining a fixed air of taking everything in around him. A fine gold ring pierces his right ear. He wears a faded plaid shirt open at the collar accentuating suntanned and well-developed pectoral muscles and exposing a smattering of chest hair. The shirt is also rolled at the elbows below which he clenches his wrists slightly and holds his hands and forearms somewhat stiffly, occasionally simply putting a thumb into a front pocket of a pair of well-worn and tightly fitting button-fly jeans. His thighs and buttocks are well-defined and a trained eye for detail will notice that he wears no underwear and that the lower buttons of the fly are left open exaggerating large genitalia. A coloured handkerchief hangs from his left hip pocket together with a large cumbersome set of keys on a ring that jangles noisily and almost rhythmically in time with the deliberate and set step of his tastefully scuffed western boots that seem to permanently and persistently stomp. He neither speeds up, nor slows down, turns around, stops, starts, interacts, or changes direction. He walks with a quite silent intention. He is cruising . . .

Cruising

> Two men passing on the street may momentarily glance at each other, drop cues that each is homosexual and interested in the other, hesitate for confirmatory signals and, within a half hour, consummate 'spontaneous' love in the many available niches that are legion in congested New York City.
>
> (Delph, 1978: 9)

Cruising has acquired new meanings. The invention of cruising is, moreover, a modern phenomenon, centred on the separation of sex from procreation. Thus, it is not surprising that it should originate with gay men whose sexual activity is necessarily already separated from procreation. Cruising, like all sexual activity, requires codes, definitions and identities to communicate sexual access and sexual preference. These codes, definitions and identities are, as we shall see later, quite extraordinarily developed and sophisticated.

In addition, cruising also requires the development of a city environment which provides sufficient opportunity and anonymity for the processes of sexual interaction to take place. In particular, the city street is reconstructed as a kind of catwalk allowing people to present themselves visually to other people, publicly. Cruising next requires nooks and crannies for sexual activity to take place, privately. This process of simultaneous exhibitionism and voyeurism is central to all public sexual activity.

This exhibitionist–voyeurist distinction is also located in public and private sphere definitions and is of colossal significance for it illustrates the simultaneous importance of modern developments in inventing the distinction and the continued consignment of sexual activity to the private sphere. This may seem unclear. Thus, to illustrate this: public sexual activity constantly crosses the public–private distinction in practice as one goes out to get sex (private to public) conveying covert (private) signals of sexual availability (public) to retreat into invisibility for the actual sexual activity (public to private). Gay men, in being publicly controlled through the lack of more socially approved and overt sexual accessibility and opportunity at the level of the local cafeteria, workplace or disco, are particularly caught up in this dichotomous process as their private and covert sexuality necessarily requires public and overt display in heterosexual culture.

Much emphasis has also been placed by some writers on the homosexual male 'pick-up system' as an escape from sexual repression or as being liberationary (Hocquenghem, 1972; Lee, 1978; Rechy, 1977). This liberation works on several levels: first, individually, as the idea is that public sex liberates personal hang-ups and inhibitions about sexuality; and second, collectively as 'every fuck is a fuck for freedom', a sign of community, and an opposition to the heterosexual monogamous and familial sexual ideology motivating state surveillance.

Quite clearly, such sexual activity does confront and overturn certain ideas concerning sexuality including heterosexist ideology; yet it is also clearly questionable as to whether this is 'liberationary' as this depends, problematically, partly on an essentialist notion of a re-pressed, as opposed to oppressed, sexuality and partly on a notion of sex and sexuality as intrinsically value free. This is, perhaps, profoundly fallacious as Pollak states:

> The homosexual pick-up system is the product of a search for efficiency and economy in attaining the maximisation of 'yield' (in numbers of partners and orgasms) and the minimisation of 'cost' (waste of time and risk of one's advances being rejected).
>
> (Pollak, 1985: 44)

Opponents of this position, then, point out that the sexual pick-up system is deeply set in a series of modern developments, including capitalism, that limit and shape sexual practices (Adam, 1987; Delph, 1978; Pollak, 1985). The homosexual pick-up machine is, in fact, equally accurately seen as a reflection of the internalisation of industrial, capitalist values of efficiency and productivity in turn defined in terms of primarily male sexuality. Sexual access and activity is rationalised through processes of specialisation and diversification along the lines of the division of tasks. It is, in short, a sexual production system. The difficulty of this perspective, though, is that there is very little appearance of agency or meaning in this situation and, in addition, there is the glaring underlying issue of gendered as opposed to simply capitalist construction. Cruising sexuality as instrumental, unemotional and orgasm-oriented is indeed male sexuality, *par excellence*.

Clones and culture

While heterosexual men were relaxing into a new androgyny in the 1970s, adopting longer hair, brighter colours, and softer fabrics, gay men and lesbians were making a mass commitment to denim, plaid, and leather.

(Adam, 1987: 97)

Cruising is the linchpin of public sex. Importantly, for the process to succeed, it is dependent upon dress codes and identities. These codes and identities are sometimes merely minor adjustments to dress though ultimately constitute complete identity cultures. Consequently, identities and definitions in fact create a complex means of conveying detailed individual sexual information and facilitate sexual access in codes of sexual signification. One of the clearest and oldest indicators of male sexual orientation was the wearing of an earring, usually worn on the right ear to indicate homosexuality and on the left ear to indicate heterosexuality.[3] However, signifiers of homosexuality in the 1970s took on a whole new level of sexual sophistication as shown in Table 1.

What Table 1 demonstrates is that gay public sexual activity is both considerably more variable and diverse than might be supposed and very creatively communicated; yet is still tightly structured around active–passive distinctions. Various individual preferences are of course practised and these are not necessarily static indicators of identity as individuals can and do develop or drop different codes, definitions and associated activities. However, the active–passive distinction isn't dead yet, despite protests that any given individual practises a variety of sexual activities. The point is that these activities at any one time are still structured according to active–passive distinctions and still take on certain sexual associations of virility and masculinity (activity) and receptivity and femininity (passivity) as: 'Gender orders sexuality' (Person, 1980: 619).

Similarly, in particular, clone culture constructs an identity of

Table 1 The key and hanky code[4]

Worn on:		left	right	centre/meaning
Keys		passive	active	either/both
Hanky:	black			whipping/beating
	red			fist fucking
	dark blue			fucking
	light blue			sucking
	yellow			piss
	dark green			military
	light green	buying	selling	hustling
	pink			dildoes
	grey			bondage
	brown			scat

apparently complete uniformity: individual differences, even physical differences, are undermined in a self-conscious attempt to appear completely 'masculine', partly as a development of the 1970s attempts to create a counter- or alternative culture and partly as an attempt to oppose stereotypes of effeminacy.[5] Most importantly, then, clone culture is essentially a 'masculine' construction. The various identities are all related to occupations traditionally defined as 'masculine' or 'real man's work': the western cowboy, the construction worker, the military, motorcyclists, sportsmen or policemen. These costumes or uniforms reinforced or reflected the overall 1970s 'masculinisation' of male homosexual culture as previously outlined in Chapter 2.

However, writers are divided over its merits and limits, for some: 'it may be an attempt to show that masculine or "ordinary" men can be homosexual too – a breaking down of the stereotyped image of the homosexual' (Blachford, 1981: 200) or vice versa: gay men are 'real men' too and what's more relate man to man, as men. What is more, the question was also raised as to what extent this construction of masculine identity was, most importantly, one of unconscious conformism or self-conscious nonconformism, acceptance or ridicule. It was clearly often the case that it was an effectively slightly silly and self-conscious exaggeration of traditional male identities: its seriousness was questioned. Equally, though, it was a semi-conscious acceptance or even an adoration of traditionally conceived male sexuality as many of these costumes or uniforms were and are worn for sexual as opposed to their original more instrumental purposes.[6]

In particular, this process of sexualisation is in itself often seen as potentially subversive, yet whether it is constructed as an instrumental or sexual reification of masculinity, it is still a reification of the masculine. Consequently, the question is also raised concerning whether such a convincing psychic split or separation of sexual fantasy from more structural reality is, in practice, practical or possible (see Bersani, 1988). Importantly, if one follows constructionist logic completely this necessarily includes individual psychological as well as social structural construction. The personal is indeed political: 'Not only does modern capitalism create the socio-economic conditions for the emergence of a homosexual identity, it creates the psychological ones as well. In short, the new homosexual could only emerge in the conditions created by modern capitalism' (Altman, 1982: 93).

More importantly, many gay men were now also perceived to have mutually co-opted themselves into consumer capitalism. Their lack of economic commitments and higher income made them excellent consumers equally effectively psychically exploited as exclusively sexually defined and inadequately attractive. The development of codes and meanings, then, is often seen more as regulation than liberation: 'The transformation of gay from outcast to cultural commodity happened very quickly, and can be seen as the triumph of the demands of consumer-orientated capitalism over one based on production' (Blachford, 1981: 209).

In conclusion to this section, codes, definitions and identities provided the gay male community with a series of useful self-defined communication devices facilitating sexual access. They also limited the gay male community in enforcing certain definitions of sexual attraction and created difficulties concerning co-option into capitalist consumer culture, in itself exploding and exploiting the same processes of sexual signification.[7]

Conduct, contexts and acts

Darkness falls as the gay male subculture gets to work, late. The thick blanket of darkness is a cover, a protector of anonymity and an erotic focus: a mantle of oppression and opposition. It heightens the danger as it provides the pleasure. This tension between pleasure and danger, dream and nightmare, is a major source of its eroticism. The straight and gay worlds start to separate. As straights tuck in the kids or turn on the TV, retreating privately, gays come out to play in cottages, parks or clubs, publicly. The pub on first appearances is simply a friendly place but something more subtle is at work: a silent communication as people appear, disappear and reappear as identities and codes, postures and gestures, and constant eye contact . . . The atmosphere may vary from a heavenly community to hell-like sexual dungeon . . . Unlike the straight bar or club, the gay bar or club tends not to have a sex distribution as lesbians are often excluded or form only a small minority. It's men only: men on the walls, men in the stalls, men in the bar, men behind the bar, men on the dancefloor. Men. On entering a gay bar one encounters an institution constructed around interaction, sexual interaction. The entrance acts as a central focus of attention and the bar itself is often placed well aside to maximise room and attendance, whilst seating is kept to a minimum. Endlessly, one stands around seeing and being seen. Pretty boys stare wide-eyed, hoping and praying to summon up powers to oppose some and appeal to others, while machos bore black-eyed holes in them and everybody bitches about the old hangers-on still cruising the same places. This process of voyeurism and exhibitionism is permanent and persistent. On top of this, it is relatively or even very dark. Consequently, if you can see any of the scenery, it's usually a sexual joke or a porn shot. Thus, the two things you tend to focus on (because you can see them) are the bar and the dancefloor. The dancing is often a trifle wild and wonderful, symbolising an abandoning of public inhibitions for a set of private constructions. The music is likely to be uncommonly loud, making it difficult, if not impossible, to hold a conversation. One focuses continually on what one can see – a forever moving stream of glamorous and not-so-glamorous male bodies while one is deafened and drawn in by the thundering drum rhythm combined with a belting vocal, usually a woman's, while lyrically it's all double entendres and men – they call it high (as in dope) n (as in men) r (ah/grr) g (gee)! The effect of dancing at 130 beats per minute plus is rather like using a drug or a jogging high and, slowly, all mental control is disappearing whilst the emotional intensity of the music is making you think you might as well . . . There is a smell of powerful colognes, poppers (amyl nitrite freely sold behind the bar with butch names like 'Thrust' and 'Bullet'), beer yeast and, faintly, sweat . . . It's also hot, very hot. As the alcohol flows one is quite literally pulsated and sucked into a world of sexual interaction and nonverbal communication – dress codes, postures, gestures, eye contact . . . Always eye contact, darkened by the lack of light into blackness. Contact . . . Various nooks, crannies and corners are provided for foreplay (or more if you prefer) with your new, anonymous partner. The pig parlour or back bar (if you get that far) is ink black and stiflingly hot as the smell of amyl and sweat increases over colognes and the music fades enough to hear the sucking sounds . . . Under and beneath all of this is a thundering silence . . . Just in case you haven't scored your trick yet (the blond denim number you were after got off with the good-looking hunk in the leather jacket), there's always the bathhouse or sauna. Here one pays yet another entrance fee for the (sexual) facilities – a locker, a room to arrange oneself in or go for wanders from, and a towel . . . One enters a twenty-four hour world of non-stop sexual activity . . . It's silent, relatively, and dim – low-coloured light-bulbs, music in the background and the constant sound of movement, water, wetness, and sex . . . It's exciting, it's risk-taking, it's 'masculine' – it's unknown: pleasure and danger. Staggering back to one's own bed or another's, somewhere (don't care), with or without (what was his name?) eventually one collapses, sleeps and is later shattered by the icy blasts of morning . . . [8]

Public sex, private contexts

Public sexual encounters can happen anywhere: in a cafeteria, at work, doing the shopping, on transport networks (particularly crowded commuter trains) or in enforced physical contact situations. Public sex is an omnipresent potential; its actual practice is, however, privately controlled. Consequently, public sexual activity (relatively private really) is constantly practised in a situation of potential private disruption through public intrusion. Hence, public sex develops within specific, private contexts. However, I would like to draw a distinction between informal, or non-institutional, non-intentional, latent functional public sex contexts (for example, public conveniences or parks) and formal, or institutional, intentional, manifest functional public sex contexts (for example, bars, clubs, or saunas). This distinction is crucial as these contexts create and construct qualitatively different sexual activities with particular social, economic, and political implications.

Informal public sex contexts

Informal public sex contexts are potentially unlimited in scope as the point is that a context intended for some instrumental purpose – shopping, entertainment or simply convenience – is converted into a site for sexual purposes. On top of this though, the scope is limited not only through state restrictions but the public–private distinction itself. Sexual activity cannot, in fact, take place 'in public'.

Cottaging

Cottaging, or the frequenting of public conveniences for sexual purposes, is probably the most established and oldest male homosexual informal institution. There are two reasons for this: first, accessibility, as for several centuries the public convenience was all there was as a legitimate means of meeting others of similar sexual preferences; and second, its maleness, as it remains the single most publicly accessible male domain defined by its male exclusivity. Consequently, there is an automatic aura of masculinity located in the walls of cottages. The activity of frequenting public conveniences for sexual purposes is called cottaging in Britain and tearoom trade in the United States though they perform the same latent 'homosexual' function.[9]

It is commonly assumed that non-identified homosexual as opposed to identified gay men primarily make use of public conveniences for sexual purposes as they offer some legitimacy for the sexual activity and: 'The homosexual can therefore attend them for the functions they serve while, at the same time, transform them into theatres of erotic activities' (Delph, 1978: 60). However, given the ready access to sexual activity, it is quite clearly incorrect to say that gay men do not also use the conveniences as well or that constant frequenting of conveniences will not eventually have an impact upon identity. Moreover, homosexually identified gay men do use public conveniences for fairly obvious sexual reasons as its sexual maleness is heightened by the definitions of the acts that take place. Many homosexual or gay men find the act of watching another man urinate slightly, or even very, sexually exciting due to the 'public' exposure of an otherwise 'private' penis in the 'active' situation of urinating in relation to a 'masculine' standing as opposed to sitting position. This is also one illustration of the association of activity and masculinity mentioned earlier. This is then equated with potential sexual activity and the implications are clear. The cottage or tearoom, then, through definition of its maleness, is an informal homoerotic institution. Delph in *The Silent Community* (1978) calls this an 'erotic oasis' implying a private, secluded dimension to a public institution and this tension is crucial to the acts that take place, in private but constantly under threat of public intrusion.

In addition, whilst the cottage or tearoom is an old institution of sorts, it is not static and it has, in fact, developed and reconstructed in its importance through the dynamic social, economic, and political processes over the last century, and indeed over the last twenty years or so in question. This includes the design and location of public conveniences that provide greater or lesser sexual opportunity and, in particular, the oppressive deployment of state-related sexually restrictive devices. These include the removal of coin-operated doors in the United States, used as a sound signal, and the now common use of lavatory attendants in Britain.

The sexual activity of cottaging or tearoom trade is, in addition, defined through these structural constraints and considerations. Masturbation and oral sex are the most likely activities being most easily operable and stoppable, whilst anal sex and sado-masochism, being more elaborate, are possible but less likely. One particular solution was the 'glory hole', a hole several inches in diameter bored into the cubicle partitions at pelvic height, allowing sight of partners and, in particular, oral sex to take place, although: 'The key element in the glory hole activity is total, anonymous sexual activity' (Delph, 1978: 91). Needless to say, local councils and police authorities have since deployed prison-like restrictions on these activities. The history of cottaging is, in fact, one of increasing sexual regulation whilst sexual activity has constantly widened and spread further into other areas.[10]

Parks, meatracks and trucks
Parks, like public conveniences, are not a recent addition to the sexual outlet list. Their development in Britain centred on eighteenth- and nineteenth-century industrialisation and urbanisation processes and the middle-class creation of 'retreats to nature' or 'oases of peace' within an urban or suburban environment. The most important point to note is that the association with the anonymous city usually allows the stigmatised minority to operate under cover as an outsider. It is therefore possible for homosexual men to be able to frequent parks anonymously and without any necessary suspicion. Thus, as in cottaging, parks provide an element of legitimation. However, use of parks for sexual activity once again centres on the public–private distinction. It permits open display and overt viewing (public) whilst offering seclusion for sexual activity (private). This is created through the very structuring of the landscape into open spaces with walkways on the one hand and hidden corners behind trees and bushes on the other. In addition, it is important to point out the potential public intrusion placed upon private activity and, in particular, the structural constraints imposed upon them through park opening and closing times and the use of attendants.

'Meatracks' are more of an American invention. As designated and defined areas of park land so well secluded and hidden you have to 'know' them to find them, they are an extension of the public–private separation. This privacy and seclusion creates, constructs, and permits extended sexual freedom. For example, Fire Island, situated near New York City, featured meatracks formed for sado-masochistic activity. Particularly common is the development of group as opposed to individually orientated sexual activity, as more and less 'risky' respectively. Meatracks usually operate quite collectively in this respect. Furthermore, they operate a closure system thus allowing or preventing entry. In short, the sexual activity is created, constructed and defined according to a fairly realistic assessment of the risk factor that in turn reflects restrictions placed upon public sex.[11]

Trucks are again a more modern construction. Container trucks are left unlocked all night at many docks when gay men may come to make use of them. They offer obvious public accessibility and opportunity for private activity. In addition, there is an interesting association in their selection for sexual activity in the already latently sexualised association of male exclusivity facilitating fantasies of machismo, sweat, labouring and all the rest of the associations. In addition, sex outside is defined as 'masculine' due to its risky or 'dare-devil' value system. In conclusion, these developments reflect the informal institutionalisation of sexual activity.

Formal public sex contexts

The homosexual subcultural network of interconnected outlets is not necessarily a new invention. In Renaissance England, molly houses performed similar functions of constructing social and sexual contacts and consolidating identities (see Bray, 1982). These still form the mainstay of the 'gay scene' today. This is composed primarily of clubs, bars, bathhouses and saunas. These facilities are, in fact, social, economic, and political constructs and they tend to reflect the development of capitalism through the simultaneous processes of diversification and specialisation. In particular, they represent the emergence of the homosexual subculture as a profitable consideration, in turn representing the increasingly formal institutionalisation of sexual activity. However, whilst this successfully accounts for the structural considerations in homosexual subcultural institutions, it does not account for their particular forms or meanings.

Clubs, bars and pig parlours
There is, of course, no one single club, bar, or pig parlour, so called because of the pig-like sexual activities they provide. However, they do have defining features. First, they are characterised through their location on the outskirts rather than in the centre of a given city or town. In addition, one generally needs to 'know' beforehand of one via an advertisement in a gay magazine or through the gay community itself. Furthermore, hours of opening and closing are sometimes restricted and tend to be 'off-beat' or later than usual.

These factors reflect the temporal and spatial segregation of the homosexual subculture which ultimately becomes a complete counter-cultural separation: ghettoisation. These centralised communities of homosexual exclusivity (for example, San Francisco's Castro district, New York's West Village, or particular parts of Amsterdam) are often seen as 'the gay haven in a heartless world', and: 'This is fine as far as it goes, but it generally does not go far enough because it fails to connect the subculture back to the dominant culture' (Blachford, 1981: 184). Clubs, bars and pig parlours vary considerably according to area, location, and individual clientele including idiosyncratic factors of social and sexual preference. On top of this though, still particularly apparent are rural–urban differences as there is clearly likely to be a far greater variety of pubs and clubs in big cities and following on from this more emphasis placed upon personal prefer-ences, particularly sexual preferences, whereas country pubs remain essentially meeting places for isolated communities. Quite clearly, in either case, the character of a pub or club is both structurally and individually determined.

Bathhouses and saunas
Bathhouses or saunas, being approximately the American and British equivalents of the same thing, occupy the unenviable position of being both publicly and openly gay and sexual to those who know them but operated ostensibly as both straight and therapeutic. Im-portantly, bathhouses also became the centre of attention during the AIDS crisis and seen as contagious institutions of high-risk sexual activity, and yet issues of quite who did what where, when and why remain shrouded in secrecy.

The issue is further complicated by both political, particularly post-AIDS, implications and by British–American comparisons. It is commonly perceived to be the case that Britain never had bathhouses and their associated sexual activities in the way that, apparently, certain American cities had, but maintained and still maintains a less institutionalised and *ad hoc* sauna network of known caterers for sexual activity. Consequently, it is quite clearly the case that the public–private distinction is particularly apparent and problematic as overt–covert and front–back aspects of sexuality are central and confusingly located in a series of social, legal and sexual sanctions. It is equally clear that such facilities did offer quite unique, collective and extensive sexual opportunities for some. More particularly, the sexual activities involved in such places offering far greater privacy were often perceived as comparatively open and unrestricted, leading to the aforementioned controversy concerning the transmission of AIDS and HIV. However, the exact outcome of these developments remains a mystery.

Formal public sex contexts consequently highlight both the creativity of the gay community, its potential co-option into corporate capitalism and its persistent, permanent and profound oppression as part of state and legal regulation of all sexuality: 'The irony of the 1970s, then, was the ease with which gay and lesbian aspirations were assimilated, contained, and overcome by the societies in which they originated' (Adam, 1987: 100). This perspective contrasts sharply with the more creative and quite clearly politically oppositional or counter-cultural aspects of the gay male community's practice of sexuality (see also Chapter 8).

The public sex debates II

A second series of public sex debates or tensions, then, arises out of the particular expansion and explosion of the gay subculture and gay sexuality in the 1970s.

Sex incarnate
The first of these tensions centres on the question of the extent to which gay sexuality and sexual activities constitute sex incarnate:

> Homosexuality is considered to represent a pure, unencumbered form of sexuality. Not engendering new life, divorced from the social and economic structures of heterosexual marriage, and apparently employing sexuality as the primary form of self-definition, homosexuality represents sex incarnate. In short,

homosexuals are obsessed with sex. This obsession, along with the impulse to personal freedom that makes sexual activity possible, is at the center of the gay sensibility.

(Bronski, 1984: 191)

Why are gay men apparently so obsessed with sex? This is a problematic question raising a second question of whether gay men are sexually obsessed or not or whether they are more sexually obsessed than anyone else and do they, in fact, practise a lot of sexual activities with a lot of sexual partners and is this promiscuity necessarily any more important than for their heterosexual counterparts?

These questions are only partly answered through the sex studies of the late 1970s including *The Spada Report* (Spada, 1979) and *The Gay Report* (Jay and Young, 1979) which do indicate significant, if not extraordinarily high, degrees of sexual activity in some cities amongst some gay communities some of the time. More insight is perhaps developed in more personal or literary studies including the American work of acclaimed writer Edmund White (1986) and the ethnography of John Rechy (1977) and John Alan Lee (1978) or the UK comparisons of Quentin Crisp (1968) and Alan Hollinghurst (1988). All of these are fairly or even very positive pro-promiscuity pieces of work; a profoundly critical polemic is provided in the work of American activist Larry Kramer (1978, 1986).

This still raises the further question, though, of why? One explanation is simply that access to sexual activities creates the activity. This is a circular analysis, though, that does not stand up to critical scrutiny. A second explanation is that the stigmatisation of sexuality leads to an explosion of sexuality when presented with plenty of opportunity to practise it. This domino theory of sexuality also rests on a series of essentialist assumptions and the problem, at least partly, seems to be one of maintaining an identity.

Promiscuity and masculinity

Sexuality, in turn, may be a mainstay for gender.

(Person, 1980: 619)

Person points to the second debate of the relationship between promiscuity and masculinity as: 'There is a celebration of masculinity that allows them to distance themselves from the stigmatised label of homosexual' (Blachford, 1981: 193). In addition, the male homosexual's

social, economic, and political definition of identity through his
sexuality, puts sexuality at the top of the list of priorities. Sexuality
creates and constructs consciousness, expressed positively or negatively, through the adoption of particular dress codes, identities and
meanings in terms of the masculinisation process discussed earlier.

Essentially, male homosexual activity is defined in 'masculine'
terms of orgasm, its complete separation from procreation, its partial
separation from some forms of affection and emotional bonding. In
addition, the affection that is involved in public sexual encounters is
still limited and male defined in terms of non-demonstrative gestures
and communal feeling, few kisses, few cuddles and certainly no tears
and: 'In men, there is such a rigid link between sexual expression and
gender that their sexuality often appears driven rather than liberated'
(Person, 1980: 620). Kimmel (1990b) has alternatively seen this situation as constructed and 'scripted' (see Chapter 2).

The difficulty still is that in each case gay male sexuality is seen as
pathological and victimised as opposed to an active perpetration of
particular sexual preferences. Importantly, the sexual activity that
ensues does tend to reflect dominant traditional male sexual values.
This is exemplified in the emphasis on silence; verbal communication
is almost non-existent in all public sexual encounters. The point is: it
won't work including talking. Talking leads to distraction and more
importantly personal communication and emotional attachment. Its
excitement comes from its lack of contact: its minimalism. For
example:

> The train from Victoria to Clapham still has those compart-
> ments without a corridor. As soon as I got on the platform I saw
> who I wanted. Slim hips, tense shoulders, trying not to look at
> anyone. I put my hand on my packet just long enough so that
> he couldn't miss it. The train came in. You don't want to get in
> too fast or some straight dumbo might get in with you. I sat by
> the window. Then just as the whistle went he got in. Great. It's
> a six minute journey so you can't start anything you can't finish.
> I stared at him and he unzipped his flies. Then he stopped. So I
> stood up and took my cock out. He took me in his mouth and
> shut his eyes tight. He was sort of mumbling it about as if he
> wasn't sure what to do, so I said, 'A bit tighter son' and he said
> 'Sorry' and then got on with it. He was jerking off with his left
> hand, and I could see he'd got a fair-sized one. I wished he'd
> keep still so I could see his watch. I was getting really turned on.

What if we pulled into Clapham Junction now. Of course by the time we sat down again the train was just slowing up. I felt wonderful. Then he started talking. It's better if nothing is said. Once you find out he's a librarian in Walthamstow with a special interest in science fiction and lives with his aunt, then forget it. He said I hope you don't think I do this all the time. I said I hope you will from now on. He said he would if I was on the train, but why don't we go out for a meal? I opened the door before the train stopped. I told him I live with somebody, I don't want to know. He was jogging sideways to keep up. He said what's your phone number, you're my ideal physical type, what sign of the zodiac are you? Where do you live? Where are you going now? It's not fair. I saw him at Victoria a couple of months later and I went straight down to the end of the platform and I picked up somebody really great who never said a word, just smiled.

(Churchill, 1979: 45)

This also demonstrates the emphasis placed upon physical appearances and enforced conformity. Codes and identities, paradoxically, while performing the function of promoting communal feeling, also enforce a conformism that is often profoundly stereotypical as well as deeply sexist, racist, and ageist: 'In this reproduction of the sexual objectification that even goes beyond that characteristic of heterosexual casual encounters, one is not challenging the ideology of male dominance in our society and its resulting homosexual oppression' (Blachford, 1981: 191).

Consequently, this sets up a sharp contrast with the more positive view of gay male promiscuity as almost revolutionary: 'Gay people are generally less inhibited about the enjoyment of playful and uncommitted sex. Sex with more joy and less guilt is something gay people can teach the rest of the world' (Lee, 1978: ii). However, Andrew Holloran writes:

Last week in the baths I was sitting in a corner waiting for Mister Right when I saw two men go into an even darker nook and run through the entire gamut of sexual acts. And when they were finished – after all these kisses . . . and moans and gasps, things that caused scandals in the nineteenth century, toppled families, drove Anna Karenina to suicide – . . . after all that, they each went to a separate bedroom to wash up. Now you may

[107]

view this as the glory of the zipless fuck, but I found it suddenly
– and it surprised me, for I'd always adored this event before –
the most reductive, barren vision of sex a man could devise.

(quoted in Adam, 1987: 100)

In sum, it seems that for some men at least some of the time, casual
sexual encounters are exciting and satisfying, whilst for others they are
simply poor alternatives to more complete relationships. Perhaps, one
might say that in practising one ought not to preach.

Pleasure and danger

Public sex is primarily conducted within the context or parameters of
pleasure and danger or eroticism and oppression due to its constant
oscillation across a series of codes of decency, order and privacy. It is
essentially socially and structurally 'risk-taking'. As a psychic dis-
position this is also essentially 'masculine' as opposed to 'feminine'
and it is also primarily, though not exclusively, men who practise
these sexual activities. Consequently, whilst promiscuity and risk-
taking sexuality are socially approved as part of masculinity, such
sexuality is all too often castigated as part of femininity; whilst for
women sexuality is at worst a situation of pleasure or danger and at
best a situation of pleasure and danger combined, for men pleasure is
danger and danger is pleasure, although whether the dangers of AIDS
and HIV will change men's attitudes still remains to be seen.[12]

Conclusion: the eroticisation of an oppressed position

The paradox of the 1970s was that gay and lesbian liberation
did not produce the gender-free communitarian world it en-
visioned, but faced an unprecedented growth of gay capitalism
and a new masculinity.

(Adam, 1987: 97)

Throughout this chapter I have constantly stressed the importance of
social, economic, and political contexts in constructing codes, identities, and sexual activities. These form the basis of the gay subculture.
Public sex is paradoxically only public to the extent that it is not
practised at home and, moreover, it is permanently regulated through

state surveillance and police activity. The story of the last twenty years or so is not one of wild, abandoned liberation but of continued and increasing sexual regulation. The stigmatisation of gay men's position through these social, economic, and political contexts unfortunately counter-reacts into a reification of the masculine: masculinisation. This creates a straitjacket of sexual objectification reinforced through actual sexual activity which can also be seen as symptomatic of the overall consumer capitalist commodification of sexuality and continued oppression of homosexuality. It also implies a problem of intermale intimacy and private love. However, homosexual men have also successfully created a subculture constantly offering the potential for profoundly erotic activity as pleasure and danger come together as 'sex incarnate' (Bronski, 1984: 191). In so doing, the homosexual subculture forms the 'eroticisation' of an oppressed position.

CHAPTER 6

Private love: an alternative?

I'd like to say gay men are different. I'd like to say they've cracked the codes of masculinity and are more caring, more intimate, and more significant than straight men in their handling of love. Having had the fantasy that coming out as a gay man would provide not only the liberation of my sexuality but liberation from oppressive forms of masculine dominance, competition, power and defensiveness; I have to say the reality was, and is, different. My earliest experiences of the gay scene treated me to some of the most blatant and blinding sexual objectification I have ever encountered. In addition, a later partner in typical masculine fashion put his career ahead of me and we split up, another said he couldn't have sex and love and, most recently, another insisted we hadn't 'done' anything as we hadn't had full anal intercourse. You might say I'm cynical or just unlucky: I would like to say, first, that I've witnessed the same situations occurring over and over again in other gay relationships; and, second, that this is of course also only half the story: I've also kissed endlessly, chatted affectionately, cuddled, cried over, and declared love with other men. The problem remains, though, and many if not all gay men, including me, find it difficult to resolve equally strong desires for sexual freedom with a profound need for love and security. The crunch always comes with the word 'commitment' that seems to send most gay men completely apoplectic. On top of this, there's the politics — shouldn't we oppose romance and monogamy as heterosexist if not capitalist constructs. I crawl and groan at the simplicity and stupidity of this this point of view — 'Right on, brother — fuck off!'

I'd like to say, despite all this, it is simply gay men's own fault and that what they need is a good dose of feminism shoved up their arses where it hits home most. I'd like to say it was that easy. However, with a society that so consistently oppresses homosexuality and structurally opposes the development of their long-term relationships with truck loads of happy families and institutional ideology, it's hardly politically fair or practically realistic. To counteract these processes or to change gay men one needs to change all men and for that matter the mothers and fathers who tell them not to cry and the societies that so consistently promote and enforce one form of masculinity and one form only.

Love versus lust: the understudy

It's so much easier, as I have discovered, to write about the transient nature of much of the gay world, which is more exotic, more colourful than the ups and downs of long-lived relationships.

(Altman, 1971: 17)

Private love, or the long-term homosexual relationship, as opposed to the transient world of public sex, is an understudied subject. It is understudied because little study has been made of the subject and it is understudied because it constantly takes second place to the study of public sex, only looming when boredom with the subject of sex sets in, which is not often.

However, there have always been two elements within homosexuality: the erotic and the romantic, the public and the private, lust and love. Nevertheless, the latter has increasingly been overshadowed by the former (see Carpenter, 1908).

There are several reasons to explain this situation. First, the overall rise of sexual discourse throughout the twentieth century has led to an acceleration in attention to the sexual as opposed to the romantic, particularly in comparison with emphasis placed upon romantic attachments and friendships in previous centuries (see Faderman, 1981; Vicinus, 1989). Consequently, whilst the Victorians did indeed produce as well as socially oppress sexuality they also produced a romantic discourse and practice that has no common parallel today as contemporary romantic fiction is not romantic practice and most of it increasingly teeters on soft-core pornography (see Foucault, 1978; Snitow, 1979; Winship, 1985).

In comparison, sexuality has exploded into an omnipresent, omnipotent deity: 'The idea of the importance of sexuality today is out of any proportion, the place it occupies is that of the new religion' (Heath, 1982: 147). This explosion of discursive sex has developed through the mass media in its many forms including films, television and magazines and through the sciences including psychoanalysis, the caring professions and medicine. A second discursive factor is that whilst sex has increasingly been seen as something to be talked about, love has been increasingly confined to a situation of silence or 'invasion of privacy'. Love is indeed private and privatised. However, none of this explains the particular position of gay sexuality.

[111]

Structural restrictions

> Most of the pangs and problems of the homosexual condition
> come from the great divide between affectivity and sexuality,
> caused by the lack of social and material cement that tends to
> make heterosexual relationships last.
>
> (Pollak, 1985: 50)

Love, far from falling out the heavens or just happening, is often in
fact constructed around and developed within particular social contexts.
In particular, this places quite definite limits upon the development of
same-sex as opposed to opposite-sex attachments. These limits are
essentially applied on two mutually supporting and perpetuating
levels.

First, on the level of institutional discrimination as same-sex meeting places do not occupy the same prevalence as their opposite-sex
counterparts and, on top of this, the workplace and often the home
are implicitly heterosexual. As a result, if one crosses these hurdles,
added difficulties ensue as same-sex relationships are not legitimated
in the same way as opposite-sex relationships and are, arguably,
stigmatised and delegitimated. This occurs over small matters such as
sending cards or flowers, making arrangements for meals out or
holidays away and, ultimately, making an emotional commitment is
also hampered through the lack of concessions concerning insurance,
taxation, mortgage arrangements and the prevention of gay men
particularly from adopting or fostering children. Consequently, all
aspects of consolidating a same-sex relationship outside of the gay
scene itself run the risk of discrimination or ostracism.

Second, the more significant factor is of course the question of
sexual mores and sexual values which create and perpetuate the
institutional situation. For example, theoretically, there is no reason
why two men cannot meet up at a local disco as easily as a man and a
woman or have a meal or set up home: the difficulty quite clearly is
first, fears of rejection and retaliation; second, interpersonal or group
pressures and conflicts; and third, actual institutional discrimination.

In addition, this sense of deviance can have its psychic consequences as the gay existence is often dominated with a sense of
distance or difference that can potentially create a psyche so con-
vinced of its isolation that relationships are put under particular stress
and intensity. This sense of otherness, outsider identity, or simply

difference, is partly the outcome of the definition of gay sexuality itself as other and different and partly the result of the practical and social parameters put around potential same-sex relationships. More positively, this may also develop into a comparatively higher level of independence and self-sufficiency as: 'Looking after oneself is simply part of life' (Dowsett, 1987: 11).

More importantly, though, the same-sex relationship does not have support from the approval of the wider society as family, friends or work colleagues are often not told and therefore cannot offer support or are told and actively disapprove or discourage the relationship. Importantly, then, gay men are caught up in a particularly oppressive Catch 22 situation as their public sex lives feel the full force of state and legal regulation; whilst their long-term relationships face countless social or structural impositions placed upon their development: 'There is thus, to say the least, a strong irony in homosexuals being accused of not forming stable relationships, when it is the social prohibitions they suffer which largely prevent them from becoming involved in such relationships' (Hoffman, 1968: 179).

This social situation or context does of course still have its individual and community counter-reaction. The gay community has creatively and positively developed a vast array of meeting places, venues and groups which offer the chance to meet people of the same sexual preference. This usually only extends to the level of café, clubs and bars and the odd bookshop that one generally has to find out about first. However, it may ultimately develop into the infamous gay ghetto where everything is organised according to a single defining feature, sexuality or sexual orientation, paralleling an ethnic minority. Consequently, one can work with other gay people, go to a gay-run supermarket, eat in a gay restaurant and have a gay landlord, dentist, doctor, accountant, solicitor, therapist or adviser.

The difficulties presented in gay ghettos are essentially the same difficulties presented throughout the gay community network. Sexual preference is only one, if important, factor in an individual's identity or personality and, consequently, conflicts are likely to occur: first, over a vast array of different individual and collective needs; and second, over an equally vast array of needs and desires not necessarily related to sexual identity. As stated in Chapter 1, an identity not only defines and connects, it limits and imposes upon the plurality of human society (see DuBay, 1987). This also creates political difficulties as adopting an identity politics tends to lead to the adopting of a separatist politics. The paradox which often develops here, though, is that in separating oneself from mainstream culture and asserting difference there is a tendency to assert sameness within that separate community whilst the opposite process operates in a politics of assimilation. The similarity with the internal fragmentation of the Left generally, often around issues in gender and sexuality, is particularly apparent. More importantly still, this process also has interpersonal implications.

Intermale intimacy

We love another man, his body, his passions and desires. We love another man's loving ourselves, our bodies, passions and desires. That love is more than sex. It is the creation and maintenance of relationships of significance. This is no easy feat for anyone, but is made more difficult for homosexuals because we lack the social support offered to heterosexual relationships by the laws, the institution of marriage, by tradition, by tax benefits and overt cultural validation. Our successes and failures here are object lessons in the relationship between social structure and personal life.

(Dowsett, 1987: 11)

As we have seen in the previous chapter, gay men's resistance to private love is partly premised upon a political opposition to heterosexual monogamous ideology. In the 1970s, monogamy in the gay community was in many ways perceived of as profoundly untrendy, and an ideology developed around the idea of the negativity of monogamy and the positivity of promiscuity or a 'monogamous negative; promiscuous positive' ideology. As a result, the story of the 1970s was one of an apparent explosion of this particular kind of sexual activity and a decline in sexuality centred on monogamous relationships (see Jay and Young, 1979; Spada, 1979).

Apart from the political implications of this position, the underlying issue was still one of intimacy and, in particular, intermale intimacy. Feminists, as we have also seen, pointed out that such promiscuous sexual activity was also very 'masculine' sexual activity centred on risk-taking and sexual attraction as ends in themselves (Dworkin, 1981; Jeffreys, 1990; Stanley, 1982).[1] The counter point of view put forward was that this sexual practice was: first, a political activity centred on consolidating a sexual identity; second, that it was not so masculinist as it seemed and involved a certain degree of intimacy; and third, that this kind of activity was frequently carried out in conjunction with longer-term, more loving relationships (see Weeks, 1985). Practical evidence was not necessarily forthcoming for these assertions and, furthermore, there were clearly conflicts surrounding the actual practice of, on the face of it, a slightly idealistic cake-and-eat-it conjunction.[2] Consequently, a certain degree of criticism of the situation also developed within the gay male community itself and, with the development of feminism and its conjunction with psychoanalysis, a further perspective developed which pointed to the importance of the maintenance of masculinity and masculine identity in opposition to developing long-lasting and intimate relationships.[3]

This point of view also developed as a primary part of the development of 'men's studies' in the 1970s which sought to assert that the male sex role had its limitations for men as well as women, in particular in creating an alienated and emotionally incapacitated male experience that emphasised sexual performance to the point of producing impotence.[4] On top of this, points were made concerning the inadequacy of men's relationships with other men due to the competitive and institutionalised nature of the worlds of work and sport where men primarily met one another. Apart from the immediate criticism that this was an attempt to create sympathy for these poor victims of masculinity and let them off the hook for the crimes of violence and oppression routinely practised upon women, this perspective also stepped straight into the trap of creating stereotypes, particularly white, middle-class, well-educated stereotypes of emotional inadequacy.[5] It was, and is, primarily a heterosexual stereotype to which gay men in general found it difficult to relate and felt excluded from and therefore effectively remained disinterested. Nevertheless, the implication that men as part of masculine socialisation had a problem with intimacy stuck like shit to toilet paper.[6]

The first point to make perhaps is that the definition of intimacy used in these assertions is a very limited one centred primarily upon opposite feminine definitions of intimacy as a demonstrative series of kisses, cuddles, tears and endless emotional salving. With stereotypes flying, the question is also perhaps raised as to the intimacy involved in 'male bonding' or the kind of sporty, homoerotic, sex-talking, back-slapping stuff of the locker room.[7] More seriously, relationships between men are an understudied and uncritically unfocused subject and quite clearly men do constantly have long-lasting friendships with one another that quite clearly do something or the other for them and are a lot more intimate than the stereotypes might indicate. Men do indeed perhaps develop relationships that are equally intimate though quieter, less demonstrative and more mentally than emotionally centred than with women.

Second, the study of intimacy has developed since the pioneering of stereotypes primarily through the development of psychoanalysis and, in particular, object-relations theory. Nancy Chodorow's *The Reproduction of Mothering* (1978) has been a very influential thesis both for psychoanalysis and sexual politics as it appears at least to lend itself more successfully to social political interpretation than most psychoanalytic theory. The theory primarily states that males and females are created into different gender men and gender women through the processes of parenting and, in particular, mothering. The most important point is that females and males are mothered, that is parented primarily through female interaction and consequently develop different personality characteristics due to their different relation to the same mother, thus: 'Masculinity becomes an issue as a direct result of a boy's experience of himself in his family – as a result of his being parented by a woman' (Chodorow, 1978: 181).

To fully understand these ideas practically requires a degree in psychoanalytic theory. Nevertheless, to put it in lay terms, males through virtue of their anatomical maleness are treated differently and as different by their mothers who, consciously or unconsciously, effectively 'push' males further away from themselves than females who they perceive as more like themselves. This harder 'push' into the Oedipus Complex leads to a distancing of the male from his mother and indeed the mother from the male, whose identity crucially depends upon the whole notion of his difference, of his non-femaleness and non-femininity. Masculine identity is therefore 'not feminine' and, what is more, premised upon emotional distance and separation as opposed to closeness and attachment to the mother: 'Masculine personality, then, comes to be defined more in terms of denial of relation and connection (and denial of femininity), whereas feminine personality comes to include a fundamental definition of self in relationship' (Chodorow, 1978: 169).

This process of separation *per se* and, on top of this, its implications for disassociation from all forms of femininity is seen as primarily continuing and developing in its importance throughout life. Significantly, it is also seen to develop personality traits of splitting sexuality and love, of greater rationality and emotional distancing, and prepares the male for a leading role in public rather than private life. The implications of this process of splitting emotionality and sexuality also potentially leads to a splitting simply of men and men, particularly on a level of sexual and emotional conjunction. The theory is more convincing than many primarily for its greater connection of the structural situation where women institutionally mother with the personal emotional position and unconscious implications of the processes of the relationship:

> Women's mothering, in the isolated nuclear family of contemporary capitalist society creates specific personality characteristics in men that reproduce both an ideology and psychodynamic of male superiority and submission to the requirements of production. It prepares men for participation in a male-dominant family and society, for their lesser emotional participation in family life, and for their participation in the capitalist world of work.
>
> (Chodorow, 1978: 181)

Nevertheless, Chodorow's work is criticised for its victimising of male development and its overemphasis upon the mother. Thus, first, the absence of the father is seen as equally critical; and second, a whole series of social and institutional factors also teach males to be 'masculine': 'The problem stems from the fact that feminist object-relations theory looks at only one aspect of the formation of masculinity – infantile attachment to the mother' (Segal, 1987: 151). This also creates the question of variation not only individually but also over time and place as: 'There is no "universal" masculinity, but rather a varying masculine experience of each succeeding social epoch' (Tolson, 1977: 13).

Third, the question is also raised concerning homosexuality, usually explained psychoanalytically as a mixture of innate 'polymorphous perversity' linked with an unsuccessful resolution or irresolution of the Oedipus Complex leading to stereotypes of dominant mothers and distant fathers (Freud, 1977). This is not convincing precisely due to the fact that it is stereotyped and that the majority of males have distant fathers and dominant mothers and yet the majority are not, one assumes, homosexual: 'Heterosexual masculinity is also defined according to what it is not – that is, not feminine and not homosexual' (Herek, 1987: 73). However, what is interesting is that this theory also posits a relationship of homosexuality and intimacy, perceived of as effeminacy, and generally rejected as part of heterosexual masculinity:

[117]

From a very early age little boys are carefully watched for any symptoms of 'effeminacy'. They must play with guns not dolls; must excel above all in sports, not ballet (even musical instruments are suspect); must play football, not skipping; enjoy fighting, not cooking. They must not be too affectionate ('boys don't kiss') and not too emotional ('boys don't cry'). Boys do not hug one another, they shake hands. (They may roughly slap each other on the back, or happily punch each other in the arm. Only after a goal has been scored may teammates slap the scorer on the bum: to do so at any other time would be a 'violation' of his young manhood, calling for an immediate physical fight.)

(Hoch, 1979: 80)

If the masculine is the 'not feminine' and therefore the 'not intimate' and 'not effeminate' it is also the 'not homosexual'. This association of homosexuality and effeminacy was, of course, challenged through the development of the 1970s 'masculine' gay identity. In addition, if one accepts that men are less emotionally 'intimate' than women, then this would seem to pose potentially particularly difficult situations for gay male or dual male relationships where there is, on one level at least, no 'feminine' party or factor. Nevertheless, the association of effeminacy and intimacy was, equally, not rejected and therefore one could say that on rejecting effeminacy gay men also rejected intimacy, or at least certain kinds of intimacy.

Importantly, though, gay men do apparently still develop lasting relationships and it is important not to overestimate the personal as opposed to political implications of the masculinisation process in which only a minority of gay men took part. Evidence for this point is primarily provided in qualitative in-depth small sample studies of gay sexuality that are hardly representative, yet are consistent in stressing gay men's promiscuity and long-term relationships as an overall part of life history or life cycles (see Babuscio, 1988; Hall Carpenter Archives Gay Men's Oral History Group, 1989; Norris and Reed, 1985; Weeks and Porter, 1991). The nature of these relationships, though, is often slightly different from their straight counterparts and is characterised through more openness, particularly sexually, displaying again a splitting of sex and love; and, more positively, an awareness of fluidity that leads to a less heavy emphasis on love for ever more.

It is also commonly felt that gay men commonly oscillate from phases of promiscuous sexual activity to long-term relationships as part of developing an acceptance of their sexuality and processes of emotional maturation and the maintenance of identity.[8] The difficulty still is that they do so under significant institutional and individual duress in the context of societal discrimination and, indeed, the codes of masculinity as the separation of sex and love is a deeply masculine construction:

> Men defend themselves against the threat posed by love, but needs for love do not disappear through repression. Their training for masculinity and repression of affective relational needs, and their primarily nonemotional and impersonal relationships in the public world make deep primary relationships with other men hard to come by. Given this, it is not surprising that men tend to find themselves in heterosexual relationships.
>
> (Chodorow, 1978: 196)

Consequently, one is confronted with a curious and understudied conjunction of individual and structural, psychological and social factors, gender and sexual orientation, masculinity and homosexuality in explaining the character and context of intermale intimacy or private love.

Conclusion: private love – an alternative?

> The commercial gay world could provide 'fast-food' sex, but it did nothing to nurture lasting relationships among men. It contained and marketed gay male sexuality back to gay men, but reproduced the competitive alienation among men experienced in the larger society.
>
> (Adam, 1987: 100)

Larry Kramer's scathing condemnation of gay men's promiscuity in *Faggots* (1978) made a certain point: long-term monogamous commitments were not too appealing to the 'all male' gay man in comparison with the sexual candystore offered to him in the 1970s. Private love was not an alternative.[9]

Private love primarily develops in a paradox of conflicting pressures. Personally and psychically, we all at some point need other people emotionally as well as or more than we need them sexually.

Significantly, the social as opposed to purely personal, pressure to develop relationships, conform and couple up is immense, stemming from the maintenance of an ideal typical nuclear family form that is primarily productive and reproductive in capitalist rather than emotional terms, and flowing through everything from sitcoms and advertising to the stigmatisation of the single and social policy (see Barrett and McIntosh, 1982).[10] There is, though, in the case of gay sexuality and increasingly various younger-generation heterosexualities, an equally increasing tendency to oppose this process politically as part of rampant individualism and, more importantly in the case of the gay community, a whole series of social and institutional sanctions that work against the formation of long-term personal relationships.

Importantly then, it is hardly surprising that the outcome in the gay community is slightly contradictory as they do and they don't, it seems, succeed at personal relationships. The situation is worsened through an overwhelming lack of in-depth qualitative study conducted in the area and, what is more, a whole series of heterosexist stereotypes. These stereotypes also have an overly important part to play in the nagging issue of gender that necessarily enters the discussion and, in addition, it is an issue that is still stuck at the start gate in relation to gay sexuality. Consequently, what is still clear is that if one is to facilitate the development and study of long-term relationships, one clearly needs to address a whole series of social and structural issues and sanctions, inside and outside of the gay community, surrounding and impeding the development of intermale intimacy if one is ever to make private love an alternative to gay sexual recreation. In addition, it is difficult to see how the nature of gay male relationships or, more simply, any form of intermale intimacy, can alter or develop without undermining many institutions in society, increasing social acceptance of gay sexuality *per se* and all intermale emotionality, and changing the nature of childhood socialisation. This situation, though, was to come under threat from a new and wholly unexpected development that forms the discussion in Chapter 7.

CHAPTER 7

The AIDS dialectic

My first awareness of AIDS came whilst sitting with a group of gay men in a classroom at Oxford Polytechnic in 1983. It was the weekly meeting of the gay society and a doctor from the Radcliffe hospital had come to talk and give advice on AIDS. I had heard the word AIDS and had an extremely vague notion of its connection to homosexuality and gay sex; it had not registered, yet. He gave a slightly overly technical overview of its medical history and showed some slides. These consisted of pictures of American gay men transformed from the most gorgeous men imaginable flaunting every erotic meaning on the sunlit streets of San Francisco or New York into hideous and scarred skulls cocooned in hospital hygiene. I was at once fascinated and appalled: fascinated as fantastic visions of exotic locations, erotic displays and overwhelmingly attractive men swirled in front of me; and appalled as this suddenly slid into the sick, the hideous and the dead. Discussion centred on uncertainties and risky activities, love bites and some item named 'poppers' was mentioned. I'd read about these in New Society, *though not understood the connection to AIDS and sex – my assumption was you put them on your cock or something, like a condom, as it was supposed to 'heighten the feeling' – I was fogged over.*[1]

In addition, I had seen one or two Horizon programmes on television at which again I was simultaneously mesmerised and aghast at the clashing of images – attractive, scantily clad or sexily dressed men going cruising for sex (in itself equally outrageous and fascinating) or hanging out in luridly dark discos and clubs which in themselves were at the same time tempting and terrifying, contrasted with stories of lost lovers, grief, suffering and endless gaunt and leper-like pictures of 'AIDS faces' – I was phased and fogged up completely for hours or days afterwards.

I was twenty and two factors were of concern, location and the equation of sex and death: America (it was over there) and a sense of something threatening like a gathering storm (it was over here), and you got it by doing that (over there) and I was just coming out into the gay world (over here).

All this happened over the summer period of 1983 shortly before I was to start getting on to the gay scene. When I did so, I faced it with a mixture of intoxicating fascination and sheer terror. This I recognised partly as simply part of the process of coming out, though I also thought it was more than this, there seemed to be something almost malevolent hanging in the air and the harder and harder stares of the older gay men.

When I eventually succumbed to one of these men, he asked me if he could fuck me (I had no idea of any variety of risky activity – sex itself was somehow slightly risky per se) and I said 'Yes'. He then asked me if I wanted any 'poppers' – I pointed out that I thought this was an AIDS risk – he said it was but it had been disproved – I believed him, took them, and practically blacked out.

Later, in what was to prove a short, sharp and painfully intense affair, I noticed he had a reddish mark across the right side of his chest – fearing unknown risks, I quizzed him on his sexuality and 'promiscuity' – he admitted he was, 'quite' – at that point I withdrew although I knew rationally that the mark on his chest had been caused by an abrasion from his car seat belt on long drives in very hot weather.

After this I managed to get my act further together and find the love rather than sex that I was looking for. My partner, who was at that point in a similar position to me, had previously been involved with someone 'promiscuous'. It was now 1985 and we were newly aware of an 'AIDS test' and also Terrence Higgins Trust safe sex information: we had both been penetrated and done 'risky things', and he decided that he wanted to take the test to make sure he was clear and so went to a local clinic. I was less certain but being pressured by my mother and obligated to my partner (we also wanted to know our risk to each other) I took the test through my general practitioner. A doctor came to my home, wore surgical gloves and generally acted like a nervous cat. I sat tense and waited two weeks until I had to contact the hospital to get the same (negative) result.

Since then I split up with that partner but have continued having various sexual relationships and casual contacts according to the increased and detailed information of risks involved and my own independent decisions. In addition, the validity of HIV testing was later undermined and I decided not to take the test again.

I am no longer 'fogged over' although I have felt hampered, frustrated and depressed that I somehow missed out on something . . .

At the end of the 1970s, the gay male community, particularly in the United States of America and parts of Northern Europe, was alive. Alive, kicking and high on gay pride, sexual exploration and expression, a new sense of identity and a strong sense of community. Gay men from all over the world were emigrating to the great ghettos of San Francisco's Castro and New York's Greenwich Village, while similar scenes of sexual freedom and community were developing in London and many of the major cities of Europe. Into this positive, proud and over-spilling pool of self-expression, dropped a virus, source and name unknown. What was known was that this virus was spreading rapidly through densely populated communities, killing young apparently healthy people unexpectedly and without explanation. The impact of such an epidemic is perhaps most simply explained in psychological terms of shock, denial, anger and grief and this is indeed approximately the pattern of impact of AIDS on the gay male community who were initially shocked, denied sexual transmission and were furious at the accusations of causality, until the loss of friends and lovers to AIDS, dying in their tens and dozens, led to widespread grief and intensive activism.[2] This move from a community devastated and shocked to a community consolidated and activated has happened at colossal speed, dizzyingly quickly, and one of the difficulties lies in trying to analyse this process slowly with due care and attention to detail. It is, then, the intention of this chapter to explain and explore this rapid development of management of the AIDS epidemic.

The construction of the contemporary AIDS epidemic

AIDS was barely conceived of in Britain before 1983 or 1984. The first few cases of AIDS in 1983 crept in under a shadow of doubt and uncertainty and national attention was not drawn to the issue until 1986 when the Conservative Government became concerned about the predictions of infection into the heterosexual population and created its media-wide 'Don't Die Of Ignorance' campaign to attempt to stop the spread of AIDS. It is an insidious discourse. AIDS was, and is, defined as a deadly disease, and as an epidemic of unparalleled scope when it is neither of these things. It is a syndrome not a disease, it is not necessarily deadly, and compared with other similar epidemics in the past such as cholera or syphilis, it is not particularly contagious or rapid in its spread through the population overall. The number of AIDS cases in Britain remains relatively small compared with other infections or causes of death such as heart attacks, cancer, or accidents. It is also, incidentally, not a contemporary AIDS epidemic as the gay community was aware of a new disease in the 1970s and some evidence suggests that it is not necessarily new to us.[3]

[123]

So why all the fuss? First, there are issues of practical concern relating to the statistical projections of infection in the future, the considerable costs involved in health care, and, in particular, the lack of a cure. However, second, and far more importantly, it is the symbolic meanings attached to AIDS which account for its significance: its juxtaposing and explosion of sex and death, of homosexuality and promiscuity, of intravenous drug use and racial/ethnic variation. AIDS can be seen to mean everything concerning life and death, from eros to thanatos. Consequently, it is crucially necessary to distinguish AIDS as a medical condition from AIDS as the myriad of meanings and representations.

Moreover, AIDS has been constructed as a discourse emphasising and amplifying all these meanings, symbols and representations through the media, through advertising, through campaigns, through reports, through conferences, through surveys, through speeches, and through research. Such is the concern with these meanings and symbols that AIDS has become big business, an industry, particularly in certain sections of society: advertising campaigns, condom manufacture, medical research, and epidemiological surveys of its spread and development.

However, what is curiously lacking are investigations into the effects of AIDS on attitudes and identities, behaviours and lifestyles, feelings and thoughts, especially those extending beyond purely sexual behaviour. In particular, this creates a curious and insidious contradiction as it includes a profound lack of national concern for those groups or factions defined as 'at risk' for contracting infection: the intravenous-drug-using population, haemophiliacs, and homosexual men. Few people seem to have asked them what they might think of how AIDS as a medical condition or a series of meanings may affect them.[4] Instead, all these factions of society have been falsely and crudely categorised into two distinct camps: 'innocent victims' (haemophiliacs and children) versus 'guilty perpetrators of the deadly epidemic' (promiscuous homosexuals, prostitutes, pimps and pushers).

Added to this is a divisive distinction between 'undeserving' and 'deserving' persons with AIDS (PWAs), a label with a more than coincidental connection to prisoners of war (POWs). This particularly applies to promiscuous gay men who are seen as suffering or paying the price for their sins in more literal terms by some religious fundamentalists, and more symbolically or metaphorically by the rest of mainstream society as AIDS is commonly seen as a disease of the permissive society by British Conservatives and American Republicans.

In particular, the historical development of the AIDS epidemic is commonly seen as falling into three or four phases or stages of development, medically and socially (see Weeks, 1989).

Silent spread (pre-1981)

Here the epidemic spread silently through particular populations without demonstrating symptoms systematically and without medical diagnosis. In addition, any early symptoms were easily confused with routine sexually transmitted diseases or, more simply, influenza. Due to the discovery of the potentially very long time taken for development of symptoms post-exposure to HIV, the AIDS epidemic is assumed to have primarily spread 'silently' throughout the 1970s or even earlier.

Panic (approximately 1981–1986)

A second phase developed as symptomatic patients started to appear in hospitals and, in particular, people started dying without medical explanation. Attempts were made to provide diagnoses, the earliest of which was GRID (Gay Related Immune Deficiency), as the earliest cases in western society were sexually active gay men.[5] Moreover, media hysteria and mass discrimination ensued as cases came to light and misleading analyses of causes and outcomes were made including the metaphor of the 'gay plague', use of poppers and recreational drugs. In addition, patients were mistreated, suspected tenants evicted, and there was an overall increase in violence against the gay population particularly.[6]

Crisis control (1986–present)

Third, a phase of crisis control or consolidation and health education was created as causes of AIDS were clarified and risk categories shifted to risk activities. The eventual involvement of central government in forming campaigns and funding health education was central in this process.[7] This phase is clearly still in evidence today as health education dominates local and national governmental agendas.

Complacency (1988–present)[8]

Fourth, a phase of complacency or information overload is rapidly coming into focus and overlapping the previous phase as various reports into sexual practices particularly in the straight population imply that campaigns have failed to penetrate the practices of the population as a whole. Similarly, the spread and development of the epidemic appears less severe than anticipated and many people still assume they are immune, or that AIDS is simply a moral or media panic.

This model of the historical development of the AIDS epidemic is, then, essentially located in moral panic theory and the main criticism is that these apparent phases repeat, overlap and do not really separate in any linear way.[9] An alternative viewpoint of the development of the epidemic, perhaps more accurate, is a wave model where the various elements endlessly repeat, mutate and then retreat, reaching different points or parts of the population each time.[10]

The other main aspect of the development of the epidemic is the massive explosion of studies, theories, and perspectives taken to explain its development. Few topics in contemporary history have developed such a tidal wave of literature and study exploding with the magnitude of a mushroom cloud. Critical discussion of this literature and study is consequently difficult, easily outdated and anachronistic, and what follows is necessarily selective.

The seven wonders of AIDS

The seven wonders of AIDS are seven perspectives or stories of the development of AIDS. In addition, the seven wonders or stories of AIDS are, of course, to a greater or lesser extent, social or sociological stories of AIDS, as set apart from or opposed to the primarily medical story of AIDS as disease. In addition, they are told as 'wonders' or 'stories' of AIDS so as to hold their validity or correctness at a critical distance. They are, of course, also essentially false distinctions or crude categories as 'the story of AIDS' is ultimately a mixture and a conjunction of all these and other stories. These stories or wonders are also ordered chronologically according to the development in importance of particular perspectives, and act as a heuristic device for studying the significance of the AIDS epidemic.

Aids as personal loss

If this article doesn't scare the shit out of you we're in real trouble.

(Kramer, 1983: 14)

The story of AIDS as personal loss primarily points to the importance of its personal and emotional, as opposed to social or political, impact. It is a story often told in a slightly melodramatic format including plays and films: for example, in Larry Kramer's play *The Normal Heart* (1986), or films like *Longtime Companion, Buddies,* or *An Early Frost.* The American focus of the perspective is a case in point as it is primarily America's more widespread exposure to the epidemic in the western world which has motivated, developed and promoted the perspective, and this also ties in neatly with typical American mom-and-apple-pie patriotism and sentimentality.[11] Importantly, though, the perspective does help to personalise the epidemic and make its significance clear to outsiders who would otherwise distance themselves from it or have successfully avoided its significance so far.

Aids as deadly tragedy

> The bitter truth was that AIDS did not just happen to America – it was allowed to happen by an array of institutions, all of which failed to perform their appropriate tasks to safeguard public health.
>
> (Shilts, 1987: xxii)

The story of AIDS as a deadly tragedy is also primarily an American development and promotes the idea of AIDS as super-scope tragedy generally driven along and derived from American journalistic frenzy (see Black, 1986; Shilts, 1987). It does, however, expose widespread discrimination and clumsiness in handling the development of the epidemic, nationally and internationally, particularly in the early days.

AIDS as social history

> Acquired Immune Deficiency Syndrome – AIDS – has stimulated more interest in history than any other disease of modern times.
>
> (Fee and Fox, 1988: 1)

The story of AIDS as social history is a cooler, considered discussion of the significance of AIDS as part of a whole series of modern social and medical developments. It divides into two main points: first, an emphasis placed upon the AIDS epidemic as a particular historic moment in terms of social and political history and health policy (see

[127]

Brandt, 1985; Mort, 1987); and second, an emphasis upon AIDS as a social problem in terms of its immediate costs and implications, practical and political (see Aggleton and Homans, 1988; Aggleton et al., 1989, 1990). Its clarity and difficulty lies precisely in this distancing process as insights into the epidemic develop alongside a lost sense of its particular contemporary, personal or political significance.

AIDS as discursive crisis

> AIDS does not exist apart from the practices that conceptualize it, represent it, and respond to it.
>
> (Crimp, 1988: 3)

The story of AIDS as discursive crisis is perhaps the most theoretically advanced of the perspectives seeing AIDS as a crisis in signification and representation or primarily as a contemporary symbolic phenomenon. Most importantly, it is opposed to media and medical perspectives on the epidemic as these are seen as politically suspect or simply systematic misinformation (see Boffin and Gupta, 1990; Crimp, 1988; Sontag, 1989; Watney, 1987). It also develops into a highly political perspective upon which the ideas of most AIDS activism are often premised, though it consequently frequently misses the implications of AIDS outside of activist and academic circles.

AIDS as sexual politics

> It provides what is currently lacking: a clear and informative account of the issues which AIDS raises for women.
>
> (Richardson, 1987: 2)

The story of AIDS as sexual politics primarily points to the importance of the impact of the AIDS epidemic upon women as a sexually oppressed group and, on top of this, the importance and significance of gender in structuring discourses and practices around AIDS and sexuality (see Patton, 1985, 1990; Richardson, 1987). The perspective tends to develop into two directions: one empowering women's sexuality (Patton and Kelly, 1987) and one seeking to protect it (Kaplan, 1987), centred on the 1970s tension of pleasure and danger (see Chapter 2).

[128]

AIDS as racial exploitation

> Like a misery-seeking missile, AIDS is homing in on a global underclass.
>
> (Sabatier, 1988: 149)

The story of AIDS as racial exploitation primarily develops a perspective of opposition to stories of AIDS seen as racist or ethnocentric in their emphasis upon Africa, black sexuality or green monkeys as 'causal' of AIDS. In addition, it also points to the particular suffering of black communities through medical discrimination and/or poverty (see Chirimuuta and Chirimuuta, 1989; Sabatier, 1988). It does not, however, provide an alternative explanation of the development of the epidemic.

AIDS as practical problem

> Each person with AIDS is someone's child, perhaps someone's brother or sister, someone's husband/or wife, someone's lover or friend – even someone's parent.
>
> (Martelli et al., 1987: xiii).

The story of AIDS as primarily a practical as opposed to a political or academic problem points particularly importantly to the widening pragmatic impact of AIDS and provides safer sex manuals, legal advice and so on (see Gordon and Mitchell, 1988; Tatchell, 1987). It is also a perspective adopted and developed in health education.

These seven wonders or stories of AIDS demonstrate a wide diversity of discussions and issues and there are equally connections and conflicts arising out of this. Thus, whilst historical, sexual political, racial and discursive perspectives tend to interlink, these perspectives also tend to conflict with personal, journalistic or practical perspectives. In particular, the conflict centres on recurrent tensions of liberalism and radicalism and academic and pragmatic viewpoints, and yet the overall difficulty remains the overwhelming silence of the population itself in this due to the lack of in-depth qualitative study of AIDS' social and psychological, as opposed to medical or statistical, impact. People are constantly asked to use condoms; they are rarely asked to talk of their difficulties in doing so. The difficulty is that such study is costly, time consuming and presents messy and complex, complicated and contradictory findings that do not lend themselves easily towards statistical projections and social policies.[12]

Assessing the impact of AIDS

AIDS is both a personal tragedy for those who contract the
syndrome and a calamity for the gay community.

(Rubin, 1984: 299)

Having attempted to assess the development of the AIDS epidemic as
a medical and social phenomenon, the question is raised as to the
assessment of its impact upon the groups or populations it has primarily
affected so far: gay men, ethnic minorities and black communities
and, increasingly, women. The importance placed upon children and
haemophiliacs, whilst necessary, is often over-emphasised as part of
the aforementioned discursive dualism of 'innocent victims' and
'guilty perpetrators' of the epidemic which tends to sentimentalise
and over-dramatise the impact upon the former groups. The problem
in making such an assessment is the muddling of metaphorical and
social factors with more medical implications and, in addition, the
overwhelming significance of sexual and racial discrimination in
shaping the entire study of AIDS epidemiologically, medically and
socially. To try to put this more clearly, three factors appear particularly important in attempting to assess the impact of AIDS.

The American connection

The perception of AIDS as a gay American disease easily feeds
into a particular moralistic view that depicts AIDS as a disease
of modern decadence, for which both homosexuality and
America itself can stand as convenient symbols.

(Altman, 1986: 175)

In the earliest days of its spread, the AIDS epidemic was perceived of
as primarily an American epidemic. This process developed directly
out of America's primary position in terms of the epidemic medically
and socially. First, America, in medical terms, created the first few
cases in San Francisco and New York; second, the spread of AIDS in
the USA is quite unparalleled anywhere else in the western world;
and third, America's position as a 'superpower' turned these early
developments into a media-wide, international crisis.

The importance of this process is that it links the spread of AIDS
with various value-laden cultural associations centred around the

United States. The first of these is the association of American culture with excess, and the roots of this lie in the American Dream where success is power and power lies in excess, where superlatives and stereotypes proliferate and success is simply excess. The second, and linked, association lies in the association of America with conspicuous consumption and, in particular, the media image of glamour that goes with this, including advertising, the movie industry, Beverly Hills, and Hollywood – the list is endless. This leads on, third, to the idea of American culture as sexual culture. Thus, as GI guys were perceived as oversexed, overpaid and over here, AIDS was also seen as the result of oversex, overpay and soon came over here from over there. Thus, the American connection is particularly important in comparison with British culture which is primarily perceived in directly opposite terms of prudence and restraint, industrialism and production, and the importance of mind over matter.

The American connection in relation to AIDS in the UK primarily developed through media exposure including the Horizon programmes on the epidemic including 'Killer in the Village', screened in 1983, which focused particularly on New York's Greenwich Village and San Francisco's Castro, colourfully contrasting images of cruising, promiscuous gay sexuality and disco culture with hideous skulls cocooned in hospital hygiene. AIDS was also explained aetiologically as a result of 'immune overload' theory or the idea that too much dancing, too many drugs, too much sex, and too many trips to the clinic and too many medications were destroying gay men's immune systems. Moreover, AIDS was seen as a result of an excessively exotic, excessively depraved, excessively sexy lifestyle.

The significance of such (mis)information was manifold: first, it clearly associated AIDS with gay sexuality; second, it also clearly associated AIDS with certain lifestyles; and third, it associated AIDS with American culture in itself seen as equally excessive and sexual. This quite clearly could have led to an international attack on American culture and indeed it did lead to a national attack upon certain aspects of American culture through the simultaneous rise of the New Right. However, the American Administration, clearly aware of such implications, made sure the story did not end there and started to set up a whole series of pseudo-scientific investigations into the origins of AIDS in Africa involving ethnocentric stereotypes of voodoo, sexual practices and black sexuality as causal factors. Quite clearly, this then led to an African connection in a triangulation of otherness with the American connection, in itself partly premised on Northern

European and English perceptions of sexual 'otherness' or excess (see Sabatier, 1988).

Sex and identity

> Even though AIDS is in no intrinsic sense 'a gay disease', the fact that, at least in the Western world, it has primarily been experienced by male homosexuals has shaped the entire discourse surrounding the disease.
>
> (Altman, 1986: 21)

AIDS was and still is perceived of as a disease of a particularly sexual lifestyle. The shift from a focus upon risk categories to risk activities has done little to alter this situation due primarily to the equally constant association of activities with certain groups or lifestyles including gay sexuality and anal sex, drug using and sexual permissiveness or promiscuity, and so on. Consequently, gayness, drug use or sexual activity is still seen as 'causal' of AIDS, and sexual intercourse or anal sex are still seen as risky activities associated with either the young, ethnic groups, gays, or simply promiscuity. What this adds up to is a profound insistence upon sex, identity and sexual identity as intrinsically linked to AIDS.

There is, of course, a certain correctness in this connection as AIDS is indeed a sexually transmitted condition and yet the association of sexual activity and sexual identity leads to a confusion of activity and identity as equally causal constituents. In addition, the confusion also tends to lead to the notion of certain activities as intrinsically risky. This contrasts sharply of course with the emphasis placed upon safe(r) sex through health education.

This association, in addition, leads to two tendencies in safe sex education: first, towards the safe; and second, towards the sex. The 'safe' perspective is primarily a more conservative, prescriptive approach centred on a philosophy of 'don't do it', monogamy, romance and long-term relationships as some sort of protection in themselves. Such a perspective is evidenced in campaigns which emphasise the number or newness of partners or point to the importance of communication in loving relationships. The 'sex' perspective is more positive, centred on a 'do what you can and invent the rest' philosophy. Here the emphasis is placed on eroticism and sensation, exploration and invention: use of sex aids, pornography, oils, and fantasy are crucial factors. It can also, controversially, involve the use of circle-jerk groups and telephone sex.[13] Not surprisingly, national governments have emphasised the former and local, particularly gay, groups the latter. This situation has also led to fierce controversy concerning censorship, as the latter position depends heavily on the freedom to promote safe sex explicitly every which way and this is opposed on two levels: first, through conservative moralism; and second, through certain aspects of feminism which have exposed the oppression of women in pornography. Consequently, the same sexual political theories and tensions turn up once again as sexual politics and the politics of sexuality (see Chapter 2).[14] Similarly, this also develops into difficulties concerning the differential impact of the AIDS epidemic upon lesbians who tend to be at minimal risk medically whilst still heavily involved in the social and political implications of the epidemic (see Schneider, 1992).

Importantly, the development of the AIDS epidemic raises further questions concerning sex and identity. As stated in Chapter 5, sex can form a means of maintaining an identity. This is also often seen as particularly applying to gay sexuality and gay men. More importantly, AIDS reopens tensions concerning the oppression of private love and potentially paves pathways to more positive developments or more erotic relationships as opposed to simply sexual pick-ups. The problem remains: first, partly a political difficulty as the gay male community still insists on its sexual openness as part of its political opposition; and second, sex and identity as simply put under pressure to develop in too short a time. Moreover, for the gay man cruising the city and clocking up sexual partners like cash in a till, altering his sexuality to even a series of long-term commitments is not entirely easy or likely. Consequently, a series of networks and groups have developed in the United States particularly to try to ease the situation. These include: first, eroticising safer sex workshops; second, groups developed to support grieving for a lost way of life as well as lost lovers; and third, controversially, sex addiction courses trying to 'cure' 'excessive' sexual 'needs'.[15] None of these developments has taken place to any significant extent outside of the United States due once again to the American connection culturally and socially.

AIDS activism and ACT-UP

Act-Up! Fight back! Fight AIDS!
Silence = Death

(ACT-UP slogans)

[133]

If AIDS has led to little questioning within minority and gay communities of the implications of sexual identity, this is due to the considerable political attack placed upon those identities throughout the rest of society. Significantly then, these identities are also critical in forming the overwhelming resurgence of political activism in these communities, particularly concerning ACT-UP (the AIDS Coalition to Unleash Power).

ACT-UP was formed primarily in New York where the impact of the AIDS epidemic was at its most critical in terms of medical spread, personal impact and political disorganisation and, indeed, disaster in treatment and systematic discrimination on grounds of sex, race and sexual orientation. The process of mass exposure to these problems, combined with a profoundly personal impact at the level of mourning loved ones, led to an increase in militancy. Gay groups in particular were facing a complete decimation of their communities.

ACT-UP was also formed primarily as a direct action group, opposed to simply writing letters and campaigning on the one hand/or having violent demonstrations on the other. It is primarily confrontational in its approach, taking its resistance to discrimination to the centre of decision making and treatment processes in relation to AIDS, including medical, state and religious institutions. Its ideas are not only premised on the identity and community politics of the 1970s, it also supplements these with a more academic post-structuralist emphasis upon representation and meaning, and places a centrality on a plurality of identity that comes from the work of Foucault, Lacan and Derrida as well as a whole host of other postmodernists and post-structuralists.[16] Due to the colossal emphasis placed upon prevention, AIDS activists are also keen to point to the importance of care and cures or, more simply, resources, as discrimination is now seen to manifest itself in the form of massively disproportionate expenditure on the white, privileged and heterosexual population at the expense of primarily gay men, ethnic minorities, the poor and some women who also, not coincidentally, still make up the massive majority of the population living with AIDS or at primary risk from it on social as well as medical levels. This contradictory state of affairs is currently tending to lead to a Catch 22 situation as the populations most at risk medically are also most at risk socially if a positive discriminatory targeting of resources is used instead of a non-discriminatory national policy.

The three themes mentioned also tend to interlink and it is no coincidence that the site of gay liberation should also be the site of

ACT-UP, or that America is central in AIDS activism as well as AIDS spread, or that sex, politics and identity seem to form the strongest trinity in New York. It also raises the question of a series of essentially contested terrains surrounding AIDS, medically and socially, that have no simple or predicted outcome.[17]

Conclusion: the AIDS dialectics[18]

During the course of conducting the study, AIDS came closer in my own life: a live-in-landlord died of AIDS; a close friend's brother became HIV-positive and is now on AZT; he was also a particularly rewarding interviewee like others who, although it is not confirmed, I have strong reason to think are now dead; another friend's brother worries about his casual homosexual habits and is hysterical at taking an HIV test; my mother, who works as a doctor's receptionist, tells me stories of people with AIDS or HIV on their lists and the attitudes of staff; a friend came to stay and needed to shave, so I selected a clean razor head for him to use and threw it away when he had finished . . . I have felt myself groan under the depressive weight of all of this and studying AIDS, reading about it, speaking to people about it, watching TV pro- grammes about it, going to conferences about it, conducting research into it and carrying it all about with me day in, day out, night in, night out. I have also felt myself survive all this and continue to make my own decisions, calculate risks, weigh pros and cons, and occasionally laugh and joke over it all. AIDS is simply a part of life for all of us, no more, and certainly no less.

If you drop a pebble into a pool, you may well observe the ripples spreading seemingly ever outwards. However, if you observe this phenomenon for long enough, the same ripples will appear to dissi- pate and spread inwards towards the centre, and this is the dialectic of AIDS. On intending to study the impact of AIDS upon the gay community in the UK for my PhD, the unintended and unexpected impact was the lack of impact or, put simply, the impact of the gay community upon AIDS. The study was made up of a series of in-depth interviews with a range of gay men topped up with group discussions and questionnaires within an overall framework of oral or life history. This more particularly applied to impact the personal upon the political, the present upon the past, action upon structure, as opposed to or as well as the common conception of the impact of the political upon the personal, the past upon the present, structure upon action. In addition, this then set up a two-way process or dialectic of the personal and the political, the past and the present, action and structure, reflected in four areas of awareness, identity, mortality and sexuality in dialectical relation to AIDS.

AIDS does, of course, have an impact: first, thousands of people have died and continue to die from AIDS-related diseases in the UK; and second, the number of sero-positive people is estimated to be both unknowable and unbelievably high internationally; and third, on top of all of this, there are those who know, work with, or care for those who suffer from AIDS or HIV at any level. Nevertheless, it remains true to say that the impact of AIDS is consistently opposed, resisted and undermined through a series of personal, political and social factors. This depends partly, of course, on the distinction of AIDS as a medical condition from AIDS as a social phenomenon. As the medical impact of AIDS perpetually increases; the social, economic, and political impact of the epidemic remains essentially a contested terrain of information, meaning and outcome.

This terrain is ultimately contested on four levels: first, at the level of an awareness context, or factors such as perception and negotiation of information which affect individual decisions; second, at the level of identity and life history, as people's definitions of themselves and their sexuality over a period of time lead to different outcomes in their responses to AIDS; third, at the level of denial and mortality, as people generally find it very difficult to come to terms with any terminal illness and death itself; and fourth, at the level of politics, as AIDS is of course fraught with governmental and individual political implications as part of its symbolic significance.

There are, of course, other areas and themes dialectically related to AIDS including, for example, racism and sexism and, ultimately, the impact of AIDS is unknown as a series of ripple effects throughout society. Consequently the conclusion is, in one sense, a nonconclusion as AIDS has no linear development, no cause and effect impact, no importance *per se*, as separate from the social, economic and political phenomena it taps into or encompasses. On top of this, AIDS is now a part of life for all of us and will continue as such in the future for as much as we allow the epidemic and its implications to spread.

CHAPTER 8

Politics, plurality and postmodernity

I said to a friend of mine recently in a not very postmodern restaurant over lunch that my sexuality did not matter any more, what did still matter was my identity. Consequently, gayness wasn't necessary or even necessarily the case as a sexual orientation; it was, however, still critical as a self–other organising device, a political perspective, a viewpoint on life: an identity. He, conversely, was straight in identity and yet equally open in orientation. The sexual signification and the institutional and social dimensions of sex far outweighed the significance of sex itself in either case. Prior to this discussion, I had seen postmodernism, like most people, I suspect, as some kind of lunatic arty-farty apolitical problem for the rest of us that made an awful lot of money and not a lot else. I since lived with someone heavily into it for nine months and the walls of the house fairly regularly rang to the sound of raised voices over the issue: were we or were we not 'postmodern' now, or would we, or could we be, and what would it or does it mean. Moreover, I was never the most committed of socialists until postmodernism offered itself up for attack. Consequently, the discussions over postmodernism were constantly framed in a context of socialism versus postmodernism that also, curiously, frames the whole academic discussion of the issue too. I suspect also that each of us now recognises the other had the odd point: I certainly do. The other main turning point was realising postmodernism was not quite what I thought it was and that what I was usually reading as slightly post-structuralist social constructionism was postmodernism. Moreover, I suspect the real appeal of postmodernism is that it's more fun. The real death of socialism, if there is one, I suspect is due to the fact that it's dreary, dull and, dare I say it, BORING – what would you rather do – wear your favourite pink T-shirt or a gender-free, second-hand, dishwater jersey; vogue it up to Madonna or spend rainy Saturdays selling free papers; study David Lynch at the cinema or Lenin in a crowded café? Well, I know what I'd do and I know what a lot of others do too. Either way, you can still make out it's all 'OK' as part of the politics of postmodernity. If only it were so simple . . .

Postmodernity theory has developed into something of an uncritical consensus in the study of sexuality over the past five years since post-structuralism rose simultaneously to pre-eminence in feminism, literary theory and, increasingly, gay studies. Consequently, the primary intention of this chapter is to examine and unpack the importance of postmodernity theory as an approach to oppressed and minority sexualities. It is not my intention to uncritically accept its central points or to simply swim around in its finer details, something already too common and too apparent in contemporary academe. In addition, the key question raised is whether the theory of postmodernity as applied to oppressed sexualities is an appropriate solution to that oppression. Importantly, the aptness of postmodernity theory, and the politics of plurality attendant with it, are assessed in relation to the recurrent difficulties exposed in previous chapters, particularly including the tensions of liberalism and radicalism, reform and revolution, and sexual politics and the politics of sexuality. The chapter is divided into two parts, the first considering the general applications and limits of postmodernity theory and the second part assessing its application to three empirical examples, or test cases: AIDS, Section 28, and the state.

The theory of postmodernity

There is no one theory or definition of postmodernity. This is due partly to the opposition of postmodernity theory to any grand-trend, metanarrative theory. Moreover, it is necessary to conceptually separate postmodernity (the theory of a primarily social, political and cultural transition from modernity) from postmodernism (the aesthetic analysis of a series of stylistic changes in literature, art and architecture), and indeed from postindustrialism (the study of various economic and political developments considered indicative of a postindustrial society) and post-structuralism (an anti-metanarrative theory primarily developed from Michel Foucault) though all of these trends and 'trendy' theories are related. Postmodernity, then, refers to the increasing importance of the cultural sphere of life over the economic and social in particular; postmodernism refers to the decline of modernism in art, literature and architecture through a death of 'deeper meaning' in multiple interpretation and ultimately the annihilation of aesthetic styles; whilst postindustrialism points to the importance of consumption over production, multinational capitalism and the separation of ownership and control; and post-structuralism opposes structuralist metanarrative theory, particularly Marxism and Enlightenment ideology. In addition, the theory of postmodernity developed primarily as a reaction to the reactionary politics of the 1970s and the polemicism of some forms of Marxism and feminism. For example, the problem of lesbian feminist sexual politics previously documented in Chapter 2 is profoundly 'unpostmodern' in its attempt to enforce a form of homogenised moralism. Similarly, most Marxism is opposed on the grounds of its metanarrative attempts to impose order and meaning. Moreover, one of the primarily important points of postmodernity theory is the attempt to undermine any 'standpoint' type theory. Thus, consequently, the variety of studies involved is vast, including consideration of advertising, music, cinema and sexuality, focusing on cultural as well as or more than social, economic and political theory. These, as it were, atoms of study are then thrown centripetally together through the theory of 'postmodernity'.

Put very simply, in terms of its primarily cultural focus or aspect, postmodernity theory is centred on three key concepts and thinkers: first, the importance of imagery and signification (Baudrillard, 1983); second, the cultural as opposed to social, economic or political development of society (Jameson, 1984); and third, the importance of epistemology in challenging grand-trend theory (Lyotard, 1984). In particular relation to sexuality, these three aspects of postmodernity theory can also centre on a tension or distinction of 'utopian' post-modernity theory from 'dystopian' postmodernity theory.[1] In the former case, the aim of postmodernity theory is to provide a complete collapse or implosion of contemporary meanings concerning gender and sexuality, creating a new non-dualistic and ultimately non-discursive sexuality, derived from the work of Lacan and Derrida, in: 'A critique that would no longer avoid that of discourse, and more generally the symbolic system, in which it is realised' (Irigaray, 1985: 191). In the second instance, this collapse of meaning, already in motion due to multinational consumer capitalism and certain medical technologies, is seen to lead to a death of sexuality and a vacuous, voided life of non-living nothing (see Baudrillard, 1983; Kroker and Cook, 1988). These three aspects of the theory of postmodernity and this utopian–dystopian distinction have their part to play in the application of postmodernity to sexuality and, in addition, add to the difficulties in applying postmodernity theory to sexuality adequately.

The applications of postmodernity theory (the cultural as political)

There are, I think, three primary applications of the theory of postmodernity to sexuality.

Signification

The first of these is in the issue of signification, or in the question of style as opposed to content in defining sexual meanings and actions. This is, of course, an extension of social constructionist theory taken on to a new post-structuralist dimension.[2] In addition, this is then 'translated' into the importance of representations of sexuality, premised upon the notion that there is no content to sexuality as it is a discursive and visual construction. For utopian postmodernists this also points to the importance of potential parody and pastiche or ultimately transgression and subversion of sexual meaning (see Irigaray, 1985; Kristeva, 1986; Marks and DeCourtivron, 1981; Moi, 1985).[3] This comes through the decentring of sexual objectivity and subjectivity, the inversion of masculinity and femininity, and the overall confusion of sexual categories temporally and spatially as present is past is future and heterosexual is homosexual and homosexual is heterosexual. Calvin Klein advertising, David Lynch and Madonna are cited as implicitly positive examples of this process as:

> What makes Eurythmics, Madonna, and Carol Pope with Rough Trade so fascinating is that they play at the edge of power and seduction, the zero-point where sex as electric image is amplified, teased out in a bit of ironic exhibitionism, and then reversed against itself. These are artists in the business of committing sign crimes against the big signifier of sex.
>
> (Kroker and Cook, 1988: 21)

However, for dystopian postmodernists the implications of this process are very different. For example, Kroker and Cook also point to the technology of reproduction and a twofold 'death' of sexuality: first, the death of natural sex or sex as a purely experiential reality or non-discursive event; and second, the death of discursive sex as 'panic sex' leads to a sort of non-sex of latex, or 'virtual sex' of telephones and videos, so:

Sex today is experienced most of all as virtual sex, sex without secretions, sex which is at the centre of the medicalisation of the body and the technification of reproduction, and which, if its violent and seductive representations are everywhere in rock video, in the language of advertising, in politics, this means that, like a dying star which burns most brilliantly when it is already most exhausted and already on its way to a last implosion, sex today is dead: the site of our absorption into the simulated secretions of ultramodern technology.

(Kroker and Cook, 1988: 24)

However, this is a profoundly pessimistic or negative viewpoint on the new safer sexuality and it contrasts sharply with, for example, ACT-UP's policies and positive perspective on safer sexuality:

Having learned to support and grieve for our lovers and friends; having joined the fight against fear, hatred, repression, and inaction; having adjusted our sex lives so as to protect ourselves and one another – we are now reclaiming our subjectivities, our communities, our culture . . . and our promiscuous love of sex.

(Crimp, 1988: 270)

Consequently, there are two tendencies at work within the politics of representation that constitute this part of postmodernity and its application to sexuality: the positivity of safer sexual pleasure and the danger of 'virtual' sexual annihilation.

In addition, a similar situation applies in relation to women's sexuality and feminism. For utopian postmodernist feminists, the increasing confusion concerning sexual signification can lead to a decentring of 'masculine' sexuality and a reclaiming of 'feminine' sexuality, ultimately overthrowing feminine passivity as well as masculine activity (see Butler, 1990; Marks and DeCourtivron, 1981; Moi, 1985; Nicholson, 1990). However, for dystopian postmodernist feminists, this process leads to the increasing centring of women's sexuality as a site of power or oppression (Kroker and Kroker, 1988). In particular, reproductive technology and cosmetic surgery abuse women's bodies as sites of inscribed meaning imposed upon by male medicine, and: 'The postmodern body is penetrated by power and marked by the signs of ideology' (Kroker and Kroker, 1988: 223). Thus, postmodernity theory points to the potential for opposition to oppression and the potential for the perpetuation and imposition of more oppression of particular sexualities.

[141]

Identity

A second source of application of postmodernity theory to sexuality lies in identity, and particularly in the plurality and diversity of identities. The point, put simply, is that the complexity of contemporary society produces and necessitates a plurality and diversity of identities on several levels including sexuality. In particular, gay sexuality is seen as particularly 'postmodern' in its separation from procreation, its oscillation to and from hyper-individualism and collectivism, and its emphasis and importance placed upon sexual politics and sexual signification. The self-conscious creativity of the gay community particularly constitutes its importance in postmodernity:

> Lesbians and gays have a sense of their own creativity because they are, day by day, involved in self-making, constructing their own meanings, networks, rituals, traditions, calling on the inherited traces of the past, but responding all the time to the challenges and possibilities of the present.
>
> (Weeks, 1990: 134)

The primarily important point in this process is the politics of identity, as: 'Identity is the paradoxical necessity of the post-modern world' (Weeks, 1990: 138). Consequently, identity, under the conditions of postmodernity, is primarily a political point for opportunity of opposition. In addition, this is still paradoxical as identity in itself is not postmodern as it limits and fixes; it is only the ever-increasing diversity and plurality of identities that adds to postmodernity.[4]

Localisation–internationalisation

> The simultaneity of the universal and the particular, the all-embracing and the specialised, is a curious feature of our present.
>
> (Weeks, 1990: 135)

Identities are, of course, not only sexual; they are interactively local, racial and international and this is the focus of the third application of postmodernity theory to sexuality. Postmodernity theory is quite unique in coping with the international scope of sexuality simultaneously with the localised experience of particular populations or groups, primarily due to its opposition to the grand metanarrative theory of development. The gay community is of course colossal in its parameters, an international series of communities, yet at the same time it is contextually located and localised to particular groups; and at this point the politics of identity are particularly important in simultaneously asserting the diversity and the consolidation of identity in relation to the particular needs of individuals in international society. Consequently, the three applications of postmodernity theory to sexuality are interlinked at the level of a politics of representation resisted and opposed through the plurality and diversity of identities in international society.

The limitations of postmodernity theory (the cultural as cop-out)

Still one might think it a curious turn of events when this response takes the form of a deep investment in issues of aesthetics, philosophy of art, and literary theory as the chief areas of concern among a sizable number of committed left-wing cultural activists. For it is, to say the least, far from self-evident that specialised work in these areas could eventually feed back to exert any influence on the way people live, think, feel, vote, and comport themselves in the public sphere of politically responsible action and choice.

(Norris, 1990: 1)

Similarly, there are I think three interlinked limits to the application of postmodernity theory to sexuality and these apply equally to utopian and dystopian postmodernity theory.

Institutions
The politics of representation have a particular potential at least to start to undermine the social and psychological suffering of sexual minorities as there is a tendency to deny or undermine the existence of sexuality as a social or economic, as opposed to cultural or political, phenomenon. Most importantly, the key point in this process is the role of institutions. Cultural analysis for all its clarity concerning TV, music or cinema has equal difficulty concerning crunch issues in institutions including housing, employment, and education. The difficulty centres on its post-structuralist definition of ideology as attitudes and decisions leading to discrimination are not only individual and interactive constructs, they are also seen equally accurately

[143]

as products of social and institutional relations and positions. Inventing individual or even collective inversions of attitudes and definitions is not sufficient if individual and collective positions and relations still operate to perpetuate particular and opposed attitudes, ideologies and discrimination. In addition, this is a point applicable to the oppression of women as well as sexual minorities (see Bordo, 1990).

Perspective
The second and linked limit to the application of postmodernity theory to sexuality is in the form of a potential loss of perspective, socially and economically, as opposed to politically or culturally, and in particular historically. Consequently, whilst most postmodernity theory pays lip-service to the past, in stressing the importance of the contemporary there is a tendency to lead to a lack of consideration of history. History, in the postmodern sense, is merely a series of fragments, and ultimately for Baudrillard: 'All that remains to be done is to play with the pieces. Playing with the pieces – that is post-modern' (Kellner, 1988). Consequently, for Connor:

> The problem for a postmodern politics, then, is this dual prospect, on the one hand of a transformation of history by a sheer act of imaginative will, and on the other, of an absolute weightlessness, in which anything is imaginatively possible, because nothing really matters.
>
> (Connor, 1989: 227)

Quite clearly, it is not the case that anything is truly possible but that it is still circumscribed by certain institutional, social and economic limits. The added difficulty here is that postmodernity theory, due to its counter-discursive construction, on one level at least, is overtly aloof, distant and élitist. Reading most postmodernity theory is an oddly seductive, yet critically unfocused and difficult experience that does not lend itself to easy understanding or, in addition, application.

Politics
The politics of postmodernity are perhaps its primary limit in relation to sexuality and this forms the third problematic aspect of post-modernity theory: the lack of practical and pragmatic as opposed to political and activist application. Connor points out: 'Postmodernism holds out simultaneously possibilities for the revival and widening of

a cultural politics and for its neutralisation' (Connor, 1989: 224). In constantly conjuring up images of fashion, perfume, films, Paris, shopping malls, glamour, seduction and advertising, it is at once arousing and amusing, appealing and appalling as there appears at least a total lack of concern for equality and suffering, or the fact that whilst western, white, middle-class, affluent society struts the streets of Paris, Milan, London or New York, it consumes itself senseless and sick on the work, poverty, deprivation and destruction of the rest of the world and its population. Postmodernity theory, therefore, in endorsing this development, or at least not opposing it due to its anti-standpoint perspective, is consequently quite sickeningly repugnant and contemptibly obscene.[5]

The problem becomes one of whether postmodernity theory opposes or supports these developments, an issue it only occasionally, and with difficulty, addresses as: 'Culture is not conceived as a terrain of struggle or difference; it contains no inherently progressive potentials, no radical lines of tension that outline alternative possibilities to the identity of power' (Ryan, 1988: 569). The question, of course, centres on the potential development of postmodernity theory to incorporate this, to develop a politics of diversity and identity of its own which it supports in practice. The point is, though: 'To embrace politics in a postmodern sense is to place a stake on contingency, on the insight that power, no matter now grounded in 'reality', how seemingly bound to 'material' necessity, is up for grabs, movable and therefore removable' (Ryan, 1988: 576).

Is it really so simple, so operative in practice? It seems to me, though, despite this criticism, that postmodernity theory, in application to sexuality in contemporary society, offers the opportunity and the potential for opposition, for contesting the cultural terrain, for raising the voices of sexual minorities in a radical politics of identity, including the gay community; and consequently, to make the unequal, the marginalised, the oppressed, the other – the absolute. The problem, though, is that this is still only a potential.

AIDS, Section 28 and the state (test cases)

AIDS, Section 28 and the state represent three test cases for the application and limits of postmodernity theory to sexuality.

AIDS

As stated in Chapter 7, AIDS activism is often informed through post-structuralist and postmodern theory. Consequently, Douglas Crimp says in his introduction to a collection of articles related to the activities of ACT-UP in America that AIDS does not exist, it is a discursive event and that:

> This assertion does not contest the existence of viruses, anti-bodies, infections, or transmission routes. Least of all does it contest the reality of illness, suffering, and death. What it does contest is the notion that there is an underlying reality of AIDS, upon which are constructed the representations, or the culture, or the politics of AIDS.
>
> (Crimp, 1988: 3)

whilst Paula Treichler lists thirty-eight 'meanings' of the AIDS epidemic and points out 'that no clear line can be drawn between the facticity of scientific and nonscientific (mis)conceptions' (Treichler, 1988: 37) and: 'Above all, we need to resist, at all costs, the luxury of listening to the thousands of language tapes playing in our heads, laden with prior discourse, that tell us with compelling certainty and dizzying contradiction what AIDS "really" means' (Treichler, 1988: 70).

This perspective is, of course, derived from, or at least related to, Simon Watney's discourse analysis in *Policing Desire* (1987) (see also Chapter 7). In addition, Susan Sontag's rhetorical deconstruction of *AIDS and Its Metaphors* (1989) led more self-identified postmodernists, like Arthur and Marilouise Kroker to point out:

> The rhetoric surrounding both AIDS and Star Wars focusses on the total breakdown of immunity systems: AIDS can be perceived in such frightening terms because its appearance indicates the destruction of the internal immunological system of the body (the crisis within); while the rhetoric of Star Wars creates, and then responds to, generalised fear about the breakdown of the technological immunity systems of society as a whole (the Bomb as the crisis without).
>
> (Kroker and Kroker, 1988: 13)

Colourful as all this is, there are certain contradictions here as AIDS does, in a sense, exist at the level of lives affected through it medically and/or socially.

[146]

First, the assertion that AIDS is simply a medical condition located in a panoply of practices is not particularly helpful in itself. It is potentially helpful, however, when put into political activist practice where the metaphors and discriminatory ideologies surrounding AIDS are consequently contested, leading to a potential impact upon medical conditions and treatments and indeed attitudes and discrimination. In addition, of course, this is precisely the philosophy of ACT-UP which seeks to pull apart the association of AIDS and certain kinds of sexuality, the direct linking of HIV to AIDS, and the idea that all this necessarily leads to death. Thus, institutions and ideologies are attacked at the level of countering attitudes and discrimination and at the level of intervention and confrontation.

This does lead to difficulties though: first, an assault on metaphors and representation is not, in itself, an assault on institutions; second, this kind of political attack requires collective action not necessarily catering for a full variety of individual needs, and conflict is consequently likely; and third, it tends to leave the non-activist AIDS sufferer high and dry.

Significantly, there is also the difficulty of unnecessarily criticising sufferers for lacking sufficient 'activism' against their situation, thus tending to add rather than detract from their stigmatisation: using anger against grief as opposed to anger and grief:

> There is no question but that we must fight the unspeakable violence we incur from the society in which we find ourselves. But if we understand that violence is able to reap its horrible rewards through the very psychic mechanisms that make us part of this society, then we may also be able to recognise – along with our rage – our terror, our guilt, and our profound sadness. Militancy, of course, then, but mourning too: mourning *and* militancy.
>
> (Crimp, 1989: 18)

For example, Steven Anderson in an article called 'AFRAIDS (an anti-medical science fiction for the end of the world)' which locates the psychosomatic side of AIDS, points out: 'I knew I could not afford to be depressed' (Anderson, 1988: 216). Similarly, David Ruffell's 'Scenarios of Departure', a series of AIDS-induced paintings, points to the importance of pain and suffering as well as activism. The most easy to perceive point, though, is the pain and suffering of those neither involved in nor fully knowing of AIDS, or disassociated from the activist dimensions or the politics of representation of AIDS.

[147]

In addition, international comparisons are particularly important here as only in America, the primary proponent of ACT-UP, has sufficient suffering from AIDS in concentrated activist communities led to a situation of mourning turning into militancy. Europe, unexposed so far to this level of suffering, has primarily personally assimilated the epidemic and has consequently therefore not created anything like a similar degree of militancy. ACT-UP movements in these countries remain small and comparatively powerless.[6]

The second question centres on safer sexuality. This is, quite correctly, often seen as necessarily inventive or positive. Nevertheless, there are other aspects to this situation as safer sex is also seen as part of an overall process of signification or simulation of sex as part of scientific and medical developments and media production. In dystopian as opposed to utopian terms this creates a 'panic science' in turn related to 'panic policy' or 'urinal politics' (!) of sanitised fluid control and 'cynical' or nihilistic sexuality (Kroker and Cook, 1988). Consequently, Kroker and Cook apply the politics of representation to AIDS and safe sex sexuality or policy, pessimistically: 'AIDS is postmodern to the extent that it implies a real loss of social solidarity, and nominates sex without secretions – sex without a body – as a substitute for the normal passage of bodily fluids' (Kroker and Cook, 1988). Consequently, safer sex policy is potentially equally located in utopian and dystopian aspects of postmodernity.

Section 28

Section 28 was initially seen as a hostile reaction to AIDS from the state. Designed to prevent the 'promotion' of homosexuality, particularly in schools, and the development of 'pretend families' it was quite clearly an attack on the legitimacy of homosexuality and homosexual lifestyles.[7] The question was raised as to what extent the timing of the clause was coincidental with the development of the AIDS epidemic and, particularly, the extent to which it tied in with the spread of the epidemic into the heterosexual population. Apparently, at first sight, it was simply too much like perfect timing and it is perhaps appropriate to point out that Section 28 would not have happened *when* it did without the spur of the AIDS epidemic.

Importantly, though, the legislation was clearly located and centred in a series of institutional ideologies that had a long history including the preservation of the status quo of the nuclear family, the association of homosexuality with corruption and, in particular, child molesting, and the overall perception of homosexuality as pervasive perversion:

> Section 28 is a demonstrably poor law but its significance lies primarily not in its formal legal provisions, but rather in its concentrated affirmation of neo-Conservative moral concerns. This it seeks to accomplish by an explicit attack on an ideal, possibly *the* ideal, summary symbol of those social forces perceived as most subversive to these concerns, homosexuality; whilst at the same time implicating a number of other profoundly significant ideological motifs familiar to the student of New Right philosophy; local authority power; the teaching profession; sex education; childhood innocence and suggestibility; the sanctity of the family and illness of plague dimensions.
>
> (Evans, 1990: 74)

The demonstrable problems of the law were its ambiguous terminology, particularly the concept of 'intentional promotion', the restriction to local authorities, and the profound muddling of constructionist and essentialist notions of the homosexual as a specific type of person and homosexuality as all pervasive and corruptive.

Opposition to the proposed Section took the form of mass demonstrations and 'media zaps', often premised on the essentialist idea that homosexuality is innate and therefore cannot corrupt anybody (see Marshall, 1989).[8] The abseiling of lesbians in the House of Commons and, in addition, the associated television interference, made a certain political point premised on the idea that (mis)using the media and representation was a weapon (see Carter, 1992). However, quite clearly it was not a weapon as whilst opponents won the arguments they lost the battle, and Clause 28 sailed through to its final instatement on the statutes.

The impact of Section 28 so far is curiously contradictory in inculcating fear, causing colossal activism, and yet very few prosecutions, and in fact a plethora of fairly positive representations of homosexuality in the media in particular (for example, Channel Four's 'OUT' series, Merchant Ivory productions including *Another Country* and *Maurice*, 'Oranges Are Not the Only Fruit', etc.)

What this process does still demonstrate, though, are the limits of cultural and postmodernist politics and activism, as without an added internal, institutional assault nothing would happen and indeed nothing did. In addition, this is comparable with the movements for Law Reform in the 1960s which were eventually successful (see Chapter 1). These were conducted along institutional lines playing upon internal contradictions in democracy and equality. These same issues also tend to dominate the agenda in 1992 when the European Council for Civil Rights (ECCR) looks set to provide the most significant opposition to Section 28 (see Annets and Thompson, 1992; Tatchell, 1992).[9]

The state

Since Section 28, the state has also effected a series of further measures to regulate, control and oppress gay men and lesbians. These include the Artificial Insemination by Donor (AID) Bill set to limit lesbian rights to mother, and Section 25, a blatant attack on male homosexuality and sexual activity further forcing it into the closet due to the illegalisation of all forms of public sexual encounters and sexual procurement.[10]

These developments are primarily opposed through the activities of what is now commonly called the new gay politics of Queernation and Outrage, American and European equivalents of similar movements. The aims of these movements are still primarily post-structuralist politics premised on opposition to media misrepresentation and national misperception.

Queernation attempts particularly importantly to unite minorities of gays and lesbians, women and black groups as part of a reappropriation of 'queer'ness and a 'queer' nation state. The immediate difficulty is the pre-history of 'queer' as a discriminatory term and consequently the confrontation lies in the dissolution of differences into an alternative, unificatory 'nation'.

Outrage is semantically more satisfactory, cementing coming out and coming together into a new militancy. Unfortunately, this movement is tending, at present, to merely develop or dissolve into the politics of 'outing' where prominent people, particularly in the media or politicians, are 'outed' as closet cases of homosexuality. This is criticised, correctly I think, as a kind of reactionary or retreatist politics that echoes the essentialist 'Queens of England' perspective long opposed in new social history (see Weeks, 1977).

Similarly, the methods employed still rely on demonstrations and media opposition: confrontation not infiltration. These factors are effective in creating consciousness for those paying sufficient attention; they are profoundly ineffective at the level of internal institutional decision making as power relations still tend to perpetuate the same situation. In conclusion, perhaps potentially increasingly successful is an interaction and linking of these newer-style politics with older-style democratic politics (see Tatchell, 1992). The difficulty lies in the tension of reform and revolution, liberalism and radicalism that divided collectives and groups in the early days of gay liberation. The problem and the potential solution, then, appear to be the same and after the rise and fall of gay liberation with the subcultural spending of the pink pound in the 1970s, one might say it's happening all over again . . . [11]

Conclusion: politics, plurality and postmodernity

In this chapter, I have primarily pointed to the applications and limits of postmodernity theory to sexuality and the plight of the sexual minorities. Ultimately, if we have learned anything from the 1970s, and indeed the 1980s, it is that there are vast differences in the needs of different minorities and, in addition, in different countries. Consequently, what is needed is a politics of plurality premised upon these differences rather than attempting to stamp them out. On top of this, whilst maintaining a recognition of these differences, there is also a necessity for an autonomous, non-separatist politics in attempting to maintain when necessary an artificial, perhaps, unity in the face of concerted and conservative opposition.

Postmodernity theory, which informs the newer politics of the minorities, seems to provide some of the foundations for this development. The difficulty is that a conflict still exists with the older-style socialist politics of democracy. Consequently, what is also clear is that whilst the cultural is increasingly political it is not sufficiently political solely in itself and it needs institutional support.

Significantly, there is a question of generation. For the young gay man, lesbian, feminist, or black/ethnic activist today, their immediate needs and situations are not the same as those of their counterparts twenty years ago and are not met with the same politics. Importantly, what we are witnessing is the engendering of a new generation of gay men, lesbians and black communities, possibly better able and more willing to work together and hopefully more aware of the problems of their forebears and able to overcome them.[12]

So spend your pink pound, wear your pink T-shirt, vogue it up to Madonna or discuss David Lynch sitting in a cinema – do it by all means but don't forget and spare a thought for those who can't afford to, or who are too personally or politically oppressed to do so, or simply choose not to. They do still exist, so spare a thought for them. Now that is politics . . .

Conclusion: erotic politics

Writing a book is a bit like baking a cake. You collect the ingredients, concoct a recipe and start to prepare: shopping, sorting, selecting. Then you start cooking, checking every now and then on how it's going, watching it growing in the oven. Then, finally, after letting it cool you have to add the icing . . .

Telling stories

> We think we write definitively of those parts of our nature that are dead and therefore beyond change, but that which writes is constantly changing – still in doubt. Even a monotonously undeviating path of self-examination does not necessarily lead to a mountain of self-knowledge. I stumble towards my grave confused and hurt and hungry . . .
>
> (Crisp, 1968: 217)

As stated in the Introduction, two perspectives or stories have evolved over the past twenty-five years or so primarily to explain the development and impact of gay liberation. The former is derived mostly from gay male academics asserting the positivity of a new sexualised gay identity and the latter is derived mostly from second-wave feminism in exposing the sexist implications of the masculinity of that identity.[1] As a result, this study has told a third story or developed a third perspective located in the contrasts and conflicts of these two perspectives and their debate about the merits and limits of gay liberation.

Gay liberation is debatable and problematic both in concept and practice. Conceptually, the problem lies in the very notion of liberation itself because it rests on the essentialist assumption that there is something there to be liberated, gay sexuality; whilst social constructionist theory clearly challenges the existence of a gay sexuality or any sexuality on this level. Gay sexuality is seen as essentially conceptual.[2] In practice, the difficulty is more political, for if we have learned anything from examining the last twenty-five years it is that the struggle continues, the struggle against the all-too-evident continuation of the regulation of gay and indeed all sexuality from definitions of indecency and privacy to the handling of AIDS and Section 28.

Central in this struggle is the concept and practice of identity and identity politics. The concept of identity is also itself, difficult, located in the constructionist notion of a reconstruction of self and in the essentialist notion of identity as a specific and separate type of person. This paradox of identity in addition has implications conceptually and in practice as, conceptually, there is still no convincing theory of sexuality that accounts for its development, its outcome and, in particular, its oppression or experience and, in practice, the more one asserts the positivity of gay sexuality and the gay identity as an alternative lifestyle and self-organisation device, the more one is caught up in a process of limiting that development, putting parameters on it and, in fact, creating the gay person.[3] It is this process of limiting and parametering, or forming and creating, that is at the centre of concerns here for it is not simply the concept of identity itself which is under scrutiny, rather the quite extraordinarily narrow definition and form of that identity that underlies its development and practice.

Significantly, it is also the specific and limited form of gay identity which is challenged through feminism, which highlighted so successfully its inherent sexism. That sexism, rather than forming a mainstay for the oppression of women, was more a mainstay in forming the oppression of gay men themselves. Whilst many gay men were personally liberated by gay liberation, many others were hampered and frustrated by its limits and imposition of another set of conformities physically, psychically and socially. Most of these limits were centred on the definition of the sexuality itself, gay sexuality as sexual, and indeed gay sexuality as young, white, stereotypically physically and psychically 'masculine', swinging weights, grunting in locker rooms and separating love and sex. Feminism assumed, wrongly, that all gay men were going along with all of this, whilst gay men themselves often missed the point in asserting the importance of one form of gay sexuality and one form only.[4] These difficulties were further compounded by the processes of ageism, domination and inequality that underlay intergenerational gay sexuality and sadomasochism.

The gay male community was also perhaps simultaneously co-opting itself into the already exploding development of capitalist consumerism through the expansion of a profitable subculture. In particular, the emphasis placed upon promiscuity and the positivity of sexuality and sexual pleasure *per se*, missed the importance of masculinist ideology and attitudes in these practices, and indeed missed many other areas of concern to the gay community including the continuity of its inequality, discrimination and oppression in society. The gay male community's resistance to these issues, when apparent, was often one of self-protection and not one of political conviction. Public sex successfully formed the ultimate expression of this masculinist value system; it equally successfully failed to develop and support an alternative: private love.

However, in the final analysis, all of these developments were threatened and undermined through the rise of AIDS as a socially, economically and politically constructed disease that hit many 1970s gay men at the heart of their identity, their sexuality. It also formed the manifestation of the latent hostility towards homosexuality that had lain dormant for twenty years. AIDS represented, and still represents, a potentially volcanic eruption of social, economic and political processes of heterosexism and discrimination. Identity remains to the gay community what the state is to communism; a necessary means to an end and ultimately useless yet currently essential. It is, therefore, still vital to preserve a positive identity or at least identities and maintain and develop the strength of the gay and lesbian communities to resist these processes.

These processes of heterosexism and discrimination are presently opposed through the adoption of a postmodernist politics of opposition or a politics of culture attacking misrepresentation, demonstrating against discrimination, and exploiting the media. The difficulty here is that this opposition is still stuck in asserting the cultural as political and fails to tap into institutions and structures that successfully continue to sanction or oppress any form of sexuality that is not white, male, heterosexual, procreative and preserves the sanctity of the family.

Importantly, still underlying all of these processes of development are the three tensions of liberalism and radicalism, reformism and revolutionism and sexual politics and the politics of sexuality. These tensions translate into heated exchanges concerning the significance of law reform or alternative lifestyles, the level of diversity and difference or sameness and continuity, and the significance of gender or sexuality in constructing central inequalities. There are no easy answers and no one-sided solutions. In addition, the difficulty and the solution lie in trying to create reconciliations in the light of the recognition of these tensions: the recognition that it is not either or, more or less, yes and no; rather neither and both, possibly and probably, undeniably and uncertainly. It is this sense of uncertainty and contradiction that dominates the current climate of sexuality and society in so many ways, the family as sanctity or root of all evil, sexuality as way in or out of oppression, and the sense that the future is in our hands yet completely out of our control: telling sexual stories that are as real as they are fantasies.[5]

Problems, limits and implications

The primary problem that besets this book is one of boundaries, or a problem of scope and setting limits which in turn set out some of the implications.

I have primarily concentrated my analysis upon the gay male community as a way of focusing a whole series of issues of interest to me, to the gay community generally, to many women, feminists and sexual-politically interested straight men. The primary purpose in so doing was to expose some of the connections across these groups and provide a critique of central perspectives on gay male sexuality via an interface with feminism and vice versa.

However, in focusing on the gay male community particularly and its attendant literature, two or three issues stand out as neglected to a greater or lesser degree. The first of these issues is lesbianism which, although considered in detail in Chapter 2, tends not to receive an equality of consideration to gay male sexuality. The reasons for this situation are as follows: first, I feel the differences between lesbians and gay men are well enough established and documented to make the idea of writing a book about both simultaneously more or less impossible; second, there is now a vast, but equally very different, lesbian feminist literature, including a black lesbian feminist literature, that I simply did not have room for, without excluding other central issues such as intergenerational sexuality or sado-masochism; and third, I am not a lesbian and I am simply uncomfortable both personally and politically with the idea of a man writing a book about women's relationships with women. The comment that this is a cop-out does not stand up as I specifically chose to make significant incorporations of feminism, and the feminist critique of gay male sexuality particularly, which, it seems to me, is more rather than less challenging to gay men than a book which tells them about the differences and similarities between them and lesbians.

The second, and interconnected, limit concerns problematically black or ethnic sexuality and racism. The problem here is that whilst there is a black lesbian feminist literature there is as yet no fully developed, and in particular sociological, black gay male literature of any real significance.[6] This factor is of course an issue in itself revealing the exclusion of black issues and ethnicity in gay male theory and practice. The issue is increasingly less neglected due to the activism of black gay men themselves. However, this activism primarily appears in the form of films and representational art that are difficult to consider successfully in writing critical sociology.[7]

A third and singularly difficult area of neglect is that of sexual violence. There are several reasons for this: first, the area of sexual violence is in itself vast and contentious and, on looking at the text as a whole, I felt it would have tipped the scales of contentiousness and academic critique, already delicately levelled, into a potentially explosive controversy; and second, there is as yet little study of gay male sexuality and sexual violence as opposed to sexual violence and women.[8] Moreover, in relation to all three issues, I do not wish to imply that I consider any of them less important or less significant in relation to the issues I have included and would recommend their immediate redress and consideration in any future study of gay, or any, sexuality.

The implications of the analysis as it stands are, I think, threefold. First, theoretically, without wishing to promote the tiresome dualism of constructionism and essentialism, the text does, I think, expose some of the limits of social constructionist theory as it currently stands. In particular, this applies to a need to address the social construction of gender and sexuality and, what is more, address them, simultaneously unpacking their connections. It is, I think, quite clearly a mistake to say that in making such connections one is implying some form of essentialism.[9] It is equally quite clear from the consideration of sexuality presented in the text as a whole that gender and sexuality are connected conceptually and in practice and that this does not mean that either, or their connections, are anything other than socially constructed. In addition, this does also mean though that the definition of social construction is in need of expansion and indeed the term 'social' is misplaced on processes of construction that are equally psychological, economic or political. Until such factors of learning sexuality psychologically, economic and environmental impacts upon

CONCLUSION

sexual practice, and sexual-political negotiations of the whole issue are taken into account, there can, I think, be no theory of sexuality. Particularly importantly, there is a profound need to address the social construction of all sexualities and, in particular, heterosexuality. If we are to really assault the notion of the naturalness of sexuality, it is the 'unnaturalness' of heterosexuality that needs asserting and not the 'naturalness' of homosexuality.

Second, methodologically, this process of analysis implies a more interdisciplinary approach encompassing feminist theory, social psychology and political theory in particular, as well as sociology. It also implies a simultaneously more ideographic and nomothetic approach as the study of sexuality is often far too distant from personal and individual experience on the one hand and misses far too many connections across time and space on this level.[10] Experiential writing needs extending a good deal to include gay men and indeed men in general under a recognition that the personal is indeed political for all of us as oppressed and oppressors. In particular, this applies to men as well as women and an awareness of sexual as well as gender oppression in this context.[11]

Third, politically, there is clearly a need for a greater recognition of alliances, albeit artificial, across various factions or groups and a far greater recognition that belonging to one oppressed group does not create exclusion from oppressing others and this includes gay men's sexism, racism and ageism, women's as well as men's heterosexism and racism, and black and ethnic communities' heterosexism. Ultimately, this also implies that if socialism is to survive at all in an era of postmodernity, it needs to recognise a far greater degree or significance of gender, racial and sexual issues not easily reducible to class analysis.[12]

Erotic politics

Ultimately, it is equally vital to construct an alternative politics that is fully aware of all the issues involved. These include: sexism, racism and ageism, as well as heterosexism. First, it is partly a question of reconciling the increasing diversity of (post)modern society, requiring a constructive series of evaluative criteria concerning inequality and discrimination, and a recognition of the processes of their historical construction. In order to do this, a new analysis of sexuality is needed, linking sexuality and gender with power and inequality. The sexual politics of the 1970s and 1980s all too often failed to achieve this, either through ignoring it altogether or utilising a conservative, moral stamping of one set of issues, gender, over the other, sexuality.

Second, there is also the continued question of the persistence of oppression of sexuality. This applies not only politically, as part of conservative campaigns against AIDS and HIV or the rise of statutes on sexuality, including Section 28, but also socially and economically, as there are still no measures even comparative to those measures taken against sexism and racism, to protect lesbians and gay men from the manifold and, one suspects, increasing tide of discrimination in housing, employment and simply on the streets where gay men in particular fear assault or attack.

As a result, there is a need for what I would like to call an 'erotic politics' or a politics of sexuality that recognises racism, sexism and ageism as part of sexuality, as opposed to separate issues and, in addition, recognises and supports the rights of sexual minorities. More simply, this means talking in terms of racial, aged, and gendered sexualities not race, age, gender and sexuality. Many more recent feminist and gay studies have gone some way to doing this, as does the new politics of postmodernity. The process still has to move much further forward in defining and developing connections across categories of race, age, gender and sexuality and not in reinforcing their minority differences. There are still differences, though, and this means the place homosexuality occupies in this process is particularly critical. Whilst heterosexuality is the absolute, the assumed, the accepted and the oppressor; homosexuality remains the other, the unknown, the unaccepted: the oppressed. This must still be recognised, in all the severity of its implications, and be fully accepted before the process of constructing an erotic politics can begin.

During the writing of this book I have felt increasingly torn: torn between seeing gay men as profoundly oppressed yet equally creative opposers, victims and survivors of (post)modern society; and seeing gay men as more like men than straight men themselves, swilling around, literally sometimes, in undiluted misogyny. Yet it is a misogyny full of self-loathing, long-lost yearnings and grovelling, not some swaggering, patriarchal trip over women. I suspect some gay men will loathe this book for dragging up all those uncomfortable issues they hoped they had buried years ago and no doubt some women will groan that it doesn't go nearly far enough. The frustration and the grief lies in listening to these shouting voices who just cannot or will not listen. It's high time they started.

Notes

Introduction

1 Compare here recent European collections including Altman et al., 1989 and Plummer (ed.), 1992; with the theoretical foundations of Dannecker, 1981; Foucault, 1978, 1984a, 1984b; Hocquenghem, 1972; Mieli, 1980.
2 This point is raised in some areas of feminist study; see particularly the work of Liz Stanley (Gilligan, 1982; Stanley, 1990; Stanley and Wise, 1983).
3 I am thinking here particularly of Jeffrey Weeks' work which provides chapters out of whole books on lesbianism and feminism combined (Weeks, 1977, 1981, 1985), David Greenberg's monumental *Construction of Homosexuality* (1988) which excludes lesbianism, and the overall sliding round the issue of gender in most of Dennis Altman's writing (Altman, 1971, 1982, 1986).
4 Men's studies in the 1970s included David and Brannon, 1976; Hoch, 1979; Pleck and Sawyer, 1974; and Tolson, 1977. More recent studies include: Connell, 1987; Hearn, 1987, Hearn and Morgan, 1990; and Kimmel, 1987. See also Chapter 6.
5 I refer here to the demise of 1970s sex-role studies, including Maccoby and Jacklin (1974), since criticised as inadequate, though lacking in more recent replacements other than that provided through second-wave feminism.

1 Coming out, coming together

1 The distinction of sexual acts from sexual identities is now well-known in the sociology of homosexuality and is a vital component of social constructionist theory which seeks, perhaps unhelpfully, to completely separate the two (see Gagnon and Simon, 1973; Plummer, 1975; Weeks, 1977, 1981, 1985). The question is consequently raised as to their reconnection, an issue discussed in Chapters 5 and 6.
2 I refer here particularly to the earlier histories of homosexuality – see Altman, 1971, 1982; D'Emilio, 1983; Weeks, 1977, 1985.
3 The 'new' social history is primarily an often more politically motivated history that has questioned the 'facts' and 'categories' used in more

traditional historical analysis. There is consequently a strong connection with social constructionist theory.

4 Sources on homosexuality and Christianity include: Aries and Bejin, 1985; Boswell, 1980; Foucault, 1978, 1984a, 1984b; Greenberg, 1988; Hunt, 1989; Menard, 1989.

5 See Hester (1992) for a recent address of this issue.

6 Murphy (1988) provides an illustrative study of the regulation of male homosexuality in the North American Navy.

7 The evidence concerning the Third Reich and female as opposed to male homosexuality, already fraught with difficulties, is even more specious and sparse. It is, perhaps, a case in point though that male homosexuality, as the more visible and public phenomenon, felt a larger part of the brunt of the Third Reich's wrath against homosexuality.

8 Agents provocateurs: plain-clothes policemen 'dressed up' and/or 'acting' as homosexuals in order to procure arrests in cruising grounds and so on.

9 There is, of course, considerable current debate about this issue.

10 Section 28, Section 25 and the AID (Artificial Insemination by Donor) Bill have all been added to the legal regulation of gay men and, increasingly, lesbians in England. However, the Stonewall Group has recently been campaigning for a lowering of the age of consent for gay men and overall legal parity for gay men and lesbians with heterosexuals across the whole of the British Isles, including the Isle of Man which still technically held the death penalty for male homosexuality until 1992. See also Chapter 8.

11 An article by Jeff Hearn and Antonio Melechi entitled 'The transatlantic gaze: masculinities, youth and the American imaginary' in S. Craig (ed.) (1992) *Men, Masculinity, and the Media* (Sage) provides a more 'postmodern' or cultural focus on this issue.

12 A good example of the contrasts to be found between the Gay Liberation Front and the Campaign for Homosexual Equality can be found by consulting Aubrey Walter's counter-cultural collection of essays from GLF in *Come Together* (1980) with Bruce Galloway's more pragmatic and rights-oriented CHE collection *Prejudice and Pride* (1983).

13 Evidence and ideas surrounding some of these issues to do with gay sexuality and socialism are located in two collections: first, the more academically Marxist *Homosexuality: Power and Politics* (Gay Left Collective, 1980); and second, in the more activist socialist *Pink Triangles* (Mitchell, 1980).

14 See also Chapter 8.

15 William DuBay in *Gay Identity: the Self under Ban* (1987) provides a severely critical view of gay identity as a functionally necessary device in deviant role enforcement.

2 Sexual politics and the politics of sexuality

1 An attempt to illegalise lesbianism was made in 1921 under the Criminal Law Amendment Bill but was defeated in the House of Lords. In

addition, Section 28 which seeks to prevent the 'promotion' of homosexuality and 'pretend' families as well as the AID (Artificial Insemination by Donor) Bill directly affect lesbianism. It might be said that as lesbianism in combination with feminism has begun to become more public and visible over the last twenty years or so, it has also begun to suffer similar prohibitions to gay male sexuality. In addition: 'According to an internal memo, Female Homosexuality in the Army, lesbianism is punishable by dismissal' (Tatchell, 1985 cited in Hearn and Parkin 'Sex' At 'Work' (1987: 76).

2 Joan Nestle (1984) provides an added analysis of the butch–femme dichotomy in lesbianism.

3 This factor is of course offset by the vilification suffered by gay men and lesbians in the second world war in other ways, from stigmatisation to extermination (see Chapter 1).

4 Sheila Jeffreys (1990) provides an analysis of the Purity Campaigns as an attempt to oppose the social control of women's sexuality from a revolutionary feminist viewpoint. The purity campaigns have alternatively suffered critical attack for sexual essentialism and perpetuation of stereotypes of male vice and female virtue (see Hunt, 1990; Vance, 1984; Walkowitz, 1984; Weeks, 1977, 1981).

5 I refer here of course to Virginia Woolf's highly influential work *A Room of One's Own* (1929), perhaps seen as a culmination of women's critical writing at the time, following on from or with the similar work of Vita Sackville-West, with whom Woolf had a passionate friendship and whose explosive affair with Violet Trefusis (previously Keppel) was a further example of the development of interfemale sexuality primarily in literary circles. In fact, this literary aspect to the development of interfemale sexuality appears primary. The point to make perhaps is that it provided opportunities for women to voice opinions in the late nineteenth and early twentieth centuries whilst male-dominated science otherwise omitted, medicalised or marginalised women's sexuality. Similarly, many women were also not part of this literary circle, unless upper class, as education offered them primarily few opportunities at the time.

6 Coveney et al. (1984) provide a scathing attack on Havelock Ellis in particular as well as Freud and Masters and Johnson from a revolutionary feminist perspective which sees sexology and sexual liberation as male supremacist concepts and practices.

7 This point is made forcibly by Annabel Faraday in 'Liberating lesbian research' (1981).

8 Aubrey Walter's *Come Together* (1980), a collection of writings from the Gay Liberation Front, provides some illustrative detail on these points.

9 See Eisenstein (1984) for a clear discussion of these and other radical-separatist issues.

10 Gender oppression primarily refers to the manifold oppression of men over women and the valorisation of masculinity over femininity; the oppression of sexuality refers primarily to the oppression of sexual minorities. Sexual politics and the politics of sexuality apply to the opposition to these oppressions respectively. These perspectives and their respective tensions are partly derived from Carole Vance's influential edited

collection *Pleasure and Danger* (1984) and are comparable with Ferguson et al.'s (1984) commentary in 'Signs' (10, 1, pp. 106–135).

11 The distinctions of radical, cultural and revolutionary feminism are not entirely clear and it is often a question of degree. Radical feminism primarily stresses the importance of patriarchy or male supremacy as opposed to capitalism (socialist feminism) in the oppression of women. Cultural or separatist feminism takes this point further and states that the creation of a feminist society centred on female values of care and nurturance is necessary to prevent sexism or even save the world, whilst revolutionary feminism primarily attempts to put this into oppositional political praxis. On top of this, the more 'extreme' the feminism becomes, the more lesbianism becomes a political imperative rather than simply a sexual preference. Moreover, Mackinnon's (1982, 1987a, 1987b) work is a case in point. In asserting 'Radical feminism is feminism' (1987a: 137) she implies an essentialist determinism in an ill-defined (practice or category?) concept of 'sexuality' in saying, for example: 'Sex as gender and sex as sexuality are thus defined in terms of each other, but it is sexuality that determines gender, not the other way round' (Mackinnon, 1987a: 17) – a point picked up on by Irene Diamond and Lee Quinby in Ferguson et al. (1984: 124). In so doing, she also exposes the theoretical weaknesses of Dworkin's (1981, 1987) work with whom she has campaigned and drawn up an ordinate to outlaw pornography. One might, more correctly, analyse the situation of gender and sexuality as two interactively connected, yet conceptually distinct, socially constructed and hierarchical categories.

12 The lack of effective terminology to explain the full variety of fears, hatreds and discriminations against gay men and lesbians is a case in itself. Therefore, I use the terms homophobia and misogyny to mean, in the first instance, male hatred and fear of women and irrational fear and loathing of homosexualities respectively and, in the second instance, wish to imply a more multidimensional array of fears, prejudices and discriminations against gay men and lesbians. In addition, I have bracketed misogyny with the dualism of lesbianism and feminism and homophobia with the dualism of homosexuality and masculinity to imply that these are the *primary* paradigmatic mechanisms through which they are oppressed. I wish to point out though that either mechanism of oppression can apply to both lesbians and gay men as, for example, evidenced in the erotophobia surrounding some forms of interfemale sexuality and the backfiring of sexism against gay men explored more in later chapters.

13 These are points I shall explore more in Chapters 3, 4 and 5.

14 Owens' (1987) ideas are derived heavily from Eve Kosofsky Sedgwick's influential *Between Men: English Literature and Male Homosexual Desire* (1985), also a central text in connecting homophobia and misogyny under the rubric of homosociality or social enforcements upon the bonding between men.

15 These quotations are provided solely for the purpose of illustrating, in part conclusion, the vast difference in feminist perspectives on gay male sexuality.

3 Gender and generation

1 See Ennew (1986) for a full explication of the international consent law situation.

2 Bleibtreu-Ehrenberg (1990) also provides further anthropological evidence on this point. It is also perhaps important to point out that whilst social constructionist theory correctly locates the development of a specific homosexual identity as an invention of the advanced industrialised societies, to locate this as also the central source of the oppression of all same-sex sexualities is quite clearly incorrect as same-sex sexuality as sexual pleasure *per se* was and is universally socially unacceptable and prohibited.

3 The important point here is the development of an extended dependent population. A population group called 'children' or an equivalent has of course existed and still exists universally in time and space. The stereotypes of innocence and dependence, though, partly enforced through the withdrawal of children from any kind of productive work, are a peculiarly white, western and modern tradition. In addition, the question of inequality is consistent across time and space for when children have or do gain some independence they do so at the expense of severe exploitation (see Ennew, 1986).

4 All these stories, although their derivations are vast and various, soared in popularity in the nineteenth and twentieth centuries as part of the developing ideology of childhood innocence.

5 See Freud (1977) as his essays on sexuality were centred on case studies of childhood traumas laying dormant in the adult unconscious. Such factors still constitute significant influence in current thinking concerning childhood sexuality and the corruption of childhood innocence.

6 John Bowlby is particularly infamous for his concept of maternal deprivation and many of these developments disproportionately affect women. More importantly, perhaps, paternal deprivation is raised as an issue of concern in current thinking in parent–child sexual relations: is paternal deprivation the cause or the effect of sexual violence particularly as some evidence increasingly supports a cyclical hypothesis in victims turning into violators?

7 This conflict is echoed in the sharp contrasts of the work of many gay male academics including Ken Plummer, Theo Sandfort and Jeffrey Weeks with the more feminist critiques of Florence Rush and Diane Russell explored in this chapter.

8 Plummer (1990) also successfully explodes the idea of children as repressed 'sexual beings' as retrospective essentialism.

9 It also echoes the conflicts and confusions of constructionist and essentialist logic once again.

10 This point is premised on the frequent lesbian feminist bashing some gay male writers engage in (see previous chapter).

11 The problematic status of statistics on abuse is abundantly obvious given the taboo on the subject but see LaFontaine (1990) for a full unpacking of the problems.

12 Similarly, Andrea Dworkin asserts: 'It is unlikely that male–male sexuality will be or can be tolerated by men as a class until the very nature of masculinity is changed, that is, until rape is no longer the defining paradigm of sexuality' (Dworkin, 1981: 62). In her chapter 'Men and Boys' in Pornography (1981) Andrea Dworkin also asserts that male homosexual rape is a lesser crime than heterosexual rape and collapses the issues into an overly simplistic viewpoint on sexuality. Sheila Jeffreys (1990) makes much the same mistake in conflating gay sexuality with paedophilia. Despite this, most feminists have more sophisticated perspectives, and it is also important not to collapse and conflate the whole of feminism into such perspectives, and to do so is to avoid a series of very fundamental issues as already illustrated.

13 This also includes rent-boy abuse and increasing evidence concerning rape and sexual exploitation of adult males.

14 There is, of course, colossal discussion concerning sex education in relation to high rates of HIV infection in adolescent populations. The preposterous idea that information, particularly concerning homosexuality, 'puts ideas in young people's heads' leading simultaneously and automatically into practice, adds to the essentialist domino theory of sexuality and looks likely to prevent sex education ever creating effective protection or empowerment.

15 Jeffrey Weeks (1985) falls into this trap as does most of the collective on the Journal of Homosexuality (1990, 1/2).

16 This opens up several points: first, the status of male sexuality as stereotypically omnipresent, ever ready and never saying 'no'; and second, sexual exploitation in relation to AIDS and HIV as recent evidence points to the young as a potentially very high-risk group given currently high sero-conversion rates; and third, if passivity does still play an important part in young gay male sexuality then this compounds the previous risks.

4 Sado-masochism, masculinity and the problem of pornography

1 There is something of a political problem here as since the rise of AIDS, sometimes associated with sado-masochistic sexual activity, attempts at self-protection of premises and services have meant that one is not entirely supposed to say such places existed and certainly not that they may still exist. Suffice it to say, those who know, know . . .

2 These contrasting perspectives are illustrated in the controversially positive SAMOIS Coming to Power (1982) and the downright damning Linden et al. Against Sado-masochism (1982).

3 Mains (1984) in fact provides a very graphic, though confused, anthropological account of sado-masochism as a self-confesed sado-masochist. His unfocused and photographic revelling in everything from leather and

NOTES

muscle to piss, whips and 'the flowers of pain' have led others to condemn his work as 'a celebration of claptrap' (Rutledge, 1985: 60).

4 This first also echoes the conflict over the effects of sado-masochistic sexual activity and AIDS or HIV as the activities involved vary from virtually no risk (role playing) to the very risky (fist fucking). Second, in addition, the constructionist factor in sado-masochistic sexuality makes it potentially more open to dynamic development than naturalistic or vanilla sexuality.

5 See Plummer (unpublished work with Annabel Faraday). Education is particularly significant as sado-masochistic activity relies heavily on a strong sense of nonconformity reinforced in education and, at the same time, this necessarily stimulates the sexual imagination as sado-masochism, conversely to its stereotype, is a profoundly intellectual activity. The class factor is also significant as most sado-masochistic images are working-class or working-male images.

6 This also raises the issue previously discussed in Chapter 3 as consent implies the right to say 'no' as well as 'yes'. This creates conflicts for sado-masochists who often confuse this issue in sexual activities as a masochist saying 'no, please' may mean 'yes, please' to a sadist and one wonders how a masochist can say 'no' and mean 'no'. The solution to this situation usually lies in the use of a particular code word or action strictly interpreted as 'stop'.

7 Operation Spanner involved the trial of fifteen gay men and the prosecution of eight of them in late 1990. An appeal in early 1992 failed and went to the House of Lords later that year and so the future of the case, and the status of sado-masochistic sexual activity itself, centres on the European Convention on Human Rights (ECHR).

8 This dualistic need is primarily conceptual as, for example, in sexual fantasy.

9 The source of people's, particularly men's, sexual turn-ons centred on inequality is, it seems, limitless. Some recent developments in the gay male community include, for example, slapstick or humiliatingly messy pursuits and mud wrestling as a public spectacle in bars and clubs not dissimilar to current media interest in gunge tanks . . .

10 It is important to point out that, in the UK particularly, some censorship of pornography is currently already practised, particularly in relation to gay and intergenerational pornography, as well as in heterosexual pornography which is stratified into hard and soft variants, the former being less freely available, defined according to the degree of sexual violence and detail involved and, in particular, the visual exposure of the erect male penis.

11 An example of these problems put into practice is also provided in Richard Dyer's 'A Conversation about Pornography' (1989).

12 This analysis is, on one level at least, limited to one particular dominant form of gay male pornography, the American video. In addition, though, most European and sado-masochistic videos still play upon the same inequalities, and even the valorised passivity of youth is eroticised primarily through the opposite part it plays in the same system of values. The values of gay male pornographic magazines are, however, necessarily

slightly different, often due to the primacy of the single, non-relational nude, though the significance of the transgressive context (caught in the act of un/dressing, etc.), eroticisation of inequality (viewer's valorisation of viewee) and masculinity (muscles and heavy emphasis on cock size) mean the pornography is still locked within a similar system of values. I suspect strongly, then, that one can expect no development of gay male pornography in any format until the overall value system surrounding gay sexuality at large changes. Images of ageism and racism also undermine gay male pornography's potential, as, for example, in the specialist emphasis upon the passivity of youth and the phallocentric ethnocentrism in images of black men's above averagely large genitals (see Mercer and Julien, 1988).

5 Public sex: the eroticisation of an oppressed position

1 These three tensions are comparable with those cited in Chapter 4 in particular and are also located in similar tensions of constructionism and essentialism, liberalism and radicalism, and sexual politics and the politics of sexuality that run throughout the text (see Introduction).

2 This question of co-option is located in a wider question of connections of gay culture to mainstream or malestream straight culture. The gay community is often frequently accused of co-opting itself into such cultures from socialists and feminists respectively when it may more accurately reflect a question of structure and action. In addition, a second question concerns the extent to which gay culture is hijacked into straight culture as, for example, the masculinised image of Levi's jeans, leather jackets and musculature that dominated gay male culture in the 1970s, started to dominate more mainstream images of sexualised masculinity in the 1980s and continues to do so in the 1990s.

3 The diversity and variety of indicators of sexuality is, of course, vast and ever-increasing, including rings on certain fingers, pink triangles, pink generally, collarless jackets, cropped hair and moustaches – the potential for confusion is consequently colossal.

4 The key and hanky code in its complicated sophistication is also occasionally confusing as gay men from time to time 'get it wrong' – see, for example, Martin Humphries (1985). There is also some confusion with forms of sado-masochism. The meanings of activity and passivity also apply to the hanky as well as key code as, for example, a light blue hanky worn on the left indicates a preference to suck whilst the same hanky worn on the right indicates a preference to be sucked. Scat refers to defecation.

5 There was also an opposition in the 1970s towards the prettiness or dressed-up 'piss elegance' of the 1950s particularly and the clone image also has connotations of masculinity in terms of scruffiness. Significantly, there is some evidence to suggest that this image is now changing, as

does fashion generally, with the increased emphasis upon smartness and power dressing that developed in the 1980s (see also note 7).

6   A curious distinction is created here of 'naturalistic' versus 'constructed' masculinity as the *done* is essentially a copy of the 'natural' original. This also led some gay men to say that the macho clone was as camp as the effeminate homosexual. The important point, then, is the constant separation of the homosexual from the masculine: a 'real' man is still a self-(un)conscious STRAIGHT man.

7   There was, and is, a vast array of sexualised identities adopted in the gay male community. The important point, though, is that they all cost money to maintain. In addition, critics of clone culture cite it as out-of-date and comic. More importantly, mutations of clone culture have taken place as cropped and flat-topped hair is frequently adopted, particularly in London culture. The moustache and suntan, and sometimes even the leather, are dumped in favour of a dreary and unflattering image of 'fascism meets the holocaust', a sanitised look of no hair, sickly faces and skinny bodies clad in dirty T-shirts, old denim and militant DM's. This grim image seems partly related to the development of the AIDS epidemic and a desexualised emphasis on death.

8   This is of course only one example of such environments and there is significant variation. In addition, in the age of AIDS, much of the heavy sexual intensity or emphasis has lifted and many of the sexual facilities are closed. This has caused some serious moans of loss and some particularly mindless complaints concerning young gay men's more romantic yearnings (see Crimp, 1989; Patton, 1985; Shilts, 1987).

9   I do not wish to imply essentialism in making this point; the associations of toilets are of course socially constructed. Significantly, female toilets have a similar 'women's room' association.

10 A frequent factor in this is the life history of a particular cottage or tearoom. For example, as one site comes under attack another is often frequented. The difficulties and complexities of such activities, though, are equally positive, as a powerful form of opposition, and negative, as a representation of an overwhelmingly limited sexual emphasis that appeals so persistently to so many gay men.

11 The term 'meatrack' is often confusingly used to refer to any context of sexual selling including prostitution districts. The concept of course implies both a capitalist bartering of sexuality and an emphasis upon the body as commodity.

12 Evidence so far indicates gay men are considerably more flexible in their sexual practices, despite their apparent promiscuity, than straight men, with some reservations (see Chapter 7). In addition, renewed discussion of the rights and wrongs of non-private declarations of sexual preference is taking place in relation to the activism of movements including Outrage and Queernation and the role of the state is central in all of this (see Chapter 8).

6 Private love: an alternative?

1 See also Chapter 2 for a full discussion of the feminist critique.
2 Bell and Weinberg (1978) do provide some evidence for this hypothesis with the development of the 'open couple' concept where each partner had added sexual partners outside the relationship. This set-up is, apparently, more popular and perhaps successful in the gay male community than in other population groups (see also Pollak, 1985).
3 Juliet Mitchell's *Psychoanalysis and Feminism* (1974) was fundamental in forming this relationship through a rereading of Lacanian psychoanalysis. This is now continued primarily through post-structuralist New French Feminisms (see Marks and DeCourtivron, 1981; Nicholson, 1990). Nevertheless, it was Chodorow's work which later provided insights into masculinity as well as femininity through object-relations theory (Chodorow, 1978).
4 Sources here are vast, though all make similar sex-role-related points with some more socialist, Marxist or psychoanalytic variations (see Bell, 1982; Connell, 1983; David and Brannon, 1976; Farrell, 1974; Hoch, 1979; Ingham, 1984; Pleck, 1981; Pleck and Sawyer, 1974; Reynaud, 1983; Tolson, 1977).
5 Hearn and Morgan's (1990) edited collection provides various evidence on this point.
6 In some cases, literally. A recent resurgence of a men's rights movement in America and, in particular, explorations of intimacy in 'Wild Man' weekends has led to, on occasions, quite ludicrous considerations of sex and love, infancy and intimacy.
7 The biologically based theory of male bonding made popular primarily by Lionel Tiger (the name says it all!) in *Men in Groups* (1969) though also lurking in studies of sport and adolescence (see Willis, 1977; Willmott, 1969) is now widely laughed at in sexual political circles, partly due to its political conservatism and mostly due to its essentialism.
8 See Edwards, PhD thesis – Essex University, 1991.
9 Similarly, Larry Kramer in his play *The Normal Heart* (1986) which documented the AIDS crisis in New York, vociferously attacked heterosexist discrimination and, indeed, the gay male community's defensiveness over its promiscuity and sexual activity.
10 Social policy does not necessarily discriminate directly against gay men and lesbians but does so indirectly through its lack of support for anything other than the nuclear family.

7 The AIDS dialectic

1 Poppers: amyl nitrate, a recreational drug inhaled to heighten sexual sensation.
2 I refer here to the influential work of American psychoanalyst Elizabeth

NOTES

Kubler-Ross whose *On Death And Dying* (1969) is a classic text on individual handling of mortality, interestingly updated in *AIDS: The Ultimate Challenge* (Kubler-Ross, 1987).

3 Various sources suggest AIDS. is only semantically contemporary, perhaps starting at different points in time in different parts of the world; see Chirimuuta and Chirimuuta, 1989; Panos Institute, 1990; Shilts, 1987; Watney, 1987. However, the exact origins of AIDS are, of course, not known.

4 Nungesser (1986) is one exception. On top of this, various small-scale studies are also constantly conducted into different social aspects of AIDS though with an increasingly quantitative emphasis and use of the health belief model (see Aggleton et al., 1989, 1990).

5 Importantly, it was at this point that AIDS was increasingly defined as 'AIDS' medically through a conflicting and often contradictory series of competitive scientific investigations conducted at the Pasteur Institute in France and the CDC (Center for Disease Control) in the United States. See Shilts, 1987.

6 See reports of the Gay London Police Group (GALOP), Greasley (1986) and Herek and Burrell, 1992.

7 The turning point in the UK came with the appallingly crude 'Don't Die of Ignorance' campaign, and the death of Hollywood heart-throb Rock Hudson in the USA led to former President Ronald Reagan finally recognising the existence of AIDS.

8 This phase is primarily one of my own formulation premised primarily upon my PhD study conducted during the years 1987 to 1990. See note 18.

9 See Cohen, 1972 for the definitive use of moral panic theory, and Weeks, 1985 for an application of the theory to the AIDS epidemic. The phase model is partly my own and partly adapted from Weeks, 1989.

10 The wave model is also partly my own and partly adapted from Watney, 1988.

11 Barbara Peabody's *The Screaming Room* (1986) subtitled 'A Mother's Journal of Her Son's Struggle with AIDS, a True Story of Love, Dedication and Courage' is a case in point.

12 Numerous health authority and hospital initiatives are caught up in this process of investigating such contradictions. The difficulty is that funding is often misdirected into medical–epidemiological models of sexuality and is frequently short term and/or small scale.

13 Circle-jerk groups are primarily a gay American development and refer to ritual group masturbation. Telephone sex not only refers to contentious 0898 listings, but also to the development of mutual sexual practice over the phone. Interestingly, the relative success of these developments points to the importance of the plastic and mental as opposed to fixed and physical aspects of sexuality.

14 The politics of sexuality primarily point to the rights of sexual minorities who are often first in line on censorship lists whilst sexual politics point to the importance of gendered inequality in much sexual information and pornography, which is caught up in promoting more explicitly safer sexual practice.

15 The controversy is partly political, following on from a similar point

made earlier, and partly a question of sexual essentialism and over-individualisation of the problem. As particularly apparent in Chapter 5, contexts have an all-too-important part to play in constructing 'promiscuity', the concept and the practice.

16 The work of ACT-UP is collected in Boffin and Gupta, 1990 and Crimp and Rolston, 1990. It is also controversial in its use of highly confrontational techniques often seen as threatening or alienating the less politically activist, particularly in oppressive contexts outside of activist circles.

17 Another factor here is the relative lack of analysis of AIDS as a death-rather than sex-emphasising phenomenon (see Bronski, 1989; Crimp, 1989; as well as the thanatological literature, including Becker, 1973; Elias, 1985; Glaser and Strauss, 1965; Lifton, 1973, 1979, 1986).

18 Much of this chapter and this section in particular is premised upon my PhD thesis (Essex University – 1991). See also my article of the same title in Ken Plummer (ed.) (1992).

8 Politics, plurality and postmodernity

1 This distinction is partly derived from E. Ann Kaplan's (1988) 'utopian' versus 'co-opted'/'commercial' separation of postmodernism. I call the latter category 'dystopian' as, it seems to me, it depends upon a profoundly pessimistic view of the future; see Kroker and Cook, 1988; and Kroker and Kroker, 1988 particularly.

2 Social constructionist theory sees sexuality as socially shaped and created in concept and practice, primarily through cultural learning and institutions (see Introduction). Postmodernist theory takes this analysis further and says that sexuality is only a discursive, and increasingly not even a discursive and only a visual, event or fiction: a signifier signifying nothing, a signifier without a signified subject, a shaping process without a shaped product. To put it more simply, a standpoint of post-structuralism not structuralism.

3 Jameson (1988) provides full definitions of parody and pastiche as value-free or neutral parody.

4 This is a distinction that Simon Watney and Jeffrey Weeks, in their almost manic insistence upon the positivity of identity *per se*, consistently miss; compared with, for example, DuBay's complex questioning of the issue (see DuBay, 1987; Watney, 1987; Weeks, 1986, 1990).

5 This is, of course, the crunch objection to postmodernity theory from socialists.

6 These points are premised upon comments made in Channel Four's series of 'OUT' in 1991.

7 Section 28 states:

(1) A local authority shall not a) intentionally promote homosexuality or publish material with the intention of promoting homosexuality, b)

promote the teaching in any maintained school of the acceptability of homosexuality as a pretend family relationship; (2) Nothing in subsection (1) above shall be taken to prohibit the doing of anything for the purpose of treating or preventing the spread of disease.

(See Evans, 1990: 78)

8 It is worth comparing this with points made in Chapters 1 and 3 particularly.

9 Conservative Party resistance in the UK to European policy is of paramount importance in this.

10 Section 25 seeks to control street-level sexual encounters and raises once again connections of male homosexuality to prostitution (see Chapter 1). The point put simply is that many non-sexual and non-monetary street meetings of gay men may still invoke suspicion in the ill-informed onlooker, or prosecution from the police.

11 One factor here is the conflicts of Queernation and Outrage with such organisations as the Stonewall Group which emphasise parliamentary and democratic reform. For example, the recent meeting of Sir Ian McKellen and Conservative Prime Minister John Major to press for a Bill of Rights echoed these conflicts as the question was raised as to whether this was or was not a worthwhile exercise. Curiously, these two aspects of political activism seem to come together as this meeting was also something of a media event.

12 This change of generation is increasingly crucial academically as well as politically as the work of gay liberation writers is equally increasingly and necessarily challenged.

Conclusion: erotic politics

1 For the former see Altman, 1971, 1982; D'Emilio, 1983; Weeks, 1977, 1981, 1985, and for the latter see most radical and revolutionary feminists, for example, Dworkin, 1981, 1987; Jeffreys, 1990; Stanley, 1982, 1984. Adam, 1987, and most socialist feminists, for example Patton, 1985; Segal, 1987, 1990; Vance, 1984, are more mid-way located.

2 See in particular Plummer, 1981, also Altman et al. (1989) for an exposition of the position, and for an exposé of the contradictions see also Epstein, 1987, 1988: Fuss, 1989.

3 The literature on the development of identity particularly is fairly vast; see Cass, 1979; DeCecco, 1984; Herdt, 1989; Ponse, 1978; Troiden, 1988.

4 See Chapter 2 for full referencing of the whole issue.

5 The issue here is not narratology, rather the whole critique of meta-narrative theories of sexuality (see Chapter 8).

6 Exceptions include Gupta's (1989) and Mercer and Julien's (1988) articles. See also Isaac Julien's cinematic work and James Baldwin's novels.

7 There is, of course, a vast array of representational analyses, particularly in cultural studies and the feminist analysis of pornography. The point put simply though, is that the text in question is a critical review neither intended as a representational analysis nor part of cultural studies.

8 The feminist literature on sexual violence is vast, however; see Brownmiller, 1975; Dworkin, 1981; Griffin, 1981; Hanmer and Saunders, 1984; Kelly, 1988; Mackinnon, 1987; Russell, 1984. Evidence for male rape is increasing (see McMullen, 1990) yet in its infancy often due to added difficulties in the compounding of the maintenance of masculine identity and homosexuality for male sexual violence victims.

9 This point is put forward interestingly in itself by sexual liberals including Jeffrey Weeks and Ken Plummer who seem to throw the word 'essentialist' at anything that does not fit their limited theories (see Stanley, 1984).

10 See Stanley and Wise, 1983; and Stanley, 1984 particularly for a full exposition of these perspectives.

11 Some of the more recent men's studies already do this to a certain extent; see Cohen, 1990; Jackson, 1990. The difficulty is still the failure to address the masculinity of heterosexuality and the heterosexuality of masculinity; see Carrigan et al. (1985).

12 Socialism's long-term difficulty in doing so is a primary factor affecting its survival (see Cynthia Cockburn 1983, 1988).

Bibliography

Adam, B. D. (1987) *The Rise of a Gay and Lesbian Movement*, Boston, Massachusetts: Twayne Publications.

Aggleton, P. and Homans, H. (eds) (1988) *Social Aspects of AIDS*, Lewes, East Sussex: Falmer Press.

Aggleton, P. et al. (eds) (1989) *AIDS: Social Representations, Social Practices*, Lewes, East Sussex: Falmer Press.

Aggleton, P. et al. (eds) (1990) *AIDS: Individual, Cultural and Policy Dimensions*, Basingstoke, Hants: Falmer Press.

Alhonte, M. (1981) 'Confronting ageism' in D. Tsang (ed.) *The Age Taboo: Gay Male Sexuality, Power and Consent*, London: Gay Men's Press.

Altman, D. (1971) *Homosexual: Oppression and Liberation*, Sydney: Angus & Robertson.

Altman, D. (1980) 'What Changed in the Seventies?' in Gay Left Collective (ed.) *Homosexuality: Power and Politics*, London: Allison & Busby.

Altman, D. (1982) *The Homosexualization of America, the Americanization of the Homosexual*, New York: St Martin's Press.

Altman, D. (1986) *AIDS and the New Puritanism*, London: Pluto Press.

Altman, D. (1988) 'The impact of AIDS in the developed world' in *British Medical Bulletin*, 44, 1, pp. 170–182.

Altman, D. et al. (1989) *Homosexuality, Which Homosexuality?* London: Gay Men's Press.

Anderson, S. (1988) 'AFRAIDS (an anti-medical science fiction for the end of the world)' in A. Kroker and M. Kroker (eds) *Body Invaders: Sexuality and the Postmodern Condition*, London: Macmillan.

Annets, J. and Thompson, B. (1992) 'Dangerous activism?' in K. Plummer (ed.) *Modern Homosexuality: Fragments of Lesbian and Gay Experience*, London: Routledge.

Aries, P. and Bejin, A. (eds) (1985) *Western Sexuality: Practice and Precept in Past and Present Times*, Oxford: Basil Blackwell.

Atkinson, T. (1974) *Amazon Odyssey*, New York: Links Books.

Babuscio, J. (1988) *We Speak for Ourselves: the Experiences of Gay Men and Lesbians* (2nd edn), London: SPCK.

Barrett, M. et al. (1979) *Ideology and Cultural Reproduction*, London: Croom Helm.

Barrett, M. (1980) *Women's Oppression Today: Problems in Marxist Feminist Analysis*, London: Verso.

Barrett, M. and McIntosh, M. (1982) *The Anti-Social Family*, London: New Left Books.

Baudrillard, J. (1983) *Simulations*, New York: Semiotext(e).

Becker, E. (1973) *The Denial of Death*, New York: Free Press.

Becker, H. S. (1970) *Sociological Work: Method and Substance*, Chicago: Aldine Publishing Company.

Becker, H. S. (1986) *Doing Things Together: Selected Papers*, Evanston, Illinois: Northwestern University Press.

Bell, A. and Weinberg, M. (1978) *Homosexualities: a Study of Diversity among Men and Women*, New York: Simon & Schuster.

Bell, A. et al. (1981) *Sexual Preference: Its Development in Men & Women*, Bloomington: Indiana University Press.

Bell, D. H. (1982) *Being a Man: the Paradox of Masculinity*, London: Lewis Publishing Company.

Benjamin, J. (1984) 'Master and Slave: the Fantasy of Erotic Domination' in A. Snitow et al. (eds) *Desire: the Politics of Sexuality*, London: Virago.

Berger, P. and Luckmann, T. (1967) *The Social Construction of Reality*, Harmondsworth, Middlesex: Penguin.

Bersani, L. (1988) 'Is the rectum a grave?' in D. Crimp (ed.) *AIDS: Cultural Analysis, Cultural Activism*, London: MIT Press.

Blachford, G. (1980) 'Looking at pornography: erotica and the socialist morality' in P. Mitchell (ed.) *Pink Triangles: Radical Perspectives on Gay Liberation*, Boston, Massachusetts: Alyson Publications.

Blachford, G. (1981) 'Male dominance and the gay world' in K. Plummer (ed.) *The Making of the Modern Homosexual*, London: Hutchinson.

Black, D. (1986) *The Plague Years: a Chronicle of AIDS: the Epidemic of Our Times*, London: Picador.

Bleibtreu-Ehrenberg, G. (1990) 'Pederasty among primitives: institutionalised initiation and cultic prostitution' in *Journal of Homosexuality*, 20, 1/2, pp. 13–30.

Boffin, T. and Gupta, S. (eds) (1990) *Ecstatic Antibodies: Resisting the AIDS Mythology*, London: Rivers Oram Press.

Boogaard, Van Den, H. (1989) 'Blood furious underneath the skins . . . on anti-homosexual violence: its nature and the needs of the victims' in D. Altman et al. (eds) *Homosexuality, Which Homosexuality?* London: Gay Men's Press.

Bordo, S. (1990) 'Feminism, postmodernism, and gender-scepticism' in L. J. Nicholson (ed.) *Feminism/Postmodernism*, London: Routledge.

Boswell, J. (1980) *Christianity, Social Tolerance and Homosexuality: Gay People in Western Europe from the Beginning of the Christian Era to the Fourteenth Century*, Chicago: University of Chicago Press.

Brake, M. (ed.) (1982) *Human Sexual Relations: a Reader in Human Sexuality*, Harmondsworth, Middlesex: Penguin.

Brandt, A. (1985) *No Magic Bullet: a Social History of Venereal Disease in the United States since 1880*, New York: Oxford University Press.

Bray, A. (1982) *Homosexuality in Renaissance England*, London: Gay Men's Press.

Bristow, J. (1989) 'Homophobia/misogyny: sexual fears, sexual definitions' in S. Shepherd and M. Wallis (eds) *Coming on Strong: Gay Politics and Culture*, London: Unwin Hyman.

Bronski, M. (1984) *Culture Clash: the Making of a Gay Sensibility*, Boston, Massachusetts: South End Press.

Bronski, M. (1989) 'Death and the erotic imagination' in E. Carter and S. Watney (eds) *Taking Liberties: AIDS and Cultural Politics*, London: Serpent's Tail.

Brownmiller, S. (1975) *Against Our Will: Men, Women and Rape*, New York: Simon & Schuster.

Butler, J. (1990) 'Gender trouble, feminist theory, and psychoanalytic discourse' in L. J. Nicholson (ed.) *Feminism/Postmodernism*, London: Routledge.

Califia, P. (1981) 'Man/boy love and the lesbian/gay movement' in D. Tsang (ed.) *The Age Taboo: Gay Male Sexuality, Power and Consent*, London: Gay Men's Press.

Campbell, D. (1989) 'AIDS: the race against time' in *New Statesman & Society*, 2, 1, pp. 9–14.

Campbell, D. (1989) 'Living positively' in *New Statesman & Society*, 2, 4, pp. 13–16.

Cant, B. and Hemmings, S. (eds) (1988) *Radical Records: Thirty Years of Gay and Lesbian History, 1957–1987*, London: Routledge.

Caplan, P. (ed.) (1987) *The Cultural Construction of Sexuality*, London: Tavistock.

Carpenter, E. (1908) *The Intermediate Sex: a Study of Some Transitional Types of Men*, London: Mitchell Kennedy.

Carrigan, T. et al. (1985) 'Toward a new sociology of masculinity' in *Theory & Society*, 14, pp. 551–604.

Carter, E. and Watney, S. (eds) (1989) *Taking Liberties: AIDS and Cultural Politics*, London: Serpent's Tail.

Carter, V. (1992) 'Abseil makes the heart grow fonder' in K. Plummer (ed.) *Modern Homosexualities: Fragments of Lesbian and Gay Experience*, London: Routledge.

Cass, V. C. (1979) 'Homosexual identity formation: a theoretical model' in *Journal of Homosexuality*, 4, 3, pp. 219–235.

Chapman, R. and Rutherford, J. (eds) (1988) *Male Order: Unwrapping Masculinity*, London: Lawrence & Wishart.

Charmaz, K. (1980) *The Social Reality of Death: Death in Contemporary America*, London: Addison-Wesley.

Chirimuuta, R. C. and Chirimuuta, R. J. (1989) *AIDS: Africa and Racism*, London: Free Association Books.

Chodorow, N. (1978) *The Reproduction of Mothering: Psychoanalysis and the Sociology of Gender*, California: University of California Press.

Churchill, C. (1979) *Cloud Nine*, London: Pluto Press.

Cockburn, C. K. (1983) *Brothers: Male Dominance and Technological Change*, London: Pluto.

Cockburn, C. K. (1988) 'Masculinity, the Left and feminism' in R. Chapman and J. Rutherford (eds) *Male Order: Unwrapping Masculinity*, London: Lawrence & Wishart.

Cohen, D. (1990) *Being A Man*, London: Routledge.
Cohen, S. (1972) *Folk Devils and Moral Panics: the Creation of Mods and Rockers*, London: Martin Robertson.
Connell, R. W. (1983) *Which Way Is Up? Essays on Sex, Class and Culture*, London: George Allen & Unwin.
Connell, R. W. (1987) *Gender and Power: Society, the Person and Sexual Politics*, Cambridge: Polity Press.
Connell, R. W. et al. (1989) 'Facing the epidemic: changes in the sexual lives of gay and bisexual men in Australia and their implications for AIDS prevention strategies' in *Social Problems*, 36, 4, pp. 384–402.
Connor, S. (1989) *Postmodernist Culture: an Introduction to Theories of the Contemporary*, Oxford: Basil Blackwell.
Coulson, M. (1980) 'The struggle for femininity' in Gay Left Collective (ed.) *Homosexuality: Power and Politics*, London: Allison & Busby, pp. 21–37.
Coveney, L. et al. (1984) *The Sexuality Papers: Male Sexuality and the Social Control of Women*, London: Hutchinson.
Coward, R. (1982) 'Sexual violence and sexuality' in *Feminist Review*, 11.
Crimp, D. (ed.) (1988) *AIDS: Cultural Analysis, Cultural Activism*, London: MIT Press.
Crimp, D. (1989) 'Mourning and militancy' in *October*, 51, pp. 3–18.
Crimp, D. and Rolston, A. (1990) *AIDSDemographics*, Seattle: Bay Press.
Crisp, Q. (1968) *The Naked Civil Servant*, Glasgow: Collins.
Daly, M. (1979) *Gyn/Ecology*, London: Women's Press.
Dannecker, M. (1981) *Theories of Homosexuality*, London: Gay Men's Press.
David, D. S. and Brannon, R. (eds) (1976) *The Forty-Nine Percent Majority: the Male Sex Role*, Cambridge, Massachusetts: Addison-Wesley Publishing Company.
De Beauvoir, S. (1953) *The Second Sex*, New York: Alfred A. Knopf.
DeCecco, J. (1984) *Bisexual and Homosexual Identities: Critical Clinical Issues*, New York: Haworth Press.
Delph, E. W. (1978) *The Silent Community: Public Homosexual Encounters*, Beverly Hills, California: Sage Publications.
Delphy, C. (1984) *Close To Home*, London: Hutchinson.
D'Emilio, J. (1983) *Sexual Politics, Sexual Communities: the Making of a Homosexual Minority in the United States 1940–1970*, Chicago: University of Chicago Press.
Dexter, L. A. (1970) *Elite and Specialised Interviewing*, Evanston, Illinois: Northwestern University Press.
Douglas, J. D. (ed.) (1972) *Research on Deviance*, New York: Random House.
Dowsett, G. (1987) 'Queer fears and gay examples' in *New Internationalist*, 175, pp. 10–12.
DuBay, W. H. (1987) *Gay Identity: the Self under Ban*, Jefferson, North Carolina: McFarland and Co.
Duberman, M. B. et al. (eds) (1989) *Hidden from History: Reclaiming the Gay and Lesbian Past*, New York: New American Library.
Dworkin, A. (1981) *Pornography: Men Possessing Women*, London: Women's Press.

Dworkin, A. (1987) *Intercourse*, London: Women's Press.
Dyer, R. (1989) 'A conversation about pornography' in S. Shepherd and M. Wallis (eds) *Coming on Strong: Gay Politics and Culture*, London: Unwin Hyman.
Easlea, B. (1981) *Science and Sexual Oppression: Patriarchy's Confrontation with Women and Nature*, London: Weidenfeld and Nicolson.
Easthope, A. (1986) *What a Man's Gotta Do: the Masculine Myth in Popular Culture*, London: Paladin.
Edwards, J. N. (ed.) (1972) *Sex and Society*, Chicago: Markham Publishing Company.
Edwards, R. (1979) *Contested Terrain: the Transformation of the Workplace in the Twentieth Century*, London: Heinemann.
Edwards, T. (1990) 'Beyond sex and gender: masculinity, homosexuality and social theory' in J. Hearn and D. Morgan (eds) *Men, Masculinities and Social Theory*, London: Unwin Hyman.
Edwards, T. (1991) *The AIDS Dialectics*, PhD thesis: University of Essex.
Edwards, T. (1992) 'The AIDS dialectics: awareness, identity, death and sexual politics' in K. Plummer (ed.) *Modern Homosexualities: Fragments of Lesbian and Gay Experience*, London: Routledge.
Eglinton, J. Z. (1971) *Greek Love*, London: Neville Spearman.
Eisenstein, H. (1984) *Contemporary Feminist Thought*, London: Unwin.
Elias, N. (1985) *The Loneliness of the Dying*, Oxford: Basil Blackwell.
Ellis, H. (1897) *Sexual Inversion*, London: Wilson and Macmillan.
Ennew, J. (1986) *The Sexual Exploitation of Children*, Cambridge: Polity.
Epstein, S. (1987) 'Gay politics, ethnic identity: the limits of social constructionism' in *Socialist Review*, 17, pp. 9–54.
Epstein, S. (1988) 'Nature vs. nurture and the politics of AIDS organising' in *Out/Look*, 1, 3, pp. 46–50.
Erikson, E. H. (1965) (2nd edn) *Childhood and Society*, Harmondsworth, Middlesex: Penguin.
Evans, D. (1990) 'Section 28: law, myth and paradox' in *Critical Social Policy*, 9, 3, pp. 73–95.
Faderman, L. (1981) *Surpassing the Love of Men: Romantic Friendship and Love between Women from the Renaissance to the Present*, New York: William Morrow.
Faraday, A. (1981) 'Liberating lesbian research' in K. Plummer (ed.) *The Making of the Modern Homosexual*, London: Hutchinson.
Faraday, A. and Plummer, K. (1979) 'Doing life histories' in *Sociological Review*, 27, 4, pp. 773–798.
Farrell, W. (1974) *The Liberated Man beyond Masculinity: Freeing Men and Their Relationships with Women*, New York: Random House.
Fee, E. and Fox, D. M. (1988) *AIDS: the Burdens of History*, California: University of California Press.
Feldman, D. A. and Johnson, T. M (1986) *The Social Dimensions of AIDS: Method and Theory*, New York: Praeger.
Ferguson, A. et al. (1984) 'Forum: the feminist sexuality debates' in *Signs: Journal of Women in Culture and Society*, 10, 1, pp. 106–135.
Finkelhor, D. (1990) 'Response to Bauserman' in *Journal of Homosexuality*, 20, 1/2, pp. 313–315.

EROTICS & POLITICS

Firestone, S. (1970) *The Dialectic of Sex: the Case for Feminist Revolution*, New York: Bantam Books.
Fitzpatrick, M. and Milligan, D. (1987) *The Truth about the AIDS Panic*, London: Junius.
Ford, D. and Hearn, J. (1988) *Studying Men and Masculinity: a Sourcebook of Literature and Materials*, Bradford: University of Bradford. [repub. 1991]
Foucault, M. (1978) *The History of Sexuality – Volume One: an Introduction*, Harmondsworth, Middlesex: Penguin.
Foucault, M. (1984a) *The Use of Pleasure: the History of Sexuality – Volume Two*, Harmondsworth, Middlesex: Penguin.
Foucault, M. (1984b) *The Care of the Self: the History of Sexuality – Volume Three*, Harmondsworth, Middlesex: Penguin.
Friedan, B. (1963) *The Feminine Mystique*, London: Victor Gollancz.
Freud, S. (1977) *On Sexuality: Three Essays on the Theory of Sexuality and Other Works*, London: Penguin. [orig. pub. 1905]
Freidman, S. and Sarah, E. (eds) (1982) *On the Problem of Men: Two Feminist Conferences*, London: Women's Press.
Fuss, D. (1989) *Essentially Speaking: Feminism, Nature and Difference*, London: Routledge.
Fuss, D. (ed.) (1991) *Inside/Out: Lesbian Theories, Gay Theories*, London: Routledge.
Gagnon, J. H. (1977) *Human Sexualities*, Glenview, Illinois: Scott, Firesman and Company.
Gagnon, J. H. and Simon, W. (1973) *Sexual Conduct: the Social Sources of Human Sexuality*, Chicago: Aldine Publishing Comapany.
Galloway, B. (ed.) (1983) *Prejudice and Pride: Discrimination against Gay People in Modern Britain*, London: Routledge & Kegan Paul.
Gamson, J. (1989) 'Silence, death, and the invisible enemy: AIDS activism and social movement "Newness"' in *Social Problems*, 36, 4, pp. 351–367.
Gay Left Collective (ed.) (1980) *Homosexuality: Power and Politics*, London: Allison & Busby.
Gay Left Collective (1981) 'Happy families? Pedophilia examined' in D. Tsang (ed.) *The Age Taboo: Gay Male Sexuality, Power and Consent*, London: Gay Men's Press.
Gilligan, C. (1982) *In a Different Voice: Psychological Theory and Women's Development*, Cambridge, Massachusetts: Harvard University Press.
Glaser, C. (1989) 'AIDS and A-bomb disease: facing a special death' in P. O'Malley (ed.) *The AIDS Epidemic: Private Rights and Public Interest*, Boston, Massachusetts: Beacon Press.
Glaser, B. and Strauss, A. (1965) *Awareness of Dying*, London: Weidenfeld and Nicolson.
Goetz, J. (1987) 'Interrupting homophobia' in *Achilles Heel*, 8, pp. 5–7.
Gordon, P. and Mitchell, L. (1988) *Safer Sex: a New Look at Sexual Pleasure*, London: Faber & Faber.
Gough, J. (1989) 'Theories of sexual identity and the masculinization of the gay man' in S. Shepherd and M. Wallis (eds) *Coming on Strong: Gay Politics and Culture*, London: Unwin Hyman.

BIBLIOGRAPHY

Gough, J. and Macnair, M. (1985) *Gay Liberation in the Eighties*, London: Pluto Press.

Greasley, P. (1986) *Gay Men at Work: a Report on Discrimination against Gay Men in Employment in London*, London: Lesbian & Gay Employment Rights.

Greenberg, D. F. (1988) *The Construction of Homosexuality*, London: University of Chicago Press.

Greig, N. (1987) 'Codes of conduct' in G. Hanscombe and M. Humphries (eds) *Heterosexuality*, London: Gay Men's Press.

Griffin, S. (1979) *Rape: The Power of Consciousness*, San Francisco, California: Harper & Row.

Griffin, S. (1981) *Pornography and Silence: Culture's Revenge against Nature*, New York: Harper & Row.

Grosz, E. (1987) 'Feminist theory and the challenge to knowledges' in *Women's Studies International Forum*, 10, 5, pp. 475–480.

Gupta, S. (1989) 'Black, brown and white' in S. Shepherd and M. Wallis (eds) *Coming on Strong: Gay Politics and Culture*, London: Unwin Hyman.

Hall Carpenter Archives Gay Men's Oral History Group (1989) *Walking after Midnight: Gay Men's Life Stories*, London: Routledge.

Hancock, G. and Carim, E. (1986) *AIDS: the Deadly Epidemic*, London: Victor Gollancz.

Hanmer, J. (1990) 'Men, power and the exploitation of women' in J. Hearn and D. Morgan (eds) *Men, Masculinities and Social Theory*, London: Unwin Hyman.

Hanmer, J. and Saunders, S. (1984) *Well Founded Fear: a Community Study of Violence to Women*, London: Hutchinson.

Haraway, D. (1990) 'A manifesto for cyborgs: science, technology, and socialist feminism in the 1980s' in L. J. Nicholson (ed.) *Feminism/Postmodernism*, London: Routledge.

Harding, S. (1988) 'The decline of permissiveness' in *New Statesman & Society*, 1, 22, pp. 25–26.

Hart, J. and Richardson, D. (eds) (1981) *The Theory and Practice of Homosexuality*, London: Routledge & Kegan Paul.

Hearn, J. (1987) *The Gender of Oppression: Men, Masculinity and the Critique of Marxism*, Brighton, Sussex: Wheatsheaf.

Hearn, J. and Melechi, A. (1992) 'The transatlantic gaze: masculinities, youth and the American imaginary' in S. Craig (ed.) *Men, Masculinity, and the Media*, London: Sage.

Hearn, J. and Morgan, D. (eds) (1990) *Men, Masculinities and Social Theory*, London: Unwin Hyman.

Hearn, J. and Parkin, W. (1987) *'Sex' At 'Work': the Power and Paradox of Organisation Sexuality*, Brighton, Sussex: Wheatsheaf.

Heath, S. (1982) *The Sexual Fix*, London: Macmillan.

Herdt, G. (ed.) (1989) *Gay and Lesbian Youth*, London: Haworth Press.

Herek, G. M. (1987) 'On heterosexual masculinity: some psychological consequences of the social construction of gender and sexuality' in M. S. Kimmel (ed.) *Changing Men: New Directions in Research on Men and Masculinity*, London: Sage.

Herek, G. M. and Burrell, K. T. (eds) (1992) *Hate Crimes: Confronting Violence against Lesbians and Gay Men*, London: Sage.

Hester, M. (1992) *Lewd Women and Wicked Witches: a study of the dynamics of Male Domination*, London: Routledge.

Hewitt, B. et al. (1987) 'The politics of AIDS' in *Newsweek*, 32, pp. 12–20.

Hoch, P. (1979) *White Hero, Black Beast: Racism, Sexism, and the Mask of Masculinity*, London: Pluto Press.

Hocquenghem, G. (1972) *Homosexual Desire*, London: Allison & Busby.

Hoffman, M. (1968) *The Gay World: Male Homosexuality and the Social Construction of Evil*, New York: Basic Books.

Holland, J. et al. (1990) 'AIDS: from panic stations to power relations – sociological perspectives and problems' in *Sociology*, 25, 3, pp. 499–518.

Hollinghurst, A. (1988) *The Swimming-Pool Library*, Harmondsworth, Middlesex: Penguin.

Howells, K. (ed.) (1984) *The Psychology of Sexual Diversity*, Oxford: Basil Blackwell.

Humphries, M. (1985) 'Gay machismo' in A. Metcalf and M. Humphries (eds) *The Sexuality of Men*, London: Pluto.

Hunt, M. (1990) 'The de-eroticisation of women's liberation: social purity movements and the revolutionary feminism of Sheila Jeffreys' in *Feminist Review*, 34, pp. 23–36.

Hunt, M. E. (1989) 'On religious lesbians: contradictions and challenges' in D. Altman et al. (eds) *Homosexuality, Which Homosexuality?* London: Gay Men's Press.

Ingham, M. (1984) *Men: the Male Myth Exposed*, London: Century Publishing.

Irigaray, L. (1985) *This Sex Which Is Not One*, Ithaca, New York: Cornell University Press.

Jackson, D. (1990) *Unmasking Masculinity: a Critical Autobiography*, London: Unwin Hyman.

Jameson, F. (1984) 'Postmodernism, or the cultural logic of late capitalism' in *New Left Review*, 146, pp. 53–93.

Jameson, F. (1988) 'Postmodernism and consumer society' in E. A. Kaplan (ed.) *Postmodernism and Its Discontents: Theories, Practices*, London: Verso.

Jardine, A. and Smith, P. (eds) (1987) *Men in Feminism*, London: Methuen.

Jay, K. and Young, A. (1979) *The Gay Report*, New York: Summit Books.

Jeffreys, S. (1990) *Anticlimax: Feminist Perspective on the Sexual Revolution*, London: Women's Press.

Joint Council for Gay Teenagers (1981) 'I know what I am: Gay Teenagers and the Law' in D. Tsang (ed.) *The Age Taboo: Gay Male Sexuality: Power and Consent*, London: Gay Men's Press.

Kamerman, J. B. (1988) *Death in the Midst of Life: Social and Cultural Influences on Death, Grief and Mourning*, New Jersey: Prentice-Hall.

Kaplan, E. A. (ed.) (1988) *Postmodernism and Its Discontents: Theories, Practices*, London: Verso.

Kaplan, H. B. et al. (1987) 'The sociological study of AIDS: a critical review of the literature and suggested research agenda' in *Journal of Health and Social Behaviour*, 28, pp. 140–157.

BIBLIOGRAPHY

Kaplan, H. S. (1987) *The Real Truth about Women and AIDS*, New York: Simon & Schuster.

Katz, J. (1976) *Gay American History: Lesbians and Gay Men in the U.S.A.*, New York: Thomas Y. Crowell.

Kaufman, M. (ed.) (1987) *Beyond Patriarchy: Essays by Men on Pleasure, Power and Change*, Toronto: Oxford University Press.

Kellner, D. (1988) 'Postmodernism as social theory: some challenges and problems' in *Theory, Culture & Society*, 5, 2–3, pp. 239–270.

Kellner, D. (1989) *Jean Baudrillard: from Marxism to Postmodernism and Beyond*, Oxford: Polity.

Kelly, L. (1988) *Surviving Sexual Violence*, Cambridge: Polity.

Kimmel, M. S. (ed.) (1987) *Changing Men: New Directions in Research on Men and Masculinity*, Beverly Hills, California: Sage.

Kimmel, M. S. (1990a) 'After fifteen years: the impact of the sociology of masculinity on the masculinity of sociology' in J. Hearn and D. Morgan (eds) *Men, Masculinities and Social Theory*, London: Unwin Hyman.

Kimmel, M. S. (ed.) (1990b) *Men Confront Pornography*, New York: Crown Publishers.

Kinsey, A. C. et al. (1948) *Sexual Behaviour in the Human Male*, Philadelphia: W. B. Saunders.

Kleinberg, S. (1987) 'The new masculinity of gay men, and beyond' in M. Kaufman (ed.) *Beyond Patriarchy: Essays by Men on Pleasure, Power and Change*, Toronto: Oxford University Press.

Kowalewski, M. R. (1988) 'Double stigma and boundary maintenance: how gay men deal with AIDS' in *Journal of Contemporary Ethnography*, 17, 2, pp. 211–228

Krafft-Ebing, R. (1965) *Psychopathia Sexualis: a Medico-Forensic Study*, New York: G. P. Putnam's Sons. [Orig. pub. 1886]

Kramer, L. (1978) *Faggots*, London: Methuen.

Kramer, L. (1983) '1,112 and counting' in *New York Native*, 59, pp. 14–27.

Kramer, L. (1986) *The Normal Heart*, London: Methuen.

Kramer, L. (1990) *Reports from the Holocaust: the Making of an AIDS Activist*, Harmondsworth, Middlesex: Penguin.

Kristeva, J. (1986) *The Kristeva Reader*, (ed. Moi, T.) Oxford: Basil Blackwell.

Kroker, A. and Cook, D. (1988) *The Postmodern Scene: Excremental Culture and Hyper-Aesthetics*, London: Macmillan.

Kroker, A. and Kroker, M. (1988) *Body Invaders: Sexuality and the Postmodern Condition*, London: Macmillan.

Kubler-Ross, E. (1969) *On Death and Dying*, London: Tavistock.

Kubler-Ross, E. (1987) *AIDS: the Ultimate Challenge*, New York: Macmillan.

LaFontaine, J. (1990) *Child Sexual Abuse*, Cambridge: Polity.

Layland, J. (1990) 'On the conflicts of doing feminist research into masculinity' in L. Stanley (ed.) *Feminist Praxis: Research, Theory and Epistemology in Feminist Research Processes*, London: Routledge.

Lee, J. A. (1978) *Getting Sex: a New Approach – More Fun, Less Guilt*, Ontario, Canada: Mission Book Company.

Lee, J. A. (1979) 'The gay connection' in *Urban Life: a Journal of Ethnographic Research*, 8, 2.

Lee, P. C. and Sussman Stewart, R. (1976) *Sex Differences: Cultural and Developmental Dimensions*, New York: Urizen Books.

Leznoff, M. (1956) 'Interviewing homosexuals' in *American Journal of Sociology*, 62, 2, pp. 202–204.

Lifton, R. J. (1973) *Home from the War – Vietnam Veterans: Neither Victim nor Executioners*, New York: Touchstone.

Lifton, R. J. (1979) *The Broken Connection: on Death and the Continuity of Life*, New York: Touchstone.

Lifton, R. J. (1986) *The Nazi Doctors: Medical Killing and the Psychology of Genocide*, London: Macmillan.

Linden, R. et al. (eds) (1982) *Against Sado-masochism: a Radical Feminist Analysis*, California: Frog in the Well.

Lyotard, J. F. (1984) *The Postmodern Condition*, Manchester: Manchester University Press.

Maccoby, E. and Jacklin, C. (1974) *The Psychology of Sex Differences*, Stanford, California: Stanford University Press.

McIntosh, M. (1968) 'The homosexual role' in *Social Problems*, 16, pp. 182–192.

Mackinnon, C. A. (1982) 'Feminism, Marxism, method and the state: an agenda for theory' in N. O. Keohane et al. (eds) *Feminist theory: a Critique of Ideology*, Brighton, Sussex: Harvester Press.

Mackinnon, C. A. (1987a) 'Feminism, Marxism, method and the state: toward feminist jurisprudence' in S. Harding (ed.) *Feminism and Methodology: Social Science Issues*, Milton Keynes: Open University Press.

Mackinnon, C. A. (1987b) *Feminism Unmodified: Discourses on Life and Law*, Cambridge, Massachusetts: Harvard University Press.

McKusick, L. (ed.) (1986) *What to Do about AIDS: Physicians and Mental Health Professionals Discuss the Issues*, California, University of California Press.

McMullen, R. (1990) *Male Rape*, London: Gay Men's Press.

Macnair, M. (1989) 'The contradictory politics of SM' in S. Shepherd and M. Wallis (eds) *Coming on Strong: Gay Politics and Culture*, London: Unwin Hyman.

Mains, G. (1984) *Urban Aboriginals: a Celebration of Leathersexuality*, San Francisco: Gay Sunshine Press.

Mangold, T. (1987) 'The plague mentality makes victims of us all' in *Listener*, 118, 3018, pp. 5–6.

Marks, E. and DeCourtivron, I. (eds) (1981) *New French Feminisms: an Anthology*, Brighton, Sussex: Harvester Press. [Orig. pub. 1980]

Marotta, T. (1981) *The Politics of Homosexuality*, Boston, Massachusetts: Houghton Mifflin Co.

Marshall, J. (1981) 'Pansies, perverts and macho men: changing conceptions of male homosexuality' in K. Plummer (ed.) *The Making of the Modern Homosexual*, London, Hutchinson.

Marshall, J. (1989) 'Flaunting it' in *Gay Times*, January: pp. 12–13.

Martelli, L. J. et al. (1987) *When Someone You Know Has AIDS: a Practical Guide*, New York: Crown Publishers.

BIBLIOGRAPHY

Masters, W. H. and Johnson, V. E. (1979) *Homosexuality in Perspective*, Boston, Massachusetts: Little, Brown and Company.

Mead, M. (1977) *Sex and Temperament in Three Primitive Societies*, London: Routledge & Kegan Paul.

Menard, G. (1989) 'Gay theology, which gay theology?' in D. Altman et al. (eds) *Homosexuality, Which Homosexuality?* London: Gay Men's Press.

Mendelson, E. (ed.) (1979) *W. H. Auden: Selected Poems*, London: Faber & Faber.

Mercer, K. and Julien, I. (1988) 'Race, sexual politics and black masculinity: a dossier' in R. Chapman and J. Rutherford (eds) *Male Order: Unwrapping Masculinity*, London: Lawrence & Wishart.

Metcalf, A. and Humphries, M. (eds) (1985) *The Sexuality of Men*, London: Pluto Press.

Mieli, M. (1980) *Homosexuality and Liberation: Elements of a Gay Critique*, London: Gay Men's Press.

Millett, K. (1971) *Sexual Politics*, London: Sphere.

Millett, K. (1984) 'Beyond politics? Children and sexuality' in C. S. Vance (ed.) *Pleasure and Danger: Exploring Female Sexuality*, London: Routledge & Kegan Paul.

Mitchell, J. (1971) *Woman's Estate*, Harmondsworth, Middlesex: Penguin

Mitchell, J. (1974) *Psychoanalysis and Feminism*, New York: Pantheon Books.

Mitchell, P. (ed.) (1980) *Pink Triangles: Radical Perspectives on Gay Liberation*, Boston, Massachusetts: Alyson Publications.

Moffett, M. (1981) 'Loving men' in D. Tsang (ed.) *The Age Taboo: Gay Male Sexuality, Power and Consent*, London: Gay Men's Press.

Moi, T. (1985) *Sexual-Textual Politics: Feminist Literary theory*, London: Methuen.

Moody, R. (1981) 'Man/boy love and the Left' in D. Tsang (ed.) *The Age Taboo: Gay Male Sexuality, Power and Consent*, London: Gay Men's Press.

Morgan, R. (1977) *Going Too Far*, New York: Random House.

Mort, F. (1987) *Dangerous Sexualities: Medico-Moral Politics in England Since 1830*, London: Routledge & Kegan Paul.

Mort, F. (1988) 'Boys Own? Masculinity, style and popular culture' in R. Chapman and J. Rutherford (eds) *Male Order: Unwrapping Masculinity*, London: Lawrence & Wishart.

Murphy, L. R. (1988) *Perverts by Official Order: the Campaign against Homosexuals by the United States Navy*, London: Harrington Park Press.

National Deviancy Conference (eds) (1980) *Permissiveness and Control: the Fate of the Sixties Legislation*, London: Macmillan.

Nestle, J. (1984) 'The fem question' in C. S. Vance (ed.) *Pleasure and Danger: Exploring Female Sexuality*, London: Routledge & Kegan Paul.

Nichols et al. (1982) in R. Linden et al. (eds) *Against Sado-masochism*, California: Frog in the Well.

Nicholson. L. J. (ed.) (1990) *Feminism/Postmodernism*, London: Routledge.

Norris, C. (1990) *What's Wrong with Postmodernism: Critical Theory and the Ends of Philosophy*, Hemel Hempstead, Herts: Harvester Wheatsheaf.

Norris, S. and Reed, E. (1985) *Out in the Open: People Talking about Being Gay or Being Bisexual*, London: Pan.

Nungesser, L. G. (1986) *Epidemic of Courage: Facing AIDS in America*, New York: St Martin's Press.

Oakley, A. (1972) *Sex, Gender and Society*, London: Temple Smith.

O'Carroll, T. (1980) *Paedophilia: the Radical Case*, London: Peter Owen Ltd.

Okely, J. (1987) 'Privileged, schooled and finished: boarding education for girls' in G. Weiner and M. Arnot (eds) *Gender under Scrutiny: New Enquiries in Education*, London: Hutchinson.

Ortner, S. B. and Whitehead, H. (eds) (1981) *Sexual Meanings: the Cultural Construction of Gender and Sexuality*, Cambridge: Cambridge University Press.

Owens, C. (1987) 'Outlaws: gay men in feminism' in A. Jardine and P. Smith (eds) *Men in Feminism*, London: Methuen.

Panos Institute, The (1989) *AIDS and the Third World*, Philadelphia, PA: New Society Publishers.

Panos Institute, The (1990) *The Third Epidemic: Repercussions of the Fear of AIDS*, London: Panos Publications.

Patton, C. (1985) *Sex and Germs: the Politics of AIDS*, Boston, Massachusetts: South End Press.

Patton, C. (1990) *Inventing AIDS*, London: Routledge.

Patton, C. and Kelly, J. (1987) *Making It: a Woman's Guide to Sex in the Age of AIDS*, New York.

Peabody, B. (1986) *The Screaming Room: a Mother's Journal of Her Son's Struggle with AIDS, a True Story of Love, Dedication and Courage*, San Diego, California: Oak Tree Publications.

Person, E. S. (1980) 'Sexuality as the mainstay of identity: psychoanalytic perspectives' in *Signs*, 5, 4, pp. 605–630.

Petras, J. W. (ed.) (1975) *Sex: Male Gender: Masculine – Readings in Male Sexuality*, Boston, Massachusetts: Alfred Publishing.

Plant, R. (1987) *The Pink Triangle: the Nazi War against Homosexuals*, Edinburgh: Mainstream Publishing.

Plant, M. (ed.) (1990) *AIDS, Drugs and Prostitution*, London: Routledge.

Pleck, J. H. (1981) *The Myth of Masculinity*, Cambridge, Massachusetts: MIT Press.

Pleck, J. H. and Sawyer, J. (eds) (1974) *Men and Masculinity*, Cambridge, Massachusetts: Prentice-Hall.

Plummer, K. (1975) *Sexual Stigma: an Interactionist Account*, London: Routledge & Kegan Paul.

Plummer, K. (1978) 'Men in love: observations on the male homosexual couple' in M. Corbin (ed.) *The Couple*, Harmondsworth, Middlesex: Penguin.

Plummer, K. (1981a) 'The paedophile's progress' in B. Taylor (ed.) *Perspectives on Paedophilia*, London: Batsford.

Plummer, K. (ed.) (1981b) *The Making of the Modern Homosexual*, London: Hutchinson.

Plummer, K. (1983) *Documents of Life: an Introduction to the Problems and Literature of a Humanistic Method*, London: Allen & Unwin.

Plummer, K. (1990) 'Understanding childhood sexualities' in *Journal of Homosexuality*, 20, 1/2, pp. 231–249.

Plummer, K. (ed.) (1992) *Modern Homosexualities: Fragments of Lesbian and Gay Experience*, London: Routledge.

Pollak, M. (1985) 'Male homosexuality – or happiness in the ghetto' in P. Aries and A. Bejin (eds) *Western Sexuality: Practice and Precept in Past and Present Times*, Oxford: Basil Blackwell.

Ponse, B. (1978) *Identities in the Lesbian World: the Social Construction of Self*, Westport, Connecticut: Greenwood Press.

Presland, E. (1981) 'Whose power? Whose consent?' in D. Tsang (ed.) *The Age Taboo: Gay Male Sexuality, Power and Consent*, London: Gay Men's Press.

Price, M. E. (1989) *Shattered Mirrors: Our Search for Identity and Community in the AIDS Era*, Cambridge, Massachusetts: Harvard University Press.

Rabinow, P. (ed.) (1984) *The Foucault Reader*, Harmondsworth, Middlesex: Penguin.

Radclyffe-Hall (1982) *The Well of Loneliness*, London: Virago. [orig. pub. 1928]

Rechy, J. (1977) *The Sexual Outlaw: a Documentary*, London: W. H. Allen.

Reeves, T. (1981) 'Loving boys' in D. Tsang (ed.) *The Age Taboo: Gay Male Sexuality, Power and Consent*, London: Gay Men's Press.

Reynaud, E. (1983) *Holy Virility: the Social Construction of Masculinity*, London: Pluto Press.

Rian, K. (1982) 'Sado-masochism and the social construction of desire' in R. Linden et al. (eds) *Against Sado-masochism: a Radical Feminist Analysis*, California: Frog in the Well.

Ribbens, J. et al. (1991) 'The use of student autobiography in teaching undergraduate sociology', unpublished paper, Oxford Brookes University.

Rich, A. (1984) 'Compulsory heterosexuality and lesbian existence' in A. Snitow et al. (eds) *Desire: the Politics of Sexuality*, London: Virago.

Richardson, D. (1987) *Women and the AIDS Crisis*, London: Pandora.

Roberts, H. (ed.) (1981) *Doing Feminist Research*, London: Routledge & Kegan Paul.

Rubin, G. (1981) 'Sexual politics, the new right and the sexual fringe' in D. Tsang (ed.) *The Age Taboo: Gay Male Sexuality, Power and Consent*, London: Gay Men's Press.

Rubin, G. (1984) 'Thinking sex: notes for a radical theory of the politics of sexuality' in C. S. Vance (ed.) *Pleasure and Danger: Exploring Female Sexuality*, London: Routledge & Kegan Paul.

Ruffell, D. (1990) 'Scenarios of departure' in T. Boffin and S. Gupta *Ecstatic Antibodies: Resisting the AIDS Mythology*, London: Rivers Oram Press.

Ruse, M. (1988) *Homosexuality: a Philosophical Inquiry*, Oxford: Basil Blackwell.

Rush, F. (1980) *The Best Kept Secret: Sexual Abuse of Children*, Englewood Cliffs, New Jersey: Prentice-Hall.

Russell, D. (1984) *Sexual Exploitation: Rape, Child Sexual Abuse, and Workplace Harassment*, Beverly Hills, California: Sage.

Rutledge, L. W. (1985) 'Have leathermen transcended the nasty shallowness of western society?' in *Mandate*, pp. 59–60.

Ryan, M. (1988) 'Postmodern politics' in *Theory, Culture & Society*, 5, pp. 559–576.

Sabatier, R. (1988) *Blaming Others: Prejudice, Race and Worldwide AIDS*, London: New Society Publications.

Sagarin, E. (1973) 'The good guys, the bad guys, and the gay guys' in *Contemporary Sociology*, 2, 1, pp. 3–13.

SAMOIS (ed.) (1982) *Coming to Power*, Boston, Massachusetts: Alyson Publications.

Sandfort, T. et al. (1990) 'Man-boy relationships: different concepts for a diversity of phenomena' in *Journal of Homosexuality*, 20, 1/2, pp. 5–12.

Schippers, J. (1989) 'Homosexual identity: essentialism and constructionism' in D. Altman et al. (eds) *Homosexuality, Which Homosexuality?* London: Gay Men's Press.

Schneider, B. (1992) 'Lesbian politics and AIDS work' in K. Plummer (ed.) *Modern Homosexualities: Fragments of Lesbian and Gay Experience*, London: Routledge.

Sedgwick, E. K. (1985) *Between Men: English Literature and Male Homosexual Desire*, New York: Columbia University Press.

Segal, L. (1987) *Is the Future Female? Troubled Thoughts on Contemporary Feminism*, London: Virago.

Segal, L. (1990) *Slow Motion: Changing Masculinities, Changing Men*, London: Virago.

Shepherd, S. and Wallis, M. (eds) (1989) *Coming on Strong: Gay Politics and Culture*, London: Unwin Hyman.

Shiers, J. (1980) 'Two steps forward, one step back' in Gay Left Collective (ed.) *Homosexuality: Power and Politics*, London: Allison & Busby.

Shilts, R. (1987) *And the Band Played On: Politics, People, and the AIDS Epidemic*, London: Penguin.

Siegel, K. et al. (1989) 'The motives of gay men for taking or not taking the HIV antibody test' in *Social Problems*, 36, 4, pp. 368–383.

Silverstein, M. (1977) 'The history of a short, unsuccessful academic career (with a postscript update)' in J. Snodgrass (ed.) *A Book of Readings: for Men against Sexism*, New York: Times Change Press.

Smith, D. E. (1987) *The Everyday World As Problematic*, Milton Keynes: Open University Press.

Snitow, A. (1979) 'Mass market romance: pornography for women is different' in *Radical History*, 20.

Snitow, A. et al. (eds) (1984) *Desire: the Politics of Sexuality*, London: Virago.

Sontag, S. (1978) *Illness as Metaphor*, London: Allen Lane.

Sontag, S. (1989) *AIDS and Its Metaphors*, London: Allen Lane.

Spada, J. (1979) *The Spada Report*, New York: Signet.

Stanley, L. (1982) '"Male needs": the problems and problems of working with gay men' in S. Friedman and E. Sarah (eds) *On the Problem of Men: Two Feminist Conferences*, London: Women's Press.

Stanley, L. (1984) 'Whales and minnows: some sexual theorists and their followers and how they contribute to making feminism invisible' in *Women's Studies International Forum*, 7, 1, pp. 53–62.

Stanley. L. (ed.) (1990) *Feminist Praxis: Research, Theory and Epistemology in Feminist Research Processes*, London: Routledge.

Stanley, L. and Wise, S. (1983) *Breaking Out: Feminist Consciousness and Feminist Research*, London: Routledge & Kegan Paul.

Stein, T. S. and Cohen, C. J. (eds) (1986) *Contemporary Perspectives on Psychotherapy with Lesbians and Gay Men*, New York: Plenum Medical Book Company.

Stoltenberg. J. (1982) 'Eroticized violence, eroticized powerlessness' in R. Linden et al. (eds) *Against Sado-masochism: a Radical Feminist Analysis*, California: Frog in the Well.

Stoltenberg, J. (1989) *Refusing to be a Man: Essays on Sex and Justice*, Portland, Oregon: Breitenbush Books.

Styles, J. (1979) 'Outsider/insider: researching gay baths' in *Urban Life: a Journal of Ethnographic Research*, 8, 2.

Tatchell, P. (1987) *AIDS: a Guide to Survival*, (2nd edn) London: Gay Men's Press.

Tatchell, P. (1992) 'Equal rights for all: strategies for lesbian and gay equality in Britain' in K. Plummer (ed.) *Modern Homosexualities: Fragments of Lesbian and Gay Experience*, London: Routledge.

Taylor, B. (1981) (ed.) *Perspectives on Paedophilia*, London: Batsford.

Tiger, L. (1969) *Men in Groups*, New York: Random House.

Tolson, A. (1977) *The Limits of Masculinity*, London: Tavistock.

Treichler, P. (1988) 'AIDS, homophobia and biomedical discourse: an epidemic of signification' in D. Crimp (ed.) *AIDS: Cultural Analysis, Cultural Activism*, London: MIT Press.

Troiden, R. R. (1988) *Gay and Lesbian Identity: a Sociological Analysis*, New York: General Hall.

Trumbach, R. (1989) 'Gender and the homosexual role in modern western culture: the 18th and 19th centuries compared' in D. Altman et al. (eds) *Homosexuality, Which Homosexuality?* London: Gay Men's Press.

Tsang, D. (ed.) (1981) *The Age Taboo: Gay Male Sexuality – Power & Consent*, London: Gay Men's Press.

Tucker, S. (1990) 'Radical feminism and gay male porn' in M. Kimmel (ed.) *Men Confront Pornography*, New York: Crown Publishers.

Valverde, M. (1985) *Sex, Power and Pleasure*, London: Women's Press.

Vance, C. S. (ed.) (1984) *Pleasure and Danger: Exploring Female Sexuality*, London: Routledge & Kegan Paul.

Vass, A. A. (1986) *AIDS: a Plague in Us – a Social Perspective – the Condition and its Social Consequences*, St Ives, Cambs: Venus Academia.

Veyne, P. (1985) 'Homosexuality in ancient Rome' in P. Aries and A. Bejin (eds) *Western Sexuality: Practice and Precept in Past and Present Times*, Oxford: Basil Blackwell.

Vicinus, M. (1989) '"They wonder to which sex I belong": the historical roots of the modern lesbian identity' in D. Altman et al. (eds) *Homosexuality, Which Homosexuality?* London: Gay Men's Press.

Walkowitz, J. R. (1984) 'Male vice and female virtue: feminism and the politics of prostitution in nineteenth-century Britain' in A. Snitow et al. (eds) *Desire: the Politics of Sexuality*, London: Virago.

Walter, A. (ed.) (1980) *Come Together: the Years of Gay Liberation (1970–73)*, London: Gay Men's Press.

Warren, C. (1977) 'Fieldwork in the gay world: issues in phenomenological research' in *Journal of Social Issues*, 33, 4, pp. 93–107.

Watney, S. (1987) *Policing Desire: Pornography, AIDS and the Media*, London: Comedia.

Watney, S. (1988) 'AIDS, "moral panic" theory and homophobia' in P. Aggleton and H. Homans (eds) *Social Aspects of AIDS*, Lewes, East Sussex: Falmer Press.

Weeks, J. (1977) *Coming Out: Homosexual Politics in Britain from the Nineteenth Century to the Present*, London: Quartet.

Weeks, J. (1981) *Sex, Politics and Society: the Regulation of Sexuality Since 1800*, London: Longman.

Weeks, J. (1985) *Sexuality and its Discontents: Meanings, Myths and Modern Sexualities*, London: Routledge & Kegan Paul.

Weeks, J. (1986) *Sexuality*, London: Tavistock.

Weeks, J. (1989) 'AIDS: the intellectual agenda' in P. Aggleton et al. (eds) *AIDS: Social Representations, Social Practices*, Lewes, East Sussex: Falmer Press.

Weeks, J. (1990) 'Post-Modern AIDS?' in T. Boffin and S. Gupta (eds) *Ecstatic Antibodies: Resisting the AIDS Mythology*, London: Rivers Oram Press.

Weeks, J. and Porter, K. (eds) (1991) *Between the Acts: Lives of Homosexual Men 1885–1967*, London: Routledge.

Weinberg, M. S. (1970) 'Homosexual samples: differences and similarities' in *Journal of Sex Research*, 6, 4, pp. 312–325.

West, D. J. (ed.) (1985) *Sexual Victimisation: Two Recent Researches into Sex Problems and their Social Effects*, Aldershot: Gower.

West, D. J. (1987) *Sexual Crimes and Confrontations: a Study of Victims and Offenders*, Aldershot: Gower.

White, E. (1986) *States of Desire: Travels in Gay America* (2nd edn), London: Picador.

Wieringa, S. (1989) 'An anthropological critique of constructionism: berdaches and butches' in D. Altman et al. (eds) *Homosexuality, Which Homosexuality?*, London: Gay Men's Press.

Willis, P. (1977) *Learning to Labour: How Working Class Kids Get Working Class Jobs*, Farnborough, Hants: Saxon House.

Willmott, P. (1969) *Adolescent Boys of East London*, Harmondsworth, Middlesex: Penguin.

Wilson, E. (1983) *What Is to Be Done about Violence against Women?*, Harmondsworth, Middlesex: Penguin.

Winship, J. (1985) '"A girl needs to get street-wise": magazines for the 1980s' in *Feminist Review*, 21.

Wollstonecraft, M. (1929) *Vindication of the Rights of Women*, London: Everyman. [orig. pub. 1792]

Woolf, V. (1929) *A Room of One's Own*, London: Hogarth Press.

Youth Liberation (1981) 'Children and sex' in D. Tsang (ed.) *The Age Taboo: Gay Male Sexuality, Power and Consent*, London: Gay Men's Press.

Index